Hiking Mississippi

Hiking Mississippi

A Guide to Trails and Natural Areas

Helen McGinnis

UNIVERSITY PRESS OF MISSISSIPPI   JACKSON

The paper in this book meets the guidelines for permanence and durability
of the Committee on Production Guidelines for Book Longevity of the
Council on Library Resources.

Library of Congress Cataloging-in-Publication Data

McGinnis, Helen.

   Hiking Mississippi : a guide to trails and natural areas / Helen
McGinnis.

     p. cm.

   Includes bibliographical references (p.) and index.

   ISBN 0-87805-704-8. — ISBN 0-87805-664-5 (pbk.)

   1. Hiking—Mississippi—Guidebooks. 2. Outdoor recreation—
Mississippi—Guidebooks. 3. Trails—Mississippi—Guidebooks.
4. Mississippi—Guidebooks. I. Title

GV199.42.M7M34 1994

796.5'1'09762—dc20   94-12156

                                        CIP

British Library Cataloging-in-Publication data available

Readers who can update or correct the information supplied in this book
are invited to write the author in care of University Press of Mississippi,
3825 Ridgewood Road, Jackson, MS 39211.

Contents

Illustrations

Acknowledgments

I am indebted to many people for information and encouragement. Some of them (but by no means all) are Allen Albritton, University of Mississippi Forest; Mark Anderson and Nell Covington, Chickasawhay Ranger District, DeSoto National Forest (NF); Keith Baca, Mississippi Department of Archives and History; David Barron, David Carter, and Evan Peacock, Tombigbee NF; Ed Bratcher, Biloxi Ranger District, DeSoto NF; Don Bolinger, Sam Brookes, Gene Jackson, and Sue Terry in the Jackson office of the U.S. Forest Service; Betty Bensey, City of Pascagoula; Linda Boulton; Bill Breeken, Bill Hamrick, Chester Hunt, Beth Lipe, and Cathy Shropshire, Mississippi Department of Wildlife, Fisheries, and Parks (MDWFP); Randy Breland, Yazoo National Wildlife Refuge (NWR) Complex; Tommy Brooks, Enid Lake; Gene Buglewicz; Mrs. Jerri Bull, Tennessee Trails Association;

Ken Carlton, Choctaw Reservation; Jim Carver, Old River Wildlife Management Area (WMA); Marcel Crudele and Del Smith, Natchez Trace Parkway; Mary Currier and Mary Page, Mississippi Department of Health; Eleanor Daly, Natural Science Museum; Mary Byrd Davis; Maurice Dantin; Mike Dawson, U.S. Fish and Wildlife Service; Mary Dent Deaton; Walter Dennis, International Paper Company; Dean Elsen, Bienville NF; Mahmoud ElSohly, Research Institute of Pharmaceutical Sciences, University of Mississippi; Frank Evans, Ward Bayou WMA;

Bill Fly, Arkabutla Lake; Ruth Gaddis and Raymond Rowland, Mississippi Endurance Riders Association; Ken Gordon, Mississippi Natural Heritage Program; Paul Govedare, Flint Creek Water Park; Jimmy Graves, Division of Recreation and Parks, MDWFP; Kent Grizzard, Mississippi Forestry Commission; Diane Hancock, Homochitto Ranger District, Homochitto NF; Mike Hobbs, Gulf Islands National Seashore; Mike Hughes, Poison Control Center, University Medical Center; Gerald Inmon, Holly Springs NF;

Roger Jones and Pat Patterson, Nature Conservancy; Ronnie Kerr, Shipland WMA; Allan Moore; Herman Murrah, Pascagoula WMA; Brian Nunnery, Legion State Park; Doug Oliver, Alvin Womack and Clinton Youngblood, Delta NF; T. Rose Parmer, Shepard State Park; James Parker, Pearl River Basin Development

District; Ellen Presson, Grand Gulf Military Monument; Tom Prusa, St. Catherine's Creek NWR; Robert Reams and Tony Tooke, Black Creek Ranger District, DeSoto NF; Bill Riecken; Rosie Rotwein, Garden Clubs of Mississippi; Jasper Sanderson, Nanih Waiya State Park; Jim Sharp; Steve Shepard; L. J. Smith, Hunter Education, MDWFP; Wayne Syron, Bogue Chitto NWR; Julius Thomas and Carol Boll, Bude Ranger District, Homochitto NF; Jim Tisdale, Noxubee NWR; Chris Wells, Crosby Arboretum; Terry Wenschel, Vicksburg National Military Park; Steve White, Lake Tiak O'Khata; and Brooke Williams, Mississippi Sandhill Crane NWR.

I especially thank JoAnne Prichard, my editor at the University Press of Mississippi, Rich Sankovich, and John Schneider and Andrea Dinep for their encouragement and assistance. Mary P. Stevens, Librarian at the Natural Science Museum in Jackson, compiled a list of recommended natural history books and helped me in other ways. Jerome Goddard, the state medical entomologist, provided me with much information on medically important arthropods. Finally, I would never have completed this project without the suggestions and continued interest of my brother, Richard P. McGinnis, and the use of his computer word processor in writing the manuscript.

Hiking Mississippi

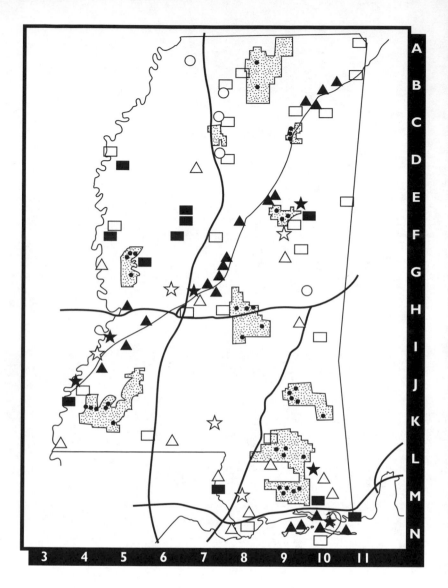

Interstate Highways

Natchez Trace Parkway. See page 107.

Areas and trails in national forests. See page 8.

National wildlife refuges. See page 68.

Areas in the national park system. See page 94.

U.S. Army Corps of Engineers reservoirs. See page 124.

State parks. See page 152.

State wildlife management areas, water parks and natural areas. See page 70.

Other public lands. See page 77.

Private natural areas and resorts. See page 231.

How to Use This Book

This is a guide to the larger areas of public land in Mississippi where natural conditions prevail—lands managed by federal agencies, including national forests, national parks, national wildlife refuges, and the reservoirs built by the Army Corps of Engineers; state lands, including state parks and selected state wildlife management areas; and areas that are the responsibility of more local agencies, such as water parks. Five privately owned areas are also included. Maintained trails ranging from half-mile trails accessible to the disabled to the 41-mile-long Black Creek Trail are included, but the guide is not limited to land with trails.

The wildest sections of the state are probably its extensive swamps and coastal marshes—places accessible only by canoe or other small boat. I have visited and read about almost all the areas described in the guide and have hiked many but not all of the trails, although I have not explored most of the swamplands personally in a canoe. I will take you to the edges of such places and let those of you who are more adventuresome and self-confident in the outdoors find your own way.

I emphasize exploration by muscle power, either your own or that of a horse. As I indicate, however, many Mississippi trails are open to wheels—a few to wheelchairs and many to mountain bicycles and all-terrain vehicles. Since the emphasis is on nature, fitness trails are not described. In addition, most trails less than half a mile long have been omitted.

Descriptions of individual areas and trails have been arranged by management area—federal, state, and other. The national forests, two of the national parks, the Corps of Engineers reservoirs, state parks, many water parks, and other areas have improved outdoor recreation facilities, ranging from a few picnic tables to rental cabins, campgrounds, swimming and boating areas, lodges, and even golf courses. Introductions to each major type of area indicate the available facilities.

Supplementary Maps

Supplementary maps are recommended for many trails and areas. Because of space constraints, I have included maps in this book only if they contain information not available elsewhere.

Official Mississippi state highway map: Free copies are available at any of the Mississippi Welcome Centers, which are on interstate highways near the state border, and also from the Mississippi Division of Tourism Development, P.O. Box 1705, Ocean Springs, MS 39566 (1-800-927-6378). The location codes printed in the margins of this book's area/trail descriptions, such as "C5," refer to the numbers and letters printed in the margin of this map. The official map shows more public land areas than other maps of Mississippi do, but if you do not have a copy, you can still determine the general location of an area on map 1.

Maps issued by state and federal agencies: Many of these maps are excellent. Addresses and phone numbers of the appropriate agencies are provided in the text of this book. Plan ahead to be sure you will have the maps you need for a weekend trip, especially in the national forests. Forest Service offices are officially open only during working hours. Like most natural resource professionals, Forest Service employees tend to come in early (about 7:30 A.M.) and are often gone by 4:00 P.M. Also, remember that most of the area managers are government workers and will not be available during public holidays. Don't expect to get maps if you decide on Friday evening or Saturday morning to go on a trip that weekend.

U.S. Geological Survey topographic maps: The entire state is depicted by 1:24,000 topo maps, also called 7.5′ maps because each takes in 7.5 minutes of longitude. Printed in color and based on aerial surveying, these maps impart an enormous amount of information to anyone who knows how to read them (see figure 1). Hikers in particular can keep track of their precise position and see what lies ahead. If you don't know how to read a topo map, it's worth a half hour of study and some practice in the field to learn. Most books on camping and backpacking devote space to topo maps.

The names of relevant topo (7.5′) maps are given for many of the areas and trails in the descriptions that follow. Some of the maps are "recommended"; others are listed as "helpful." Whether or not you need a topo map to do a trail, you might want one just to see how the area fits into the landscape.

The Mississippi Office of Geology (Southport Center, 2380 Hwy 80 West, P.O. Box 20307, Jackson, MS 39289-1307; 601-961-5523), carries all the 7.5′ topo maps for the state (they cost three dollars apiece in 1993). The office also can provide you with an index map for Mississippi and a brochure explaining the symbols. You can order through the mail or buy maps over the counter

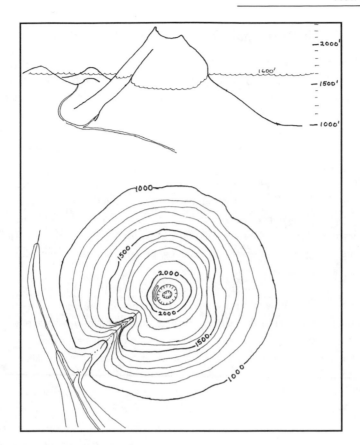

FIGURE 1. A simple topographic map
  Shown is a volcanic cone 1,000′ high with a crater on top. It stands on a plain 1,000′ above
  sea level. An intermittent stream has eroded a deep gully on one side and flows into a
  larger stream. There is a cliff on the far side of the cone. The contour lines are at 100′ in-
  tervals; the concentric lines on the topo map connect all points at each interval. If the
  mountain were gradually submerged in water and the level raised 100′ at a time, the
  water lines would correspond to the contour lines. The drawing depicts the hypothetical
  water line at 1,600′.

on weekdays during working hours. Map distributors in other cities also sell
topo maps; check the yellow pages of your telephone directory.

  The maps in this book: You don't need to carry this book with you into the
woods and swamps. If the maps for the area you plan to visit are provided in
this guide, photocopy them for use on the trail. Photocopies are lightweight
and will save your book from wear and tear. You can make an enlarged copy
and put it in a one- or three-gallon zip-lock bag with the relevant portion facing outward. Other maps can be protected in the same fashion.

Coping with Mississippi's Environmental Conditions

When to go: The best weather for trips in Mississippi is in the spring, from late February through May, and in the fall, from October to Thanksgiving. In spring you will enjoy fresh green leaves and flowering dogwoods. Low-lying areas on the Delta and along major rivers are likely to be flooded at this time—poor for hiking but good for swamp exploration by canoe. Average rainfall is lowest in October, and many of the areas that flood in the spring will be dry and easy to walk through.

Midsummer is the worst time for strenuous exertion; temperatures rarely go above 95°F, but high relative humidity makes temperatures in the low 90s feel at least 10° higher because your body is less able to cool itself through the evaporation of sweat. When you do hike in warm weather, start out early so that you can spend midafternoon relaxing, preferably near water where you can take a dip. Continue walking in late afternoon.

If meeting armed people and the sound of rifle fire disturbs you, avoid areas where hunting is allowed during the opening week of the deer (rifle) season. Hunting is permitted in the national forests, state wildlife management areas, and most national wildlife refuges. Traditionally the deer (rifle) season begins the Saturday before Thanksgiving, but the season varies on different wildlife management areas and national wildlife refuges. (See Appendix 1 for precautions.)

What to bring: Many good books on camping, canoeing, map reading and orienteering, and backpacking are available. Two good comprehensive references on nonmotorized camping techniques are the Boy Scouts of America's *Fieldbook* and Greenspan and Kahn's *Camper's Companion* (see the bibliography). Much of the latter is devoted to food, with intriguing recipes that you prepare at home and dehydrate in a home food drier. Two classics specifically on backpacking are Manning, *Backpacking*, and Fletcher, *The Complete Walker III* (see the bibliography). Most such books are written from the perspective of people who are familiar with the mountains of the West or the Appalachians.

Except in December, January, and February, you won't need a very warm sleeping bag and will be extremely uncomfortable if you bring the kind of bag you'd use in the Sierra or the Rockies. In the summer, use a very light bag or just bring a sheet.

If you have money for only one tent, select one with extensive mosquito netting and maximum cross-ventilation. When you buy hiking boots, remember that you won't find rocks larger than a grain of sand in much of Mississippi and that snow is rarely a problem. You may run into mud and puddles, however. I recommend a lightweight boot for all but midwinter hiking. Bring a second pair of light shoes or sneakers that can be fastened firmly to your feet to

FIGURE 2. Poison ivy vine
Poison ivy assumes three forms—a sparsely leaved woody plant less than a foot high on the forest floor, a vine, and occasionally thickets up to chest high. Identifying characteristics are the compound leaves with three leaflets and the adventitious roots with which the vine clings to tree trunks. These roots resemble short thick hairs.

use for wading in areas likely to be flooded in the spring. A walking stick is also helpful for flooded patches.

If you are a photographer, remember that most of the areas in this guide are in deep shade much of the year, and bring film with an ASA of at least 400.

Hazards and Discomforts: Minor discomfort is a part of almost any outdoor experience. Most can be minimized by knowing what to look for and watching for it, using preventative measures such as lotions and sprays, and having the right mind set so that little things don't (literally) bug you. Certain hazards, such as being bitten by a poisonous snake or coming down with Lyme disease, are vastly exaggerated. For further information, see Appendix 1.

One potential source of discomfort, poison ivy, needs to be mentioned up front because the reaction is delayed one to three days after your skin contacts the leaves. The plant thrives in the woods and forest margins of Mississippi. You can minimize contact with poison ivy by staying on maintained trails and in cleared areas in campgrounds and recreation sites. Temperature permitting, wear long pants and sleeves. If you are especially sensitive, you may want to hike the wider trails maintained for horseback riding and all-terrain vehicles. Launder your outer clothing frequently.

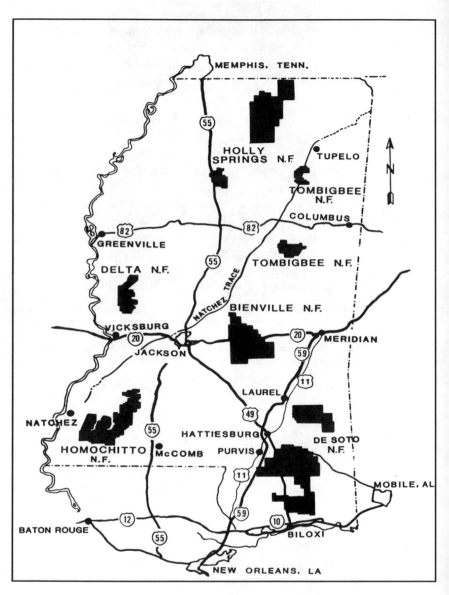

M A P 2. The National Forests in Mississippi

1. The National Forests

The six national forests, with 1,155,518 acres of federal land, are the largest holdings of public land in Mississippi. They include some of the state's wilder country, as well as 276 miles of hiking trails and 21 developed campgrounds and picnic grounds.

National forest land is in nine widely distributed blocks, each enclosed in a proclamation boundary established by an act of the U.S. Congress. About half of the acreage within each block is privately owned. About 49% of national forest lands are also state wildlife management areas. The national forests take in many different kinds of forests and landscapes.

The Mississippi national forests are managed as one national forest with 10 ranger districts. Each district is managed by a district ranger, with staff, from offices within or near the districts. The district rangers report to a forest supervisor in Jackson.

Most of the land in the Mississippi national forests was purchased from large timber companies in the 1930s after they had been stripped of their virgin forests. "Roosevelt's Tree Army," the Civilian Conservation Corps, was put to work replanting trees, stopping erosion, and building recreation areas. Old CCC barrack sites appear on some national forest maps.

People often confuse national forests with national parks, national seashores, and other areas that are the responsibility of the National Park Service, a branch of the U.S. Department of the Interior. Preservation, education, and compatible recreation are the management goals for areas under the Park Service. Mining, logging, and grazing are prohibited.

National forests, on the other hand, are the responsibility of the Forest Service, part of the U.S. Department of Agriculture. Under the Multiple Use Act of 1960, national forests must be managed to provide timber, watershed protection, grazing, wildlife, and recreation. Another use that is not formally recognized in the act but is important nonetheless is production of minerals, oil, and gas. Of course, not all of the goals can be met on every acre or even in every national forest.

TABLE 1. Facilities at National Forest Recreation Areas

National Forest	Ranger District/Unit	Recreation Area	FEE CHARGED	WHEN OPEN	BOATING	CAMPING	DRINKING WATER	FISHING	PICNICKING	SANITARY FACILITIES	SWIMMING	WATER SKIING	TRAILER SPACE	RV HOOKUPS	TRAILER DUMP STATION
Bienville	Bienville	Shockaloe Base Camp 1		a		●	●		●	P			●		
		Shockaloe Base Camp 2		A		●	●		●	P			●		
	Strong River	Marathon	●	A	L	●	●	●	●	T,S	●		●		
		Shongelo		b		●	●	●	●	T	●		●		
Delta		Blue Lake		A	L	●		●	●				●		
Homochitto	Bude	Clear Springs	●	c	●	●	●	●	●	T,S	●		●	●	●
	Homochitto	Pipes Lake		A	●	●		●	●	P					
Holly Springs	Holly Springs	Chewalla	●	d	L	●	●	●	●	T,S	●		●	●	●
		Puskus		A	L	●	●	●	●	P					
	Tillatoba	Lake Tillatoba		A	L	●	●	●	●	P					
Tombigbee	Ackerman	Choctaw Lake	●	e	L	●	●	●	●	T,S	●		●	●	●
	Trace	Davis Lake	●	e	L	●	●	●	●	T,S	●	●	●	●	●
DeSoto	Biloxi	Airey Lake		A		●	●	●	●	P			●		
		Big Biloxi	●	A		●	●	●	●	T,S			●	●	●
		Bigfoot Trail Camp		A		●			●	P			●		
		POW Camp		A	●	●			●				●		
	Black Creek	Ashe Lake		A	●	●		●	●	P			●		
		Big Creek Landing		A	L	●		●	●				●		
		Cypress Landing		A	L	●	●	●	●	P			●		
		Fairley Bridge Landing		A	L	●		●	●	P			●		
		Janice Landing		A	L	●	●	●	●	P			●		
		Moody's Landing		A	L		●	●	●	P					
	Chickasawhay	Longleaf Trail Camp		A		●		●	●	P			●		
		Turkey Fork	●	f	L	●	●	●	●	T,S	●	●	●	●	●

Note: A = all year, a = April–October, b = April 15 to October 15, c = April 15 to November 30, d = March 15 to December 15, e = March 1 to September–October, f = April to Labor Day. L = boat launch ramp. P = privies or chemical toilets. S = hot showers. T = flush toilets.

Timber production dominates the Forest Service's budget and manpower. Most national forest lands nationwide were managed under the even-aged system. After one or two thinning cuts or intermediate cuts, all trees in a given block were removed (clearcut). However, under the current ecosystem management direction, clearcutting no longer is the primary cutting method nationwide. Tree harvest methods, of which clearcutting is one, are now selected on the basis of the desired future condition for the forest. The trees may be replanted with so-called genetically superior pines (those that grow rapidly and straight) or may be reseeded naturally from adjacent uncut forests.

Even-aged management coexists uneasily with aesthetic considerations, trails, and cross-country hiking. When you hike or ride on the longer trails, you will pass along the edges of many older clearcuts and will sometimes cross them. As new forests mature, clearcuts go through an intermediate stage with dense growths of young pines and brushy hardwoods.

Facilities at developed recreation sites are summarized in table 1. The Delta National Forest and part of the Tombigbee National Forest have no improved campgrounds. Instead separate primitive campsites without any facilities are scattered along roads throughout the forests. You must have a permit (free) from the Forest Service to use them, at least during the hunting seasons.

Maps and Literature: The Forest Service sells four maps in color that encompass the six national forests. They show public land and all Forest Service roads open to general use. On national forest land, roads are generally marked only by numbered signs, so the maps are nearly essential for finding your way. Maps are available from the forest supervisor's office in Jackson and from the relevant ranger districts. The free eight-page *Mississippi National Forests Recreation Guide* is also available from all the Forest Service offices. Contact the Forest Supervisor's office, National Forests in Mississippi, 100 W. Capitol St., Suite 1141, Jackson, MS 39269 (601-965-4391). For information on specific areas and trails, it is better to contact the relevant district rangers on weekdays.

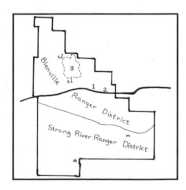

LEGEND

m = Marathon Recreation Area

s1 = Shockaloe Base Camp 1

s2 = Shockaloe Base Camp 2

sh = Shongelo Recreation Area

1 = Bienville Pines Scenic Area

2 = Harrell Prairie Hill Botanical Area

3 = Shockaloe Trail

M A P 3. Bienville National Forest

BIENVILLE NATIONAL FOREST
(178,000 acres)

All but the extreme southern portion of the Bienville NF is in the gently rolling to almost level terrain of the Jackson Prairie region. The moister areas with underlying Yazoo clay are acidic and support predominantly loblolly pine forests on higher ground, with hardwoods in the bottoms. Small natural prairies occur in drier areas with alkaline soils. Sixty-eight separate prairies, some less than an acre in size, have been identified on the Bienville.

The federal government purchased the land in 1934 from four large landowners, the Adams-Edgar Lumber Company, Bienville Lumber Company, Gardner Lumber County, and Marathon Lumber Company, after almost all the virgin forest had been cut. The national forest is named after the noted French-Canadian explorer and colonist Jean Baptiste le Moyne, Sieur de Bienville, who was responsible for the first white settlements on the Mississippi Gulf Coast and at Natchez.

The forest is divided into two ranger districts, the Bienville Ranger District in the north and the Strong River Ranger District in the south half.

H 8 ## BIENVILLE RANGER DISTRICT,
Rt. 2, Box 1239, Forest, MS 39074 (601-469-3811). The office is 3 miles S of Forest on State Hwy 35

- **Shockaloe Trail,** between Forest and Morton, Scott County. This 23-mile looped trail is one of the two longest circuit trails in the state. It makes an easy weekend backpacking trip through rolling terrain in pine woods, with several colonies of red-cockaded woodpeckers along the way.

The Shockaloe Trail goes through gently rolling terrain covered with pines (predominantly loblolly) of various ages. Stream bottoms with the typical array of bottomland hardwood trees are rather poorly defined. Some of the small clearings you will pass date from the early 1980s, when trees infested with southern pine beetles were removed to control infestation of adjacent healthy trees.

The trail is slightly elevated and resembles a small woods road. Because it is well drained, you rarely have to cross muddy spots pockmarked with sunken horse tracks. It is marked with elevated wooden posts with horse-and-rider symbols. Wooden posts also mark each mile, starting at Base Camp 1 and going east (counterwise) from there. (Some of the posts may be missing, however.) The trail crosses at least two recent gravel logging access roads between Mile Posts 14 and 11, so be on the lookout for paint blazes to stay on route on

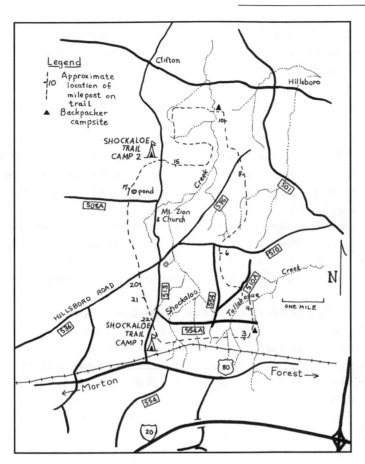

M A P 4. Shockaloe Trail. Numbers on the trail indicate the approximate location of mileposts. Filled triangles denote backpacker campsites.

this section of the trail. Several large signs along the route explain Forest Service timber management practices.

This portion of the Bienville National Forest is one of the last strongholds of the endangered red-cockaded woodpecker (RCW) in Mississippi. Near Mile Post 21 a "viewing tube" is aimed at a typical RCW cavity tree. The birds have stripped off the bark around the cavity, and it is covered with resin flowing from "wells" pecked in the sapwood. You will pass through at least one other active RCW colony (marked with signs) and near several others along the trail.

Most backpackers will be able to complete the entire trail in a weekend. The terrain is gentle, and the trail is in good condition. The best campsite for backpackers is at the crossing of the main fork of Shockaloo Creek between Mile

Posts 9 and 10, but don't drink the creek water. If you start at Base Camp 1, you can get clean water at Base Camp 2 and carry it the remaining five miles to the campsite at Shockaloo Creek.

The other campsite is just north of Mile Post 3. Water (boil it) is available from a small wildlife pond at a point where the trail makes a right angle to the north. The deeply shaded woods to the left (east) of the pond have space for several tents with a minimum of undergrowth.

Best Time to Visit: Base Camp 1 is closed and gated between November 1 and March 31, but you can park outside the gate and hike the trail. Ask the District Ranger's office when horseback riding groups have organized events on the trail, and hike accordingly.

Facilities: Base Camps 1 (larger) and 2 both offer shaded parking spots, drinking water, chemical toilets, hitching rails, and picnic tables protected by pavilions. Camp 1 has a watering hole for horses, a mowed lawn, barbecue grills, and a large pavilion. Neither camp has hookups for RVs and trailers.

H 8 • **Harrell Prairie Hill Botanical Area,** near Forest, Scott County

(160 acres). Natural prairies were once common across the Black Prairie and Jackson Prairie geographical regions. They were fertile, and so almost all were converted to agriculture. Sixty-eight small prairies, known locally as "cedar fields," have been identified in the Bienville and Strong ranger districts. The one on Harrell Prairie Hill is the largest and least disturbed prairie remaining in Mississippi. The Forest Service classified it as a botanical area in 1980.

The most common species in the botanical area is little bluestem grass. Other plants characteristic of prairies are big bluestem grass, Indiangrass, yellow coneflower, purple coneflower, and prairie clovers. Different flowers bloom from early spring into late fall. (A list of Latin names is in Jones's article in the botanical journal *Castanea*, listed in the bibliography.) An endemic species of crayfish, the Jackson Prairie crayfish, is known to occur in 24 of the 68 prairies. Deer, quail, and Bachman's sparrows find excellent habitat here.

The soil of the prairies is alkaline (pH of 7.5 or more), in contrast to the acidic soil of the loblolly pine forests that surround them. Fire is essential to these prairies. From 1934, when the Forest Service purchased the land from the Bienville Lumber Company, into the 1970s, fire was suppressed or eliminated. Aerial photos taken in 1936 and compared with recent photos show that the prairies have been shrinking with the encroachment of various species of shrubs, vines, and trees on the edges. Today the Forest Service burns Harrell Hill Prairie every three years and also cuts down invading trees on the edge, including pines that were artificially planted (fortunately the pines grew poorly). (See articles by Welland et al. and by Jones, in the bibliography, for more information.)

Apparently the prairie on Harrell Hill Prairie escaped the plow because it was in a block of timberland purchased by the Bienville Lumber Company. The company was interested in lumbering, not farming, and so the prairie remained intact.

Facilities: You will find no designated trails or any other facility in this botanical area. FS 515 runs through the area, however. You can park alongside the road or near the sign in the middle of the prairie and wander at will. (Please do not pick the flowers.)

- **Bienville Pines Scenic Area,** Forest, Scott County (189 acres, ca. two miles of trail). In 1991 the Forest Service prepared an excellent description of the area along with a guide to numbered posts on the trail, on which I have based the following account. H 8

At 189 acres, this scenic area is the largest known block of residual pine timber in Mississippi. The cover type consists of old-growth loblolly and short-leaf pines ranging generally in age from 125 to 200 years with a dense midstory composed primarily of young hardwoods.

The Forest Service has recognized the uniqueness of the area since its purchase. The salvage of storm-, insect-, or disease-damaged trees alone has been allowed. Since 1964, only insect-infested trees that threaten the remaining area or endangered species have been removed (trees along the trail that present a safety hazard have also been felled, however).

The Forest Service has sought primarily to maintain the relatively undisturbed character of this scenic area for its aesthetic and educational value. The preservation of the large, old pines is a secondary objective, since loblolly pines rarely live 300 years.

The Bienville Pines Hiking Trail wanders through the scenic area for a distance of about 1.8 miles. A shortcut is available to reduce the mileage to about 1.2. The last section of the trail is routed outside the larger pines. Along the trail, you will find numbered stops at points of interest.

Stop 1. This part of Mississippi lies within the physiographic province known as the Jackson Prairie. High shrink-swell clay, the soil visible here and characteristic of the Jackson Prairie, demonstrates extremely large volume changes between wet and dry, which often produce the small mounds and depressions you see around you here. This "loblolly prairie," whose name refers to the small basins that often retain water during winter months, is literally a mudhole. Loblolly pine is so called because of its affinity for wet areas.

Stop 2. Trees like the one before you lean primarily because of advanced age and the deterioration of the large tap root that held them firmly in younger years. Most such trees will probably die when they fall.

Stop 3. The dead pines you see in front of you here were killed by an infestation of tiny southern pine beetles. While healthy pines are usually capable of expelling small numbers of them with flowing sap, the beetle's chances of success increase if the tree is under stress due to drought, flooding, or old age. Adult beetles lay eggs just below the outer bark. The larvae later kill the tree by feeding on the inner bark.

Stop 4. This stream bottom represents an area of relatively greater moisture as evidenced by the willow oaks and switch cane growing here. This diversity in plant species is important in providing food and shelter for wildlife.

Stop 5. This old piece of logging equipment was commonly called a "go-devil," or dray. It hauled logs that were cut into long lengths. The large end of the logs was fastened underneath the cradle; the small end dragged on the ground.

Stop 6. The trees now growing where this large fallen pine once stood are small oaks. In fact, throughout the scenic area, you will find a dense midstory of hardwood trees and very few small pines. Ecologists use the term "natural succession" to refer to the order in which plant communities change from the pioneering grasses and other nonwoody plants to the mature oak-hickory cover type that, for this locality, is the climax cover type. Before Europeans arrived, fires set by lightning and Indians prevented most forests from progressing to a climax cover. Instead, stands of pine with sparse understory dominated the landscape.

Stop 7. The tall pine tree in front of you is home to a red-cockaded woodpecker. This bird is the only species that excavates a cavity and raises its young in living pine trees. Many of the trees that it selects are infected with "red heart," a fungal heart rot that makes the woodpecker's task much easier. The development of this infection to the height required for cavity construction takes many years, and so these cavity trees are often quite old. Few old pines exist in today's forests. Also the woodpecker will not nest in pines with a heavy midstory of hardwoods. The number of breeding clans has declined to such a point that the bird is on the federal endangered species list.

Stop 8. Most of the pine timber in the remaining section of the hiking trail was removed in the early 1930s. The pine stand that you see here is therefore less than a third of the age of the older trees in the scenic area. Leaning and down trees are not evident here, a hardwood midstory is just beginning to develop, and there are many more pine trees per acre. At this age, the growth on these pines has begun to slow, and the characteristics of the older pine stand will slowly begin to appear.

Facilities: Only a small parking area.

Literature: A typewritten three-page description and diagrammatic map are available from the district office.

STRONG RIVER RANGER DISTRICT,

P.O. Box 217, Raleigh, MS 39153 (601-782-4271). The district office is 0.5 mile N of Raleigh on State Hwy 35

The Strong River Ranger District includes the head of the Strong River, which flows southwest into the Pearl. Extensive hardwood bottoms surround the river and its principal tributaries in the district.

• **Marathon Lake Recreation Area,** S of Forest, Smith County (146 acres, 0.75-mile nature trail). Marathon Recreation Area is on a 50-acre lake that was the millpond of Marathon Lumber Company's last logging camp (1920–29). The recreation area was built on the site in 1962 and was improved in the 1980s.

I 9

The nature trail circles the lake. It crosses the grass-covered dam (wildflowers in season). Tall loblolly pines have reclaimed most of the area since the mill closed. As you walk on the trail on the far side of the lake, look for straight lanes with smaller-than-usual trees. These are dummy lines, abandoned rail lines that brought logs to the mill. The Forest Service plans to develop a historical display on the early logging days at the lake.

Maps and Literature: There is a Forest Service brochure on the recreation area.

• **Shongelo Recreation Area,** N of Raleigh, Smith County (0.5-mile trail). This small recreation area in rugged hills is shaded by large shortleaf and loblolly pines. The focal point is a five-acre lake on Shongelo Creek, highlighted by a white stucco bathhouse at the edge of the dam. The trail follows the edge of the lake. Local people and the Forest Service constructed the facilities between the late 1930s and the 1950s.

I 8

Shongelo is officially open between April 15 and October 15, but you can park at the gate and walk in at other times of the year. In the off season, the water is turned off and the restrooms are closed. A campground host lives year round just inside the gate.

Shongelo was a small community of white settlers between the early 1800s until 1923. The lake was originally a millpond. Remnants of the old water-powered gristmill can still be seen just below the dam.

DELTA NATIONAL FOREST AND RANGER DISTRICT

USDA Forest Service, Sharkey-Ag Bldg., 402 Hwy 61 North, Rolling Fork, MS 39159 (601-873-6256). The forest is between Rolling Fork and Holly Bluff, in Sharkey County (59,518 acres, more than 50 miles of maintained and unmaintained trails)

The Delta National Forest is the only bottomland hardwood forest in the entire national forest system. It is the low-lying land at the confluence of three major rivers of the Mississippi Delta—the Yazoo, Big Sunflower, and Little Sunflower rivers. It is threaded with an interconnecting network of bayous.

The best-drained portions of the forest floor (about 100' above sea level) are only about 15' above the lowest portions, but the minor differences in drainage and duration of flooding result in different assemblages of trees. Hardwood bottom forests occupy frequently flooded, nearly flat ground between 85'–86' in elevation. Characteristic trees are Nuttall and overcup oaks, water hickory, sweetgum, boxelder, red maple, American elm, white ash, and sugarberry. Lianas and vines are abundant, but ground herbaceous plants are confined mostly to disturbed soil.

Ridge bottom forests occupy sites above 92' in elevation. Flooding here is less frequent and prolonged. Willow oak, water oak, sweetgum, pecan, honeylocust, cedar elm, and common persimmon are characteristic. Cane, dwarf palmetto, roughleaf dogwood, and other shrubs may form dense thickets under the trees. The lowest elevations in the bottoms of swales and along the edges of bayous and oxbow lakes are the realm of swamp forests, dominated by bald cypress, often draped with Spanish moss (see Carter, *A Floristic Study of the Delta National Forest*, in the bibliography).

The Corps of Engineers has also excavated two major cutoffs across the forest, shortcutting river bends. Their purpose is to speed up drainage of floodwaters in the upper Yazoo Basin (better known as the Delta). They have little, if any, effect on drainage in the Delta NF, however.

The Corps of Engineers is also responsible for five greentree reservoirs in the national forest. Greentree reservoirs are large areas of predominantly bottomland hardwoods that are enclosed with levees and flooded with shallow water from late fall through the winter. They provide shelter where migratory ducks can rest, court, and feed. The reservoirs are drained in the early spring to avoid killing the trees. The Corps constructed them within the last 20 years to compensate partially for waterfowl habitat that had been lost because of Yazoo Basin projects, designed to reduce flooding in the Delta. Most bottomland hardwood forests in private ownership, which once flooded naturally, have been cleared and drained as a direct result of Corps flood control projects.

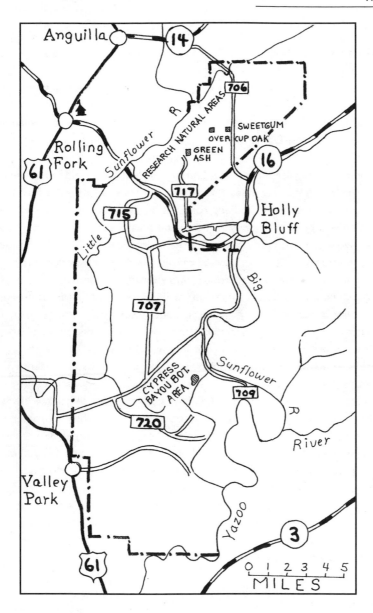

MAP 5. Delta National Forest

The Forest Service has designated 21 low standard dirt roads as trails that are closed to conventional-sized vehicles but are open to horseback riders, hikers, and ATVs less than 40″ wide. In length, the trails range from less than a mile to more than four miles. They are marked with white metal diamonds nailed on trees. Most ATV use is during the deer seasons. In addition, the

7.5' topo maps show many unmarked abandoned roads. Some are excellent for hiking and horseback riding. The trails and some abandoned roads are wide enough to keep you away from poison ivy.

The Delta National Forest is extremely popular with deer hunters, attracted by the large, well-nourished deer that live there. Also, it is one of the few areas of good deer habitat left on the Delta that is not owned or leased by private hunting clubs. During the spring, the roadside sloughs are lined with fishermen.

Flooding is a regular occurrence. During the first six months of the year you are likely to encounter at least some standing water. Usually it is less than a foot deep (but watch out for deep roadside ditches). During warm weather you can move around pretty well in shorts and sneakers if you don't mind occasional wading. The larger sloughs that have been dammed by small water control structures invite exploration by canoe. Flooding is rarely deep enough, however, for you to take a boat cross-country through the forest.

 A circuit nature trail about a mile long at Blue Lake is no longer maintained and has been disrupted by selective logging, but you can still follow the rectangular white paint blazes that mark the trail from the south end of the clearing with the wooden picnic tables to a giant hollow bald cypress.

Best Time to Visit: The extent of flooding is one of the most important considerations in planning a visit to the Delta NF. Flooding is maximum between February and May and minimal between July and November. When the Mississippi River is high, water backs up the Yazoo all the way to the national forest and spreads into it. If the level of the Mississippi at Vicksburg is 35' or less, flooding in the Delta NF will be minimal. If it is between 35' and 40', you may want to get additional information from the Forest Service. If the river is above 40', forget about hiking. For up-to-date recorded information on the river levels, call the Corps of Engineers in Vicksburg at 601-636-2900. Daily river levels are also printed in the weather sections of newspapers, including the *Jackson Clarion-Ledger*, and are given on some local television news programs. The levels of the Big and Little Sunflower rivers also influence flooding in the national forest.

The best time to visit the forest is October and November prior to the onset of the deer (gun) seasons, which begin the Saturday before Thanksgiving. The weather is pleasant, and flooding, heat, humidity, and insects are minimal. The worst times are the summer months (July-August) and the deer (gun) seasons, which usually end the first week of January.

Facilities: The only picnic area is at Blue Lake. It has tables but no restrooms or drinking water.

Instead of a campground, the Forest Service has established 87 campsites scattered along gravel roads throughout the forest. The sites, marked by numbered posts, are clearings at the ends of short spur roads. With the exception of tables at two sites at Blue Lake, none has tables, privies, or any other facilities. Camping is allowed only in these sites. Parties with horses are welcome. Many of the sites are flooded during the first half of the year. Among the highest and prettiest are the ones at Blue Lake and Barge Lake.

A map showing the campsites is available from the Forest Service and the manager of the Sunflower Wildlife Management Area, which includes essentially the same area as the national forest. You must get a free permit to occupy a campsite. You may request permits in person or by telephone at the Forest Service office on Hwy 61 in Rolling Fork during regular business hours.

Ten Mile Lodge, a nearby motel and campground with RV hookups, is in a remote setting along Old Spanish Fort Rd., at the southeast edge of the national forest at the mouth of Ten Mile Bayou at the now extinct village of Lucre. (Ten Mile Bayou is incorrectly labeled as Cypress Bayou on the provisional Lucre and Valley Park topo maps.) Call 601-828-3355 or write to Ten Mile Lodge, Star Route 73, Box 48, Holly Bluff, MS 39088.

Maps and Literature: Get the Forest Service map of the Delta NF and the free map showing campsites. The topo maps of the area show many old roads and trails that are not depicted on the Forest Service map. They are recommended to anyone seriously interested in exploring the forest on foot as well as to those who would like to explore the larger bayous by canoe. A small index map on the Forest Service map shows the extent of relevant topo maps.

RESEARCH NATURAL AREAS

Green Ash RNA (originally 60 acres), Overcup Oak RNA (40 acres), and Sweetgum RNA (40 acres) are the only uncut remnants of the 13,200 acres of nearly virgin forest that the Forest Service purchased from Houston Brothers in 1936. All are easily accessible on foot. Their boundaries are marked with light blue paint blazes and small yellow metal signs nailed in trees, facing outward from the designated areas. The boundary markings are often vague.

The Green Ash and Overcup Oak RNAs are representative hardwood bottom forests. Green Ash is dominated by old-growth green ash trees between 215 and 265 years old. Other trees include American elm, sugarberry, and bald cypress.

The giant uprooted fallen trees that you will see here are a rare sight in Mississippi's managed forests. An increasing body of research in the old-growth forests of the Pacific Northwest indicates that fallen old trees and the nutrients that are released into the forest ecosystems as they gradually decay may be essential for long-term forest maintenance (centuries, not decades). (For more on old-growth forests, see Maser's *Redesigned Forest*, in the bibliography.)

G 5

• **Green Ash Research Natural Area,** on the east side of FS 717, just S of the levee enclosing the Green Ash Greentree Reservoir. FS 717-B is on top of this levee. Park on the levee at the junction of FS 717 and FS 717-B and walk back south of Rt. 717. Cross the shallow roadside ditch on your left at a convenient spot, and walk about a hundred feet east to the vaguely marked boundary of the RNA. It is easy to get disoriented here, so bring a compass. The forest blends in well with the forest on the east side of the RNA boundary, which was selectively cut in the 1930s. Except for an occasional stump, it superficially resembles the adjacent virgin forest.

The northernmost section of the forest includes the Overcup Oak and Sweetgum RNAs. This is perhaps the nicest part of the forest for serious off-road hiking and exploration. You reach it via FS 706. From the east, the turnoff is near a prominent white tank labeled "Loch Lommond" along State Hwy 16 north of Holly Bluff.

G 5

• **Overcup Oak Research Natural Area** on FS 706-1 SE of Dowling Bayou Greentree Reservoir. This RNA is dominated by old-growth overcup oaks and sugarberry trees of approximately the same age as those in the Green Ash RNA. It is easy to walk around in both these areas because the forest floor is almost bare. Herbaceous plants are shaded out by the dense canopy overhead except where old giant trees have fallen down.

FS 706-1 is a woods trail. Park at the junction of FS 706 and 706-1 and walk west on FS 706-1 about 1.2 miles. You will know you are in or very near the RNA when there is a cypress slough (sometimes dry in the fall) on your right. The signs marking the RNA boundary are indistinct. You can continue a very pleasant and interesting walk on FS 706-1 for a considerable distance west beyond the RNA.

G 5–6

• **Sweetgum Research Natural Area,** W of FS 706 and about 0.7 mile N of the junction of the ATV trail designated 706-1. This RNA is an example of a ridge bottom forest on slightly higher ground. The dominant trees are massive sweetgums estimated to be 265 to 315 years old. Here, in contrast to the other two RNAs, the better-drained soils support a dense understory of dwarf palmettos and cane.

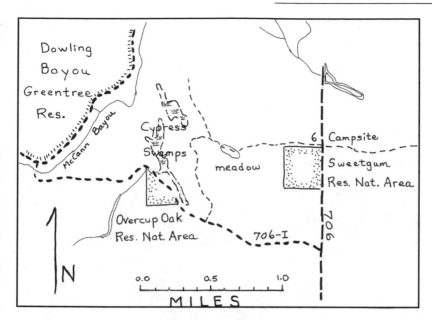

MAP 6. Overcup Oak and Sweetgum Research Natural Areas

Campsite 6 is at the northern edge of Sweetgum RNA. A trail starts behind a gate here and goes west along the RNA boundary and beyond. It may link up with ATV trail 706-I near the Overcup RNA. A side trail, not shown on the 7.5' topo map, heads north from this east-west trail. It stays on relatively high ground for an undetermined distance.

● **Cypress Bayou Botanical Area** (320 acres). This area was established in the southeastern end of the national forest in 1987. It encompasses a tract of old-growth hardwood bottom timber dominated by overcup oak. The Forest Service acquired the area in 1941. The timber was established in about 1874 and has not been cut since then. Other dominant tree species are green ash, sugarberry, bitter pecan, Nuttall oak, and sweetgum. Shrubs include swamp privet, swamp snowbell, green hawthorne, and stiffcornel dogwood. Herbaceous plants are sparse except in disturbed areas. Vines are abundant. The most common vines are poison ivy, winter grape, supplejack, greenbrier, and peppervine.

G 5

Cypress Bayou is the southwest boundary of the area. A slough structure was installed on the mouth of the bayou. Water is backed up year round to enhance wildlife habitat, especially for alligators and wood ducks.

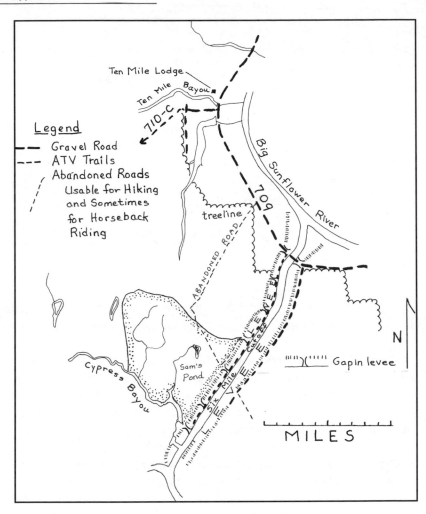

Legend
—— Gravel Road
--- ATV Trails
/ Abandoned Roads
/ Usable for Hiking
/ and Sometimes
/ for Horseback
/ Riding

Ten Mile Lodge
Ten Mile Bayou
710-C
Big Sunflower River
709
treeline
ABANDONED ROAD
Cypress Bayou
Sam's Pond
Six Mile Cut-off
L E V E E
Gap in levee
N
MILES

MAP 7. Cypress Bayou Botanical Area and vicinity

You can reach the edge of the area by an undesignated ATV trail that follows the inner side of the embankment bounding Six Mile Cut-Off, beginning on Old Spanish Fort Road about 1.6 miles south of Ten Mile Lodge. The edge of the botanical area is about 0.8 mile from the road. Beaten footpaths lead through two drainage notches into the botanical area. The second, marked in early 1993 by a plank over a roadside ditch and debris hung in trees, is less likely to be flooded. The far end of the botanical area is where the trail ends at the earthen embankment blocking Cypress Bayou.

You can also access the botanical area via an unmarked abandoned road that begins just to the left of the point where the margin of the forest comes close to Old Spanish Fort Road, about 1.0 mile south of Ten Mile Lodge.

DESOTO NATIONAL FOREST
(502,166 acres)

DeSoto National Forest, the largest national forest in Mississippi, is subdivided into three ranger district's—the Chickasawhay, Black Creek, and Biloxi. It encompasses generous portions of the rolling hills of the piney woods geographic region. Higher ground is dominated by stands of longleaf, slash, and loblolly pine. Forests recently treated by prescribed burning may have understories of grass or dead charred shrubs. Those that have not been burned for many years have dense understories of chest-high shrubs dominated by yaupon and gallberry. A variety of hardwoods grow in the wide, flat bottoms of small streams, which are called bayheads.

The DeSoto NF has four of the state's longest hiking and horseback trails, the state's first—and so far, only—national "wild and scenic river," and the only two federal wilderness areas in the national forests in Mississippi. This is also the only national forest in the state where grazing is permitted, although it is gradually being phased out. Barbed wire fences separate grazing allotments.

The land was purchased from large timber companies in the 1930s after it had been almost totally denuded of trees. Only 60 years ago the DeSoto NF was open pasture with only a few scraggly forest remnants. (For more on the history of the logging of the piney woods and the origin of the DeSoto NF, see the books and articles by Conarro and Hickman in the bibliography.)

Maps: A map of the entire DeSoto National Forest can be purchased from the office of the forest supervisor, national forests, in Jackson or from any of the three district ranger offices. Maps of specific trails are mentioned below.

BILOXI RANGER DISTRICT,
USDA Forest Service, Rt. 1, Box 62, McHenry, MS 39561 (601-928-5291). The district office is on U.S. Hwy 49 South.

The sandy soils of the Biloxi RD are less fertile than those of the adjoining Black Creek District. Pines tend to be smaller. The area has a great diversity of plant habitats, however, including pitcher plant bogs and thickets of titi, a shrub or small tree that grows in swampy hardwood bottoms. In addition to the trails described below, the Forest Service is planning a trail for mountain bicycles.

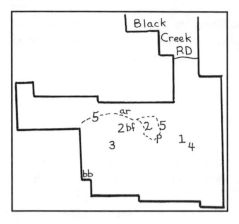

LEGEND

ar = Airey Lake

bb = Big Biloxi Recreation Area

bf = Big Foot Trail Camp

p = POW Camp

1 = Bethel ATV Trail

2 = Big Foot Horse Trail System

3 = Harrison Experimental Forest

4 = Railroad Creek Titi Swamp

5 = Tuxachanie Trail

M A P 8. Biloxi Ranger District, DeSoto National Forest

M 10   • **Bethel ATV Trail,** E of Saucier, Harrison, and Stone counties (two trail loops totaling 68 miles). The trailhead is on FS 426-C just north of Bethel Road, about 11 miles due east of Saucier and U.S. Hwy 49. A 38-mile loop is north of Bethel Road and a 30-mile loop is south of the road. Despite their length, neither loop extends more than 4 miles from the trailhead. The Biloxi Ranger District office distributes detailed maps of the trails.

M 9–10   • **Big Foot Horse Trail System,** NE of Saucier, Stone, and Harrison counties. This network, with more than 30 miles of trail, overlaps and partially shares the route of the Tuxachanie Trail. Most of it runs through longleaf and slash pine forests, some with dense understories of gallberry and yaupon, others grassy as a result of the Forest Service's prescribed burning program. The portions near streams are in the dense shade of hardwoods.

The trail is marked with brown metal horse-and-rider signs and horseshoes dipped in varied colors of paint and nailed in trees. Different trails and loops are marked with different colors. The system is likely to be further expanded. There are several water sources for horses along the trails.

 Most of the trails are within 100' of gravel roads, and some segments are occasionally routed on the roads. The only portions interesting for hikers are two trails that do not parallel roads. One, about 0.9 mile long, connects FS 440 and 420. It follows a dummy line much of the way; in one spot you may see remnants of the old ties. The other is the looped portion of the Tuxachanie Trail. Somewhere near FS 420 on the eastern part of the trail system is the site of the Carr still. Turpentine was distilled here during the railroad logging days.

Facilities: The Trail Riders Camp has hitching racks, a watering hole for horses, parking, flat spaces for camping, privies, tables, grills, and lampposts but no drinking water.

Maps: The Forest Service issued an updated free brochure on the Big Foot Horse Trail System in 1993. The trails are also shown on the large-scale 1984 DeSoto National Forest map and the 1983 Tuxachanie Trail map, but depictions of the Big Foot Trail system are out of date and do not show the western part of the network accurately. Specific errors include the following. (a) A bridge that once crossed Tuxachanie Creek about 0.8 mile north of the POW Camp is gone. Horses cannot cross the deeply entrenched creek bed. (b) No trail parallels Big Foot Creek; the trail segment depicted as doing so actually runs alongside FS 420-B.

• **Harrison Experimental Forest,** near Saucier, Harrison County, includes a 90-acre "wild tract" accessible by a short trail, which is marked along the road that begins opposite the experimental forest headquarters along State Hwy 67 about six miles east of U.S. Hwy 49 at Saucier. The wild tract is a longleaf pine forest with a palmetto understory on a relatively high sand ridge, unusual habitat for Mississippi.

M 9

• **Railroad Creek Titi Swamp,** NW corner of Jackson County. This swamp along both sides of Railroad Creek is covered with a dense growth of titi shrubs. Among them is the largest known white titi (*Cyrilla racemiflora*) in the state. Other dominant plants include black titi (*Cliftonia monophylla*) with a widely scattered overstory of cypress and slash pine. The Forest Service has considered designating it a botanical area, but it has not studied the area or proposed boundaries. The area is in T.4S, R.9W, Secs. 27, 28, 33, and 34. This is about one mile east of State Hwy 15 and north of Bethel Road. See the Beatrice 7.5′ topographic map.

M 10

• **Tuxachanie Trail,** NE of Saucier, Harrison, and Stone counties. This 19.7-mile hiking trail includes a 12.6-mile loop also open to horseback riders. The Black Creek Trail is longer and wilder, but the Tuxachanie National Recreation Trail is more varied and has more features of historic interest. Constructed in the early 1970s, it is the state's oldest long hiking trail. It is marked by white painted diamonds on trees.

M 9–10

U.S. Highway 49 to Airey Lake (4.8 miles): This part of the trail follows an old railroad grade that once carried logs and naval stores (resin) to the mill of the Dantzler Lumber Company at Howison along the Illinois Gulf Railroad track. It is Mississippi's only formally designated Rail-to-Trail, although it is by no means the only trail that follows an abandoned railroad grade (locally known as dummy lines). The railroad was built in the early 1900s by Irish immigrant laborers using hand tools and mule-powered scoops. Trestles once spanned the gaps in the elevated grade.

Rows of live oaks near the parking area along U.S. Hwy 49 were planted in 1935 by Posey N. Howell, the "Father of Mississippi Forestry." Howell was Dantzler's land manager when the Forest Service purchased 90,500 acres of cutover timberland from the company in 1935. Loggers spared occasional spike top and crooked virgin trees that Howell had marked with tags reading: "This is a Mother Tree. DO NOT CUT." They became seed trees that helped regenerate new forests.

According to Forest Service records, the first quarter mile of the trail crosses the site of a 1920s logging camp. An old millpond (now a lily pond), sites of homes and other buildings, and stands of trees that grew up after the camp was abandoned can still be seen. When funding is available the Forest Service hopes to label points of interest.

Mountain laurels, more typical of the Appalachians than of Mississippi, grow along West Creek. Farther on, the trail takes you through sand hills with cacti and palmettos. In the fall, small red flowers on the sand hills attract hordes of migrating yellow butterflies.

Airey Lake to beginning of loop (2.3 miles): The campground at Airey Lake makes a delightful base camp. The lake is a small impoundment filled with water lilies. The Forest Service provides privies, drinking water, and two picnic tables. Much of the trail passes through stands of large longleaf pines.

Along the way is a sign marking Copeland Springs. The name commemorates James Copeland (1823–57), the infamous outlaw leader of the Copeland Clan. He began his short life of adventure and crime at age 12, when he and his friends burned down the Jackson County courthouse to destroy evidence that he had been stealing pigs. They went on to loot and burn downtown Mobile and ranged from Texas to Ohio, stealing horses and cattle and bilking gullible Christians, throwing in some cold-blooded murders for good measure. Slave stealing was another Clan specialty. Actually, the slaves stole themselves when the smooth-talking clansmen convinced them that they would be led to freedom. Instead, they were taken "down the river" and sold. Copeland survived a shootout with the law at a remote log cabin on Black Creek in 1848 but was arrested the following year. He was hanged at Augusta (across the river from New Augusta). Copeland's memoirs, recorded by his jailer, J. R. S. Pitts (*The Life and Confession of the Noted Outlaw*, reprinted in 1980 and 1993), are recommended for anyone who wants to get the feel of life in the Mississippi piney woods before the era of cleancut logging.

About a quarter mile before the junction of the looped portion of the trail, you will cross a small stream on a bridge. Just beyond is a level site under large longleaf pines suitable for backpack camping.

12.4-Mile Loop: Most of the loop is open to both horses and hikers. To avoid getting sidetracked on another trail in the Big Foot Horse Trail System, watch for the painted white diamonds on trees that mark the Tuxachanie Trail. (The other Big Foot trails are marked by colored horseshoes nailed in trees.) Many parts of the loop follow dummy lines (abandoned logging railroads). Dummy lines tend to be slightly elevated, run in more or less straight lines, and are interrupted at stream crossings (once spanned by trestles).

The western half of the loop follows Tuxachanie Creek, which is deeply entrenched and overhung with trees. The creek was scoured by floodwaters in the spring of 1992 and is filled with the trunks of uprooted trees. The narrow hiking trail winds near the creek and is largely separate from the horse trail. A few hundred feet north of the bridge across Spike Buck Creek, a tributary of Tuxachanie Creek, watch for an old still. This part of Mississippi was once famous for its moonshine whiskey.

The eastern part of the loop goes through pine forests of varying ages. Before it was rerouted in about 1990, the trail went through wet savannas, habitat for yellow-flowered pitcher plants and wild miniature orchids that bloom in May and June.

The Old POW Camp: Via a side trail, the site is 0.3 mile from the Tuxachanie Trail loop. During World War II, German prisoners of war were kept near the lake. You can still see the foundations of the buildings where they stayed on the east side of the gravel access road just south of the lake. The large semicylindrical concrete structures were ammunition bunkers for a navy rifle range. The site is excellent for primitive camping under longleaf pines. No facilities are provided.

Best Time to Visit: Mountain laurels bloom along the western part of trail in early spring, pitcher plants and small orchids in May and June. Fall colors peak in late October and early November.

Maps and Literature: The Forest Service's general map of the DeSoto National Forest is adequate, but there is also a special topographic map just for the trail. The eastern part of the Big Foot Horse Trail System is not accurately depicted.

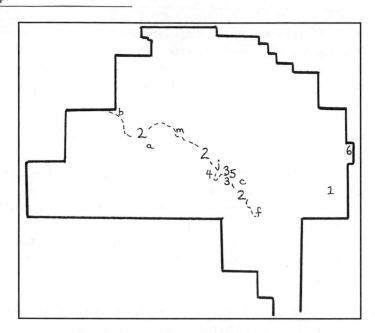

MAP 9. Black Creek Ranger District, DeSoto National Forest

LEGEND

a	=	Ashe Lake Recreation Area	2	=	Black Creek Trail
b	=	Big Creek Landing	3	=	Black Creek Wilderness Area
c	=	Cypress Creek Landing	4	=	General Jackson Trail
f	=	Fairley Bridge Landing	5	=	Howard-Breland Cemetery Trail
j	=	Janice Landing			
m	=	Moody's Landing	6	=	Leaf Wilderness Area and Trail
l	=	Big Southern Magnolia Tree			

BLACK CREEK RANGER DISTRICT,
USDA Forest Service, Box 248, 1436 Border and Frontage Rd., Wiggins, MS 39577 (601-928-4422)

Most of the district is in the watershed of Black Creek, a major tributary of the Pascagoula River. The relatively fertile soils produce large pines and hardwoods. In addition to the trails described below, the Forest Service was planning a 30-mile-long ATV trail with the cooperation of two motorcycle clubs in the fall of 1993. The trail will also be open to mountain bicycles. Camp Shelby, an installation of the Mississippi National Guard, uses much of the ranger district north of Black Creek for training maneuvers. If you spend weekends in the Black Creek area, you may hear the boom of distant artillery and perhaps the shrill roar of low-flying jet planes.

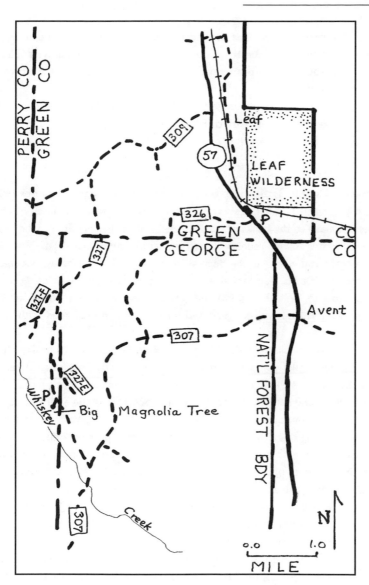

MAP 10. Big Southern Magnolia Tree and Leaf Wilderness

• **Big Southern Magnolia Tree,** W of Leaf, George/Perry County line. L 10
This is one of the largest southern magnolia trees in Mississippi. I don't have an
estimate of the age of this grand old tree, covered with decades worth of
carved initials. In 1974 it was 14′6″ in circumference (4′7″ average diameter) at
breast height, had a crown spread of 70′ and was 100′ high. No doubt it has
grown slightly since then.

As of January 1991, at least one larger southern magnolia has been discovered in Mississippi. The current state champion is in Smith County. It is 20′3″ in circumference (6′5″ in diameter), stands 122 feet tall, and has a crown diameter of 63′3″.

The tree is on the eastern edge of the Leaf River Wildlife Management Area along Whiskey Creek just east of FS 327. A short spur road ends in a small parking area. From there, a short switchback trail leads down to the tree.

L 9–10

• **Black Creek Trail,** near Brooklyn, Forrest, and Perry counties (40.8-mile hiking trail). This national recreation trail is exclusively for hikers. Sometimes it is close to the banks of Black Creek, with its banks of pure white sand and clear water stained reddish black from natural tannic acid. In the floodway of the creek you will be in the deep shade of magnolias, sweetbay, sweetgum, tulip trees, and oaks. You pass at least one oxbow lake lined with bald cypress and tupelo gum. At other points the route swings away from the creek into rolling hills forested with longleaf and loblolly pine interspersed with steep ravines.

The trail is well blazed with white paint rectangles. Eighty-two bridges, from 6′ to 42′ long, take you across streamlets and ravines. The steepest terrain along the trail is in the Red Hills near the southeastern end, but there are numerous short and sometimes steep ups and downs along the entire route.

Twenty-one miles of Black Creek, almost entirely federally owned from Moody's Landing to Fairley Bridge, constitute Mississippi's only designated national wild and scenic river. Logging is prohibited in a corridor of varying width along the stream to protect the scenery along the creek. Mountain bicycles are prohibited along the entire trail because of this corridor.

The trail was constructed between 1979 and 1982. It was intended to be the first segment of the National Bartram Historical Trail of Mississippi, which would arc its way across southern Mississippi from George County to the Pearl River opposite Bogalusa, Louisiana. The roughly 240-mile route was proposed in 1978 as part of the National Trails System, but nothing has been built except the Black Creek Trail.

Access: The trail extends from Big Creek Landing on the northwest to Fairley Bridge Landing at the southeastern end. The Forest Service has built parking areas at both landings and also at two other sites along the trail. One is at the former site of a Civilian Conservation Corps camp south of Brooklyn, and the other is on the west side of Hwy 29, 0.3 mile south of the bridge over Black Creek at Janice Landing.

The parking areas at Big Creek Landing and the CCC camp are close to Brooklyn and other rural communities and are often used by local people for activities other than camping. There are occasional reports of vandalism at these sites.

The trail crosses several other roads. You will have to watch carefully for the modest signs that guide hikers across the roads, and you may have to search for a place to park.

Notes on Major Segments of the Trail: The notes below were made in October 1992, going from west to east. Outside the wilderness area, some of the maturing forests may have been logged, and some of the recently logged areas have grown up into dense tickets of young trees and brush. You may find some changes when you hike the trail.

Big Creek Landing to Rockhill-to-Brooklyn Rd. (Rt. 335) (2.9 miles): The trail follows Black Creek closely through mature loblolly pines and southern magnolias.

Rockhill-to-Brooklyn Rd. (Rt. 335) to Point Where Trail Leaves FS 319F-1 (6.5 miles): Here the trail turns south away from the creek, taking you through loblolly and longleaf pine forests with hardwood bottoms between Rt. 335 and U.S. Hwy 49. You can explore the site of an abandoned Civilian Conservation Corps camp and find old roads and concrete foundations. This is the least wild section of the trail. It goes around the edges of several recently logged areas, and follows a road (FS 319F-1) for 0.4 mile.

FS 319F-1 to FS 319G (7.0 miles): This segment begins with a delightful walk along an entrenched meandering stream lined with impressively large trees (southern magnolia, beech, water oak, etc.) until you reach the edge of Black Creek. East of the next tributary creek crossing, you walk through the lower edge of a recently logged area. Much of this portion of the trail is on higher ground through pines. Overall, it's a pretty segment.

FS 319G to State Hwy 29 (6.8 miles): You start down a grassy lane through pines and descend to a wild section along Black Creek until you reach some recent logging. Then the trail goes through more pines and descends to a flat area with dense understory. A long part of the trail is on split-log "stepping stones." Nonetheless, plan on getting your feet wet, because shallow water may also stand in other portions that lack stepping stones or boardwalks. Next, the longest boardwalk on the trail takes you over a pretty swamp that is not shown on the map.

Finally the trail returns to the creek. Near this point, perhaps on the sharp bend of Black Creek, Joseph Mimm had a ferry in the early 1800s for travelers on the long-abandoned Old Federal Road. It went from Fort Stoddert on the

Tombigbee River in Alabama west to the John Ford house in Marion County and on to Natchez. Andrew Jackson and his army camped here on the night of November 25, 1814, on their way to the Battle of New Orleans. Between here and Hwy 29 you will cross and recross a recent low-standard logging access road.

State Hwy 29 Parking Lot to Hwy 29 Bridge over Beaverdam Creek (2.7 miles): Here the trail enters the Black Creek Wilderness. It follows the west side of Beaverdam Creek through dense woods, skirting the edges of deep, flat-bottomed ravines studded with bald cypress. The creek itself is in a trench. You see it only twice, and it is difficult to get down to the stream.

Hwy 29 Bridge over Beaverdam Creek to Spur Trail from Andrews Chapel on New York Rd. (Rt. 382) (0.4 mile): The trail leaves the Wilderness to cross Beaverdam Creek on the highway bridge and reenters it on the other side. Several cars can park off the highway on the southwest side of the bridge. The trail leads through hilly pine woods, joining the unmarked access trail from Andrews Chapel.

Spur trail from Andrews Chapel on New York Rd. to FS 382B (7.7 miles): If you don't feel secure leaving your car along Hwy 29, you can park near the wooden sign reading "Black Creek Wilderness" at the east side of Andrews Chapel. An unmarked but well-worn trail begins near the sign and leads to the Black Creek Trail, which has white paint blazes.

The Black Creek Trail descends from the pine-covered hills and follows the east side of Beaverdam Creek. This is a beautiful stream, the largest you encounter on the trail apart from Black Creek itself. It's generally in a deep, narrow trench overhung by large trees. You will see much more of the stream on this side than you will on the west side, and you can get down to the creek easily in some spots.

Eventually you reach Black Creek. There's an excellent campsite on a high sandbar overlooking the confluence of Black and Beaverdam creeks.

The route continues along the creek through mature forests in very deep shade to Mills Creek. Here you will find another excellent campsite in mature pines about 500' off the trail on the west side of the confluence with Black Creek. After crossing this rather large stream, the trail turns south and follows an old road to a gas pipe corridor at the eastern edge of the wilderness area. This is the wildest part of the trail and also the most scenic.

FS 382B to FS 318B-1 (4.3 miles): The trail descends to Black Creek, where you'll find a good campsite or lunch spot with an obvious trail leading to a sandbar favored by canoeists. Then the trail turns back and climbs into the rugged Red Hills. The route goes up and down ridgelines and crosses ravines on picturesque bridges over flowing streams. Interestingly, the hills don't seem particularly red except on recently scraped roads.

FS 318B-1 to Fairley Bridge Landing (2.5 miles): The route gradually leaves the Red Hills (each little ravine is less well pronounced) and then crosses a flat area with longleaf pine and very dense understory. The section between FS 318 and the end of the trail is pretty, with lots of rhododendron and a tree with a huge burl. There is no water along this section except where FS 374 crosses Bug Branch.

Car Shuttles: You can start your hike at either end of the trail or at a road crossing. If you have only a single car in your party and no one to meet you at another road crossing, you can turn around and retrace your steps. If you don't want to do so, you can arrange with Black Creek Canoe Rental in Brooklyn to let you off where you want to start. The livery will take your car to where you want to end your trip (Black Creek Canoe Rental, P.O. Box 414, Brooklyn, MS 39425; 601-582-8817). Call in advance to make arrangements and for up-to-date information on the level of Black Creek.

Backpacking Notes: Plan on taking at least four days to hike the entire 40.8 miles of the trail. Five days are better for most parties. If you plan on taking six days, you will have time for a layover day along Black Creek.

Some of the nicest campsites are on sandbars along Black Creek. The trail tends to approach the edge of the creek closely on the outside of bends, where the current undercuts the bank to create steep drops to the creek. It usually leaves the creek on the inside of bends, where you are most likely to find gentle terrain and sandbars. You may want to leave the trail to look for these sites.

You should have no trouble finding water for camping along the trail away from Black Creek. When I hiked the trail it had rained only once in the last month, but most of the streams marked as intermittent on the topographic map were flowing, as were some not marked on the map at all.

Combined Canoe/Backpack Trip: It's about the same distance from Big Creek Landing to Fairley Bridge landing (41 miles) by canoe or on the Black Creek Trail. You can plan a round trip, going downstream by canoe and upstream by the trail, by hiding your canoe and canoe-related equipment out of sight of roads and the stream. To lessen the possibility of losing your canoe, chain it to a tree.

Generally, it will take you less time to cover the distance by canoe than on foot. Black Creek Canoe Rental suggests allotting the following times for canoeing the creek: Big Creek Landing to Old Brooklyn Bridge (old Hwys 49, 316), 5 hours; Old Brooklyn Bridge to Janice Landing, 8.5 hours; Janice Landing to Fairley Bridge Landing, 5.5 hours. Plan on spending three whole days on the creek in addition to the five or six days on the trail to make the complete circuit from Big Creek Landing to Fairley Bridge Landing and back.

Facilities: The Forest Service has provided five boat landings for float trips along Black Creek. Starting at the northwest end, they are: Big Creek, Moody's, Janice, Cypress Creek, and Fairley Bridge. Moody's Landing is only a picnic site. The other four are good base camps for day trips. They are popular for camping and may be filled to capacity in the spring. Fairley Bridge Landing has two tables and chemical toilets. Big Creek has only one table and no privies.

The camping area near Cypress Creek Landing was improved in 1992 and has new tables, gravel tent pads, drinking water, and chemical toilets but no RV hookups. A resident campground host closes the gate to the camping area at 10:00 P.M. It's one of the few Forest Service campgrounds I've seen in the last decade that has been improved without converting it to a fee-area campground. (Cypress Creek is on the opposite side of Black Creek from the Black Creek Trail, and the only way to get across is by boat or by swimming—not advisable when the creek is high.)

Maps: The Forest Service's map of the entire DeSoto National Forest is adequate for hiking and canoeing Black Creek, but the Service has also issued a topographic map printed on water-resistant paper for Black Creek hikers and canoeists. Unfortunately, mileages are not given for the trail.

L 9   • **Black Creek Wilderness Area,** NE of Wiggins, Perry County (5,050 acres). The Black Creek Wilderness Area was established by the U.S. Congress in 1984. The entire area that is now the Black Creek Ranger District was cleancut between 1890 and 1932. The forest in the wilderness has regenerated naturally. Many of the trees along Black Creek are impressively large today. The wilderness area does include a few pine plantations on the higher ground that date from the 1970s. No logging, motor vehicles, or pedal-powered trail bikes are allowed within the wilderness.

So far, the area shows few signs of overuse or abuse by recreationists. If you backpack into the area, pack out all your trash, and build campfires only on sandbars along Black Creek or in very cold weather and in emergencies.

Fully 10.8 miles of the Black Creek Trail meander through the designated wilderness area. The Howard-Breland Cemetery Trail, an abandoned road that is now an informal trail, enters the wilderness from the north (see below).

- **General Jackson Trail** (0.25-mile loop). This level trail is barrier free with a crushed rock base. It begins and ends at the parking lot for the Black Creek Trail along State Hwy 29, 0.3 mile south of the bridge over Black Creek at Janice Landing. Large signs along the trail describe Jackson's march to the Battle of New Orleans along the Old Federal Road in 1814. For more information, see the description of the Black Creek Trail between FS 319G and Hwy 29.

L 9

- **Howard-Breland Cemetery Trail,** Black Creek Wilderness Area, NE of Wiggins, Perry County (ca. 0.8 mile). If you would like to hike into the north side of the wilderness, you can follow an abandoned one-lane gravel road that leads south 0.8 mile from FS 305 to a remote little cemetery with headstones dating from 1877 to 1907. The road is not maintained as a trail but is easy to follow. It's about a 20-minute walk one way. A couple of nongravel side roads diverge along the way; stick to the gravel path. The old road begins at a gate less than 0.1 mile west of the bridge over Cypress Creek.

L 9

- **Leaf Wilderness Area,** south of Leaf, Greene County (940 acres, one-mile hiking trail). The Leaf Wilderness is a rectangular section of the floodway of the Leaf River but doesn't get closer than 0.2 mile to the river itself.

L 10

A delightful trail about a mile long leads into the area from State Hwy 57 south of the community of Leaf. It crosses the track of the Illinois Central Gulf Railroad and follows the bluffs along the southern edge of the area. Here you will see lots of bigleaf magnolia, mature loblolly pine, white oak, and occasional beech. Then the trail descends into the floodplain. When the leaves are on the trees, this is a dark world with little or no understory, dominated by the wide, buttressed trunks of water oak, overcup oak, and other bottomland hardwoods. Flooded portions must frequently be crossed on two-plank boardwalks and small bridges. The trail then parallels a deep slough. Here you are likely to surprise a wood duck or two or to hear the splash of the tail of an alert beaver. It dead ends at the junction of another slough, which is empty in the fall, so you can continue on if you like.

According to Forest Service records, the largest water oak on the Black Creek District stands 300' to 500' off the trail. It measures approximately 60" in diameter at breast height. Its age has not been determined but is estimated to be 150 to 250 years.

The Leaf Wilderness was established in 1984 at the same time as the Black Creek Wilderness. It is undoubtedly one of the smallest designated wilderness areas in the country's national forests.

Best Time to Visit: You should be able to get into the area via the hiking trail most of the year except when floodwaters are exceptionally high. From late winter through spring much of the floodplain will be under water.

Access: The parking lot is prominently marked on the east side of State Hwy 57 1.5 miles south of Leaf.

Maps: You don't need a map to follow the trail. For cross-country walking, I recommend the Forest Service's large map of Black Creek, which includes a map of the Leaf Wilderness. The 1989 edition does not show the trail or parking area.

CHICKASAWHAY RANGER DISTRICT,

USDA Forest Service, Box 426, 481 S. Magnolia St., Laurel, MS 39440 (601-428-0594)

The district was named after the Chickasawhay River because most of its streams are tributaries of that river, which empties into the Pascagoula River. It is named after the Chickasawhay Indians, an offshoot of the Chickasaw Nation. The word means "the Indians who eat bog potatoes."

The virgin forests on the district included the finest longleaf pines in Mississippi. When Ray Conarro, Mississippi's first national forest supervisor, inspected the land in 1933, however, he reported that he had never viewed an area so large with so much devastation. Once the land had been purchased, the Civilian Conservation Corps went to work replanting the land with slash pines.

J 9–10
K 9–10
 • **Gavin Auto Tour,** SE of Laurel, Jones County (12-mile driving loop on gravel roads). The route follows FS 213, 218, 202, and 270. A number of different ways of thinning and logging slash pine are highlighted. The Civilian Conservation Corps planted them in the 1930s on the 1,800-acre Gavin Plantation, which the Forest Service had purchased from the Bently-Pope Lumber Company at Ovett. When the federal government acquired the land, it had been completely denuded of its original longleaf pine forest except for bits of scattered scrub timber. It's hard to believe today that none of the tall trees you drive through were there before 1935. You will also see impressive forests of longleaf pines.

The texts of the signs are rather technical and are likely to appeal to professional foresters and people who are seriously interested in national forest management. The "Unmanaged 40"—40 acres that have not been touched in any way since 1945—are especially interesting to naturalists.

K 10
 • **Little Tiger ATV Trail,** E of Ovett, Jones, and Wayne counties (36

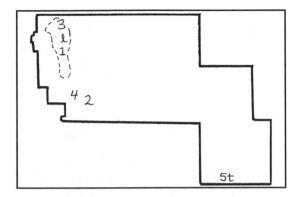

MAP II. Chickasawhay Ranger District, DeSoto National Forest

LEGEND

I	= Longleaf Trail Camp	3	= Longleaf Trail System
t	= Turkey Fork Recreation Area	4	= Tiger Creek Botanical Area
l	= Gavin Auto Tour	5	= Turkey Fork Nature Trail
2	= Little Tiger ATV Trail		

miles of trail in two loops). This broad trail goes mostly through forests of longleaf and slash pine and crosses several streams on bridges. It is designed for ATVs but is also open to hikers and horseback riders. A 23-mile loop is marked in blue and a 13-mile loop, in white. The trail was constructed by the Forest Service and Little Tiger ATV Riders Association.

Access: The official trailhead, with a parking area and signboard, is at the end of FS 220. The route to the trailhead is marked along State Hwy 15 south of Laurel.

Maps and Literature: A copy of a topographic map showing the trail is available from the Chickasawhay Ranger District office. A descriptive brochure will eventually be issued.

● **Longleaf Trail System,** Laurel, Jones County (26 miles of trail). One of the two longest looped trails in Mississippi; loops of up to 23 miles are possible. Built in the 1980s with the cooperation of horseback riders, the Longleaf Trail is not shown on most maps. Marked trails lead through open stands of longleaf and slash pines. Usually the pines rise straight up through an understory of brush dominated by gallberry, but the route also leads through grassy glades and past small fenced meadows planted with food for wildlife. At the

J 9–10
K 9–10

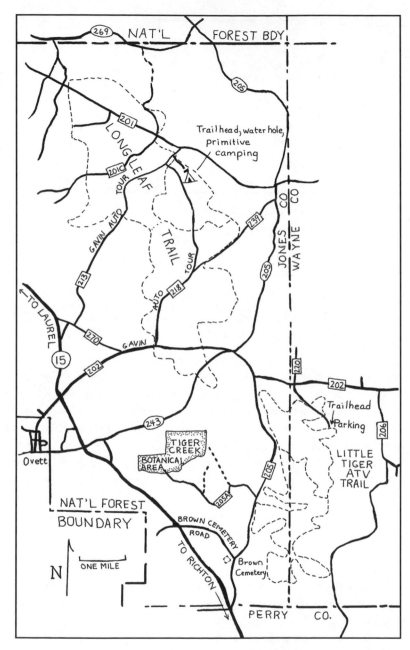

MAP 12. Little Tiger ATV Trail, Longleaf Horse Trail, Gavin Auto Tour, and Tiger Creek Botanical Area

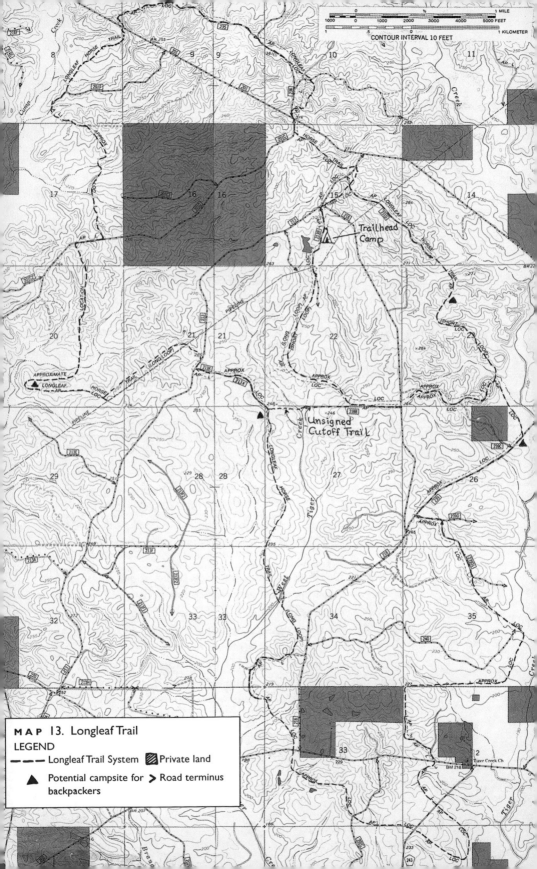

MAP 13. Longleaf Trail

LEGEND

– – – Longleaf Trail System   ▨ Private land

▲ Potential campsite for   ➤ Road terminus
backpackers

CONTOUR INTERVAL 10 FEET

Trailhead Camp

Unsigned Cutoff Trail

Tiger Creek Ch
BM 218

southern end of the route in Sec. 33 is an extensive open grassy area—the Dennis Tract. The Forest Service purchased this pasture 10 or 15 years ago and is now maintaining it as a wildlife area. In striking contrast is the deep shade along the various intermittent tributaries of Tiger Creek. The main stream of West Tiger Creek is the only perennial stream.

The trail route mainly follows old "woods roads" closed to vehicles. Only in a few spots does it follow maintained gravel roads. The trail is often a narrow "one-lane" track when it crosses bottomlands.

Two circuit routes are marked with metal diamonds nailed on trees: the 23-mile circuit marked with white, and a 6-mile circuit with orange. The circuits are irregular and cross and recross several gravel roads, inviting shorter circuits. There is also a well-used but unmarked cutoff in Secs. 21 and 22 that turns the 23-mile circuit into a crooked figure **8**.

The height and denseness of the understory depend on when the last prescribed burn took place. The Forest Service regularly burns pine forests, generally in the winter, to suppress the understory and the hardwood trees that would eventually dominate the forest if no fires occurred. The light burns char the trunks of the pines but don't otherwise harm them. Wildflowers are most abundant in stands burned a year or two previously.

The round black berries of the gallberry shrub are sour, but you will find lush blackberry thickets in some meadows and along the edges of regenerating clearcuts. Blackberries are ripe in June and July.

Colonies of endangered red-cockaded woodpeckers survive in the middle of Sec. 34 east of the bridge over the main fork of West Tiger Creek and also in Sec. 26 near the junction of FS 239 and 239D. As you walk the northwest part of the trail in Sec. 20, you will be on an old railroad grade, or "dummy line," a remnant of the network of temporary railroads built to strip the original forest.

You will also notice many barbed wire fences in the woods. These are remnants of the time when the forest was essentially a sea of grass studded with stumps and immature little pine trees after the cleancut logging was finished by the early 1930s. The Forest Service once leased the entire ranger district in grazing, but the leases are now being phased out.

Some of the best potential campsites for backpackers are shown on map 13. Most are on grassy knolls near intermittent streams. Usually you will find pools of water in these streams and also water in nearby mud puddles. Boil any water before drinking it. For a long backpacking trip, you could fill plastic jugs with water and cache them along the road/trail intersection near where you plan to camp.

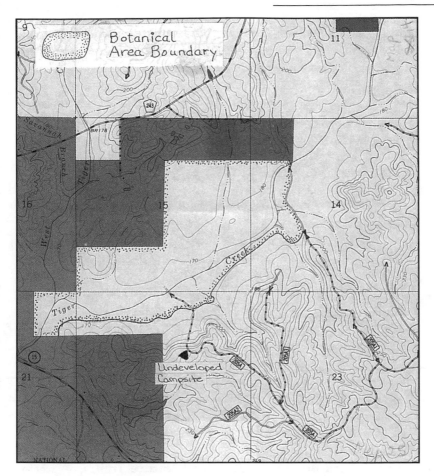

MAP 14. Tiger Creek Botanical Area. Shaded areas are private land.

Facilities: The trailhead of the Longleaf Trail is an excellent primitive camp-site, with chemical toilets, trash cans, parking spurs and hitching rails for horse trailers, and two picnic tables. Horses can water at Gator Pond adjacent to the campground, but there is no drinking water.

Maps and Literature: The 1988 edition of the Forest Service's map of the Chickasawhay Ranger District does not show the trail.

● **Tiger Creek Botanical Area,** E of Ovett, Jones County (525 acres). K 9–10
The area encompasses flat, frequently flooded hardwood bottoms on both sides of Tiger Creek, just upstream from the junction of West Tiger Creek,

and a terrace 20' high on the north side of the creek. Bottomland trees include white oak, water oak, black gum, swamp chestnut oak, beech, southern red oak, water tupelo, sweetgum, bald cypress, red maple, and spruce pine. Large loblolly and longleaf pines dominate the terrace. A rich understory of small trees and shrubs grows under the pines, which have not been burned because of the site's remoteness. A four-acre wetland in the northwest portion of the area contains pitcher plants, pipewort, and other bog species. Significant portions of the bottomland and pockets of pine may have been spared from the cleancut logging in the early 1900s.

The Forest Service plans to construct a parking area, a footbridge across Tiger Creek, and a hiking trail within the botanical area when funds are available.

Best Time to Visit: The area is worth visiting any time of year. Until the Forest Service builds a bridge across Tiger Creek, however, you may have to ford it, and this could be uncomfortable in the winter.

Nearby Primitive Campsite: The state Department of Wildlife has designated a campsite for hunters in a grassy clearing at the end of FS 205A at the point where the road becomes impassable for automobiles. It has no shade, and the only improvement is a trash can. During the hunting seasons, you must camp in this site. At other times of the year, there are other, more pleasant primitive campsites along this access road and side roads. Bring water.

Maps and Literature: The Forest Service's 1988 map of the Chickasawhay Ranger District does not show the proposed botanical area, which lies largely in the federally owned portion of T.6N, R.10W, Sec. 15.

K 10   • **Turkey Fork Recreation Area and Nature Trail,** E of Richton, Greene County (0.8-mile-long nature trail). The nature trail is one of many fea-

tures at this large recreation area, which boasts a 240-acre lake. The trail runs from the swimming/picnic area to the kiosk at the entrance to the campground. In 1991, it was not marked by a sign in the picnic area, but it starts at the edge of the woods at the west side (on your left as you face the lake). A lovely, sinuously curved boardwalk built by the Youth Conservation Corps in the 1970s takes you across a sweetbay bog. Near the campground you walk through a beautiful longleaf pine forest.

The kiosk has information on archaeological investigations in and near the campground and along the portions of the Turkey Fork now flooded by the reservoir. The earliest campsites date from the Archaic period (8,500–7,500 years ago). Native Americans of the Woodland culture had a seasonal base camp in the campground between 1,000–700 years ago.

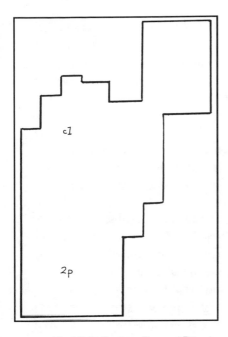

LEGEND

c   = Chewalla Lake Recreation Area

p   = Puskus Lake Recreation Area

1   = Chewalla Lake trails

2   = Puskus Lake trails

MAP 15. Holly Springs Ranger District, Holly Springs National Forest

HOLLY SPRINGS NATIONAL FOREST,

Hwy 78 East, Box 400, Holly Springs, MS 38635 (601-252-2633)(147,000 acres)

The Holly Springs National Forest includes two separate units. The smaller, the Yalobusha Management Unit, is entirely in Yalobusha County and is managed by the office of the Tombigbee National Forest at Ackerman. I know of no trails or natural areas in this unit.

The larger unit, the Holly Springs Ranger District, is filled with narrow ridges and hills. It was settled and deforested before the Civil War, mainly by small farmers. Their efforts to raise cotton and other crops failed because the soil was poor and highly erosion prone. By the 1930s much of it was abandoned. Shortleaf pines were reclaiming the land, which in places was sliced by deep red gullies. Sheep grazed the denuded slopes, exacerbating erosion. (See the Federal Writers Project *WPA Guide,* in the bibliography.)

The Holly Springs National Forest exists solely because of the efforts of one influential man, U.S. congressman Wall Doxey of Holly Springs. Doxey was committed to controlling erosion and reforesting abandoned lands in his district. Beginning in 1930, the Forest Service began to purchase land in Mississippi for national forests. Generally, the feds wanted large tracts owned by timber companies, not old farmsteads of less than 100 acres each. Mr. Doxey persuaded them to make an exception, however. Between 1934 and 1940, 110,000 acres of badly eroded land were purchased on the future ranger district, and the Civilian Conservation Corps was set to work reforesting the land. A large CCC camp at Potts Camp was open between 1933 and 1943.

The Forest Service has continued to purchase land on the district since 1940 but at a much slower rate, and it is also consolidating its holdings by swapping land with private owners. Still, public land within the national forest boundary remain scattered in isolated tracts—one reason that longer trails have not been developed and no natural areas have been designated.

B 9 • **Chewalla Lake Recreation Area and Trails,** SE of Holly Springs, Marshall County (planned 8-mile hiking trail network, partially constructed in 1992). Chewalla Lake is the largest reservoir in the Holly Springs National Forest and the only one with a fully developed recreation area, including a beach for swimming and campsites with RV hookups.

In the fall of 1992, a trail heading south from the large parking area adjacent to the picnic area had been completed. A new route below the dam has been marked with white paint squares and cleared below the dam, replacing the former hiking route across the top of the dam. The new route goes through hardwood bottoms and beside a pond with bald cypress.

The east side of the lake has an extensive network of old roads used by four-wheelers and horseback riders. Until the trails are marked, it will be easy to get temporarily lost here. The trail climbs up to the top of a hill to a clearing where a house once stood. Flowers remain at the site. You will see some deep gullies—reminders that the area was cleared, farmed, damaged by erosion, and abandoned before it was purchased by the federal government. Now the gullies barely rise above the trees and are impressive and scenic.

When a fisherman's ramp/bridge connecting the boat launch area with FS 611 on the east side of the lake is completed, you will have the option of making a four-mile circuit hike around the southern half of the lake. It's not likely that a trail making a complete circuit of the lake will be constructed because of extensive alder thickets on Chewalla Creek above the lake.

Chewalla Lake, designed for flood control, was constructed in 1966 on Chewalla Creek (in the Choctaw/Chickasaw language, "chihowa-la," meaning the Supreme Being). A small reconstructed Indian mound stands near the overlook in the recreation area. It replaces a mound predating the Chickasaw Indians that was inundated by the reservoir.

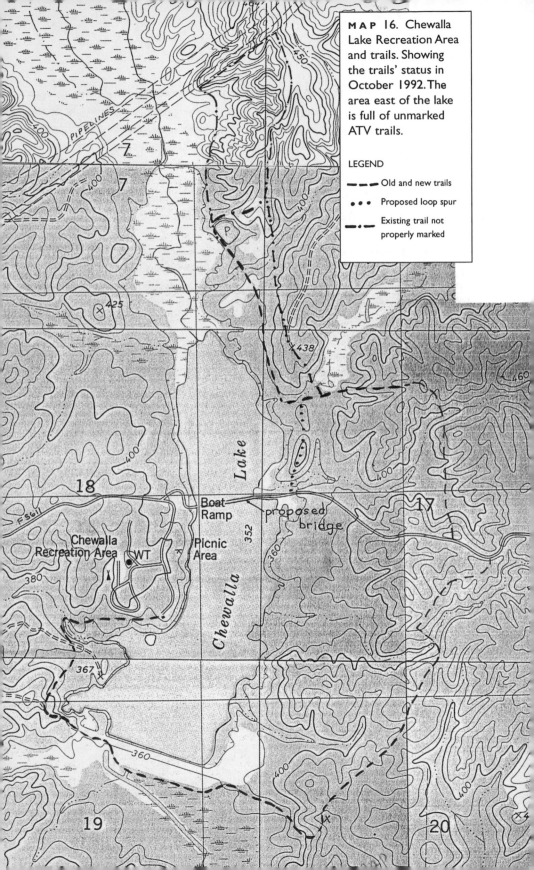

MAP 16. Chewalla Lake Recreation Area and trails. Showing the trails' status in October 1992. The area east of the lake is full of unmarked ATV trails.

LEGEND

– – – Old and new trails

• • • Proposed loop spur

–·–· Existing trail not properly marked

Facilities: The Holly Springs Lions Club has helped the Forest Service construct a ramp all the way from the boat launching ramp across the lake to the end of FS 611. It is designed to accommodate wheelchair-bound fishermen.

Access: If you are interested only in the trails and want to avoid paying an entrance fee to park in the recreation area, you can turn east on FS 634B, which leaves Higdon Road 0.4 mile south of the turnoff to the recreation area. The trail is about 100′ below the turn around/parking area at the end of the road.

Maps and Literature: As of 1992, no maps showed the trails. Use map 16.

C 9

- **Puskus Lake,** NE of Oxford, Lafayette County (2-mile interpretive trail network). Puskus Lake is a 96-acre reservoir on Puskus Creek in the southern part of the Holly Springs National Forest. The associated campground and picnic area are more remote and primitive than the recreation area at Chewalla Lake. The site is in hilly terrain, and individual campsites are perched on hillsides overlooking the lake.

The forest surrounding the lake is young and has lots of pines. A partially looped interpretive trail begins at the boat launch area. Signs identify trees and explain various aspects of plant ecology along the trail.

A nice stand of mature hardwoods is on the former meandering channel of Puskus Creek about a quarter mile below the dam. The stream has been channelized, but the old oxbows remain.

- **Mature and/or Old-Growth Timber Stands.** At least two are known in the Holly Springs National Forest. Stand 17 in Compartment 117 is designated a special study area on the recommendation of the Nature Conservancy and Mississippi Natural Heritage Program. It includes 25 acres of white oak, cherrybark oak, and other hardwoods that are as much as 114 years old. In 1993, beavers had a dam there. It's in the southwest corner of the national forest in Lafayette County north of FS 849 (T.8S, R.2W, Sec. 22).

Elsewhere in the forest are five acres of bald cypress that may be a virgin stand. The Forest Service can tell you of several other nice stands of mature hardwoods.

HOMOCHITTO NATIONAL FOREST
(187,195 acres)

The Homochitto NF, Mississippi's first national forest, is in the loess hills just east of Natchez. The national forest is divided into two ranger districts, the

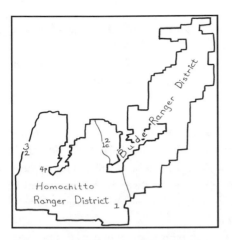

LEGEND

Bude Ranger District

c   =   Clear Springs Recreation
        Area

1   =   Clear Springs Trail

2   =   Clear Springs Nature Trail

Homochitto Ranger District

p   =   Pipes Lake Recreation Area

1   =   Brushy Creek area

2   =   Pellucid Bayou

3   =   Sandy Creek

4   =   Pipes Lake Nature Trail

MAP 17. Homochitto National Forest

Bude Ranger District in the northeastern half and the Homochitto Ranger District in the western half.

The terrain is a complicated maze of ridges and minivalleys. Most of it is in the watershed of the Homochitto River, which winds across the national forest in its wide bed of white sand.

The mantle of loess is 10′ to 15′ thick on the western side, thinning out to 4′ or less on the east. In comparison with the soil in other Mississippi national forests, it is fertile, and thus the pines and hardwoods are larger. Probably the original forest was mainly hardwoods, but loblolly pines predominate today.

From the late 1700s until the Civil War, much of what is now the western part of the Homochitto National Forest was held by large plantation owners. Initially they grew a variety of crops, including corn, wheat, rye, potatoes, and cotton. After the invention of the cotton gin, the crop shifted almost entirely to cotton. Fortunes were made, but the erosion-prone soils were exhausted in the process. Many cotton fields were abandoned just before and after the Civil War and were naturally reclaimed by pines.

The area was never subjected to the total cleancutting suffered by the piney woods region, but it did support several large lumber mills. The heyday of the logging era was between 1900 and 1910, but the last of the large mills did not close until 1940. Many small towns within the national forest boundary were once larger and much more prosperous. Appraisal of potential federal land purchases began in 1929. The first actual purchase was in 1933.

The name "Homochitto" means "red river" in Choctaw. Apparently the river was much deeper and narrower when the white man arrived. Sediment from eroding fields and slopes denuded of forests filled the riverbed with silt, making it wider and shallower.

The Homochitto NF has several oil and gas fields. You will not see any oil wells on the trails described below, but you may hear the rhythmical drone of an oil pump in the distance.

● **Old-Growth and Mature Timber Stands:** Eleven stands in the Homochitto are considered to be at least 100 years old. They include a thick 32-acre stand of bald cypress that originated in 1892, possibly after a blowdown, and a 25-acre stand of mixed pine and hardwoods that originated in 1895, from which the pines were subsequently removed. The Forest Service can tell you the locations of these stands.

Maps: Homochitto National Forest map (combined with map of the Delta NF), available from the Forest Service, is recommended.

BUDE RANGER DISTRICT,

USDA Forest Service, Rt. 1, Box 1, Meadville, MS 39653 (601-384-5876). The district office is on U.S. Hwy 84 and 98, E of Meadville

K 5

● **Clear Springs Trail,** SW of Meadville, Franklin County (10-mile loop). The trail has large pines, typical loess terrain of ridges and valleys, and a semi-wilderness setting.

Some of the loblolly pines in the forests traversed by the trail are impressively large. Here understory is sparse, and you can see a long way around you. The trail also goes past the upper edges of some clearcuts and crosses several large and small streams. It leads "across the grain" of typical loess terrain of ridges, little valleys, and box canyons. Plan on getting a good workout. It crosses roads five times in the circuit, but even so you will feel that you are in a remote place. The route is well marked with white paint blazes.

If you are lucky, you might come upon some evidence of the rare Louisiana black bear, a federal threatened species. Be on the lookout for bear sign, such as logs that have been turned over.

The existing loop is excellent for a two-day backpacking trip. The Forest Service plans to add another 15-mile loop onto the west side of the trail in the Homochitto Ranger District, so that one could hike 25 miles in a figure 8. A short interpretive trail is also planned, and the trail system will tie in with the short nature trail on the south side of Clear Springs Lake in the recreation area.

Maps and Literature: The trail was completed about 1989 and is too new to appear on maps. The Forest Service is preparing special map and brochure for the trail that should be available sometime in 1994.

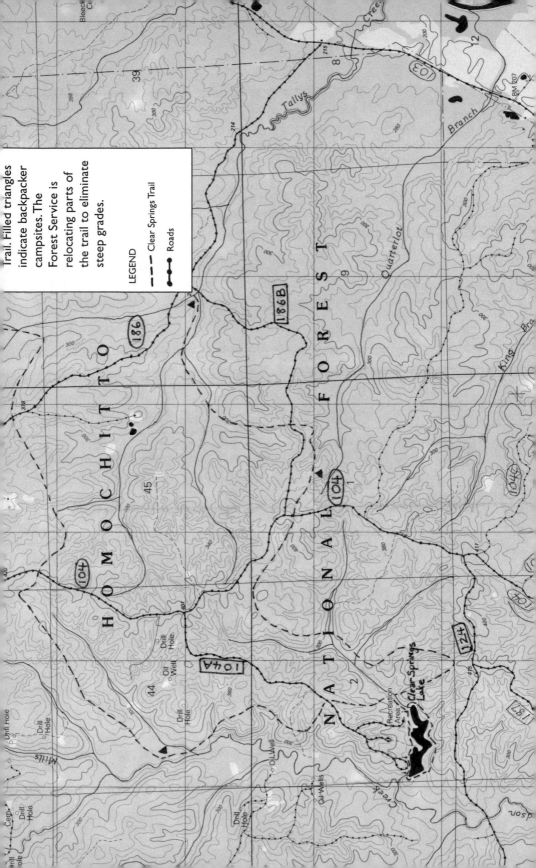

Trail. Filled triangles indicate backpacker campsites. The Forest Service is relocating parts of the trail to eliminate steep grades.

LEGEND

- - - Clear Springs Trail
•—•—• Roads

52

K 5

• **Clear Springs Recreation Area and Nature Trail,** SW of Mead-ville, Franklin County (0.9-mile loop trail). The trail circles the 12-acre lake in the recreation area, passing through maturing hardwoods and large pines. Along the way are benches and a gazebo overlooking the lake. When the 25-mile-long Clear Springs Trail system is completed, this trail will be at the middle of the anticipated figure 8 double-looped trail.

In 1927, before the national forest was established, the Homochitto Lumber Company of Bude had a logging road that ran through the center of the present lake. The recreation area was built by the Civilian Conservation Corps between 1937 and 1939. Up to 500 young men worked on the project at one time. The large log-and-stone picnic pavilion at the edge of the lake is a classic piece of CCC architecture. The campground is very popular and may be filled to capacity at the peak of the camping season in the spring and fall. A brochure with a map is available.

HOMOCHITTO RANGER DISTRICT,
USDA Forest Service, P.O. Box 398, Gloster, MS 39638 (601-225-4281). The office is on State Hwy 24, E of Gloster

K 5

• **Brushy Creek,** NE of Gloster, Amite County. This stream resembles Sandy Creek in the Sandy Creek Wildlife Management Area, with a wide bed of white sand. The creek and its tributaries—Long Branch, Brown Branch, Red Prong, and Clear Prong—all come together within a square mile and invite wading and exploration. There are no designated trails.

The area is in the southern end of the ranger district. You reach it by driving to the end of FS 106D.

K 4

• **Sandy Creek Wildlife Management Area,** SW of Roxie and NW of Crosby in Adams and Franklin counties (approximately 3,000 acres; at least five miles of unmaintained trails). The area has pockets of wild country reached by informal trails and cross-country hiking, with crystal clear streams. The trees tend to be rather large and free of understory. Sandy Creek is a braided stream in a wide bed of white sand. Pipes Lake nature trail leads under large trees at the edge of a remote small lake.

Sandy Creek WMA is so out of the way that in the late 1970s, a 2,375-acre portion centered on Pellucid Bayou was seriously studied for federal wilder-ness designation. Along with two small parcels in the DeSoto National Forest, it was one of only three candidate areas in all Mississippi's national forests. Sandy Creek was eventually dropped as a contender because several gravel

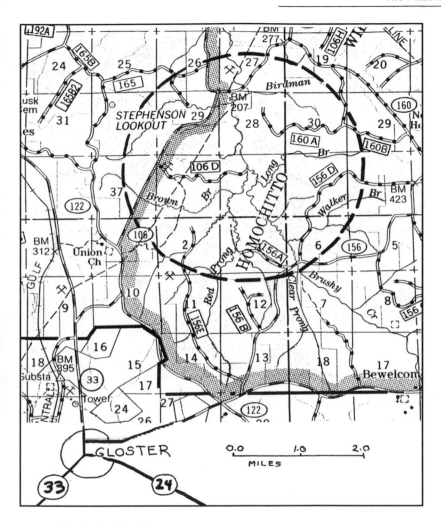

MAP 19. Brushy Creek

roads had already been built within it. Even so, remote and peaceful spots still remain along Pellucid Bayou, Pretty Creek, and the east side of Sandy Creek.

The rugged terrain is typical of the loess hills. Elevations range between 130' and 290' above sea level. Southern hardwoods predominate, with some mixed pine and hardwood forests and a few stands of pure loblolly pines.

Pellucid Bayou is a clear stream running over tan sand in a secluded hollow along Sandy Creek. Getting down to it is a beautiful walk on an abandoned road in the deep shade of hardwood forest. It begins at the intersection of FS 120 and 120B. Although the Forest Service's map of the Homochitto NF shows

FS 120B as an improved gravel road, it is actually abandoned and has a mound of earth bulldozed across the entrance to keep motorized vehicles out.

 Follow this road about 1.4 miles down to Pellucid Bayou. At the point where the old road crossed the bayou, you will see vertical posts in the streambed that are remnants of an old bridge. Trails continue on north and south in the heavily wooded flats paralleling an old railroad grade along Sandy Creek. A grove of large pines that would make a pretty, secluded backcountry campsite is near the mouth of Pellucid Bayou.

You could visit the area any time of year, but high water after prolonged periods of rain could make the streams too high for easy wading. Also, Pellucid Bayou is not pellucid then because of soil eroding from unrestrained clearcut logging that has occurred in the Sec. 16 land about a mile upstream.

 Sandy Creek is a braided stream twisting from side to side in its bed of white sand. You can walk along the east side of the creek a long way north and south of Pellucid Bayou. You can also drive almost to Sandy Creek via FS 119G and 173, both of which leave FS 120 and end just above the creek. You could probably walk the two miles from the end of FS 119G to Pellucid Bayou, walking partly in the woods on informal ATV trails and partly along the creek. You have to wade Sandy Creek from time to time, so bring shoes for comfortable walking with wet feet. If there has been a lot of rain, Sandy Creek may be too high for safe wading.

People often camp along Sandy Creek at the ends of FS 119G and 173. Chemical toilets have been set up, but no drinking water or tables are provided. The Jeannette topo map is useful for exploring the area.

 Pipes Lake Recreation Area and Nature Trail (2.2-mile loop trail) is at the end of FS 121-A at the southern end of the WMA. It is small but seems much larger than it really is because it has many arms. The high ground between the two arms of the lake has several picnic tables, a privy, and an observation platform. No drinking water is provided, and swimming is prohibited. The lake is popular with fishermen in season. Camping is permitted, but there is room only for small tents near the picnic tables.

The signs marking the beginning and end of the hiking trail that circles the lake were gone in 1992, but it is still marked with metal white diamonds nailed in trees and surveyors tape. It stays close to the edge of the lake. Your chances of seeing an egret or a heron are good. You will pass many large loblolly pines, magnolias, beeches, and oaks along the way. The outlet stream is spanned by a bridge that was in poor condition in 1992; if it is down, you will have to find your way across the steep-sided outlet stream.

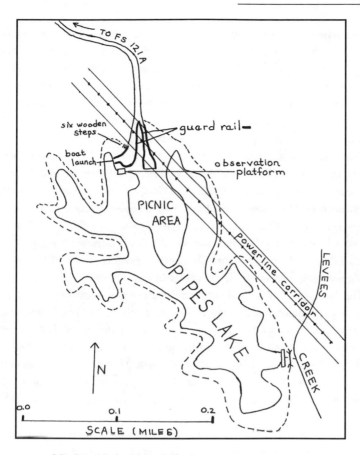

M A P 20. Pipes Lake Nature Trail

The brushy segment in the power line corridor is a problem area for people allergic to poison ivy. Consider backtracking if you are unusually sensitive.

The Forest Service removed the signs for this scenic and well-constructed trail because few people were using it or knew about it. It needs a sponsor.

TOMBIGBEE NATIONAL FOREST,

District Ranger, USDA Forest Service, Rt. 1, Box 98A, Ackerman, MS 39735 (601-285-3264). The office is 1.5 miles south of Ackerman on Highway 15 (40,000-acre Ackerman Management Unit and 26,100-acre Trace Management Unit)

The two separate management units of the Tombigbee NF are about 40 miles apart. Both units have similar histories. Both were once a mosaic of small farms in "submarginal" land, erosion prone and with poor soils. During the 1930s, some of these failed farms were purchased from small landowners under the provisions of the Resettlement Administration and other congressionally legislated programs designed to relocate poor farmers to better land and to provide them with expert advice and good equipment.

The lands thus acquired were managed by the Soil Conservation Service, which set up land utilization projects in Mississippi, Alabama, and Georgia to demonstrate good land use. The Civilian Conservation Corps was enlisted to check erosion, plant trees, and build two lakes—Choctaw Lake and Davis Lake—with adjacent recreation complexes. Between 1940 and 1950, the land was turned over to the U.S. Fish and Wildlife Service (now Noxubee National Wildlife Refuge), Mississippi State University (now Starr Memorial Forest), and the Forest Service (now the Tombigbee National Forest).

The Tombigbee NF is filled with reminders of past settlement. Small cemeteries occupy hilltops, and if you slowly cruise the gravel roads, you will find "woods roads" that are not used or maintained by the Forest Service but undoubtedly once linked the farms. (One in the Ackerman Unit diverges southwest from Sheep Ranch S Rd. [FS 956-2] about 0.5 mile south of the junction of FS 956, at the west edge of the Noxubee Crest Research Natural Area.) On private lands within the proclamation boundaries of the two units you will see steep pasturelands and abandoned cabins.

Dispersed Primitive Campsites: The Tombigbee NF has two major recreation areas, Choctaw Lake and Davis Lake. Both have associated trails and are described separately. They are highly developed fee areas and may not be appealing if you seek primitive surroundings. For you, the Forest Service has installed dispersed single party campsites along gravel roads throughout the two units of the Tombigbee NF as well as in the Yalobusha Unit of the Holly Springs NF near Oakland. Intended mainly for hunters, they offer only a flat place to camp at the end of a short road. You must bring your own water.

You can find the numbered sites by cruising the main Forest Service roads, or you can ask the District Ranger's office near Ackerman for a map of the sites. During the height of the late fall and winter hunting season, you need a permit to camp in the site of your choice, also available in the Ackerman office.

ACKERMAN MANAGEMENT UNIT

F 9 • **Choctaw Lake Recreation Area and trails,** SE of Ackerman, Choctaw County (ca. 2 miles of trail; 3- or 4-mile loop planned). Located in hills at the beginning of the Noxubee River, 100-acre Choctaw Lake is the

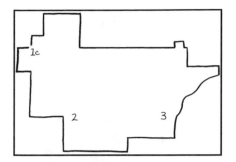

LEGEND

c   =   Choctaw Lake Recreation Area

l   =   Choctaw Lake trails

2   =   Noxubee Crest Research
        Natural Area

3   =   Old Robinson Road

M A P 21. Ackerman Management Unit in Tombigbee National Forest

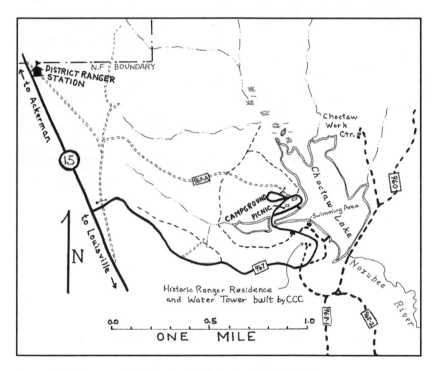

M A P 22. Choctaw Lake Recreation Area and Chata Trail

focus of one of the more highly developed recreation areas in Mississippi's national forests. Facilities are listed in table 1. The Soil Conservation Service acquired the property in the mid-1930s. The Civilian Conservation Corps built the lake and a resort complex, of which the only structures still standing are the ranger residence and, beside it, a water tower that looks like a square observation tower. They were built in 1935–36 and are now likely candidates for the

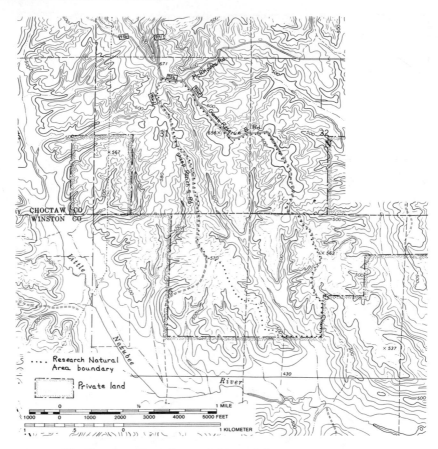

MAP 23. Noxubee Crest Research Natural Area

National Register of Historic Places. Portals displaying typical CCC stonework guard at least three road entrances. Foundations of some of the other buildings can still be seen around the lake.

The Choctaw Lake (Chata) Trail: The Forest Service plans to complete and upgrade a 3- to 4-mile loop trail on the west side of the lake. The usable portion in early 1993 is marked with white painted rectangles. It begins across the road from the swimming area, passing through a pair of stone columns flanking an abandoned road. Several species of trees in a mature forest of pines and hardwoods are identified by signs along the first half mile. After crossing a stream entering the separate lakelet, the trail climbs a hill beside a clearcut and descends through uncut mature pine forest, looping back around and ending near the restroom next to the larger of the two pavilions near the campground.

Another trail fragment is marked with a hiker symbol along the paved access road to the lake (FS 967) about 0.6 mile east of the junction of State Hwy 15. It too is marked with white rectangles, but they are widely spaced and the trail is little used and difficult to follow. It crosses several ravines in deep woods and ends up back on FS 967 in about 0.6 mile.

- **Noxubee Crest Research Natural Area,** NW of Louisville, Winston County (670 acres). This area encompasses the watershed of a tributary of the Little Noxubee River, a major tributary of the Noxubee River. The forest is relatively undisturbed mixed pine-hardwood. Much of the upland portion is old fields abandoned in the 1930s. On the steep side slopes and in the creek bottom are shortleaf pines, oaks, and hickories as much as 100 years old. The area has steep ravines that provide diverse habitats for many plants, including some on the state list of threatened and endangered species. Edward G. Roberts in the Forestry Department at Mississippi State was responsible for its special designation. (For more on the flora, see Moore's *Floristic Survey* in the bibliography.)

F 9

The public is free to enter the area, but collecting plants or otherwise disturbing the vegetation is not allowed. There are no trails, but roads bound the designated area on three sides. The Louisville North topo map is recommended.

- **Old Robinson Road.** This was one of Mississippi's earliest important roads, connecting Jackson with Columbus. In 1826, when it was improved so that stage coaches could use it, for the first time a traveler could take a stage from Washington, D.C., to New Orleans. The road lost its integrity as a single route years ago, but abandoned segments in the national forest and the Noxubee National Wildlife Refuge invite exploration. Because it was a true road, not just a trail, abandoned portions of the old roadbed are still discernible where they have not been disrupted by later earth-moving activities.

F 10

The U.S. Congress designated the route a post road (mail route) in March 1821. At that time, most of the route was probably an Indian trail or unimproved road through the Choctaw Nation. No written record of the Indians' consent can be found; presumably a few of the chiefs informally gave permission. Perhaps they came to regret their decision, because the road helped open their territory to white settlers.

One of the stage stops (or stands, as they were commonly called) was at William Kincaid's house in what became the community of Beth-Eden. Passen-

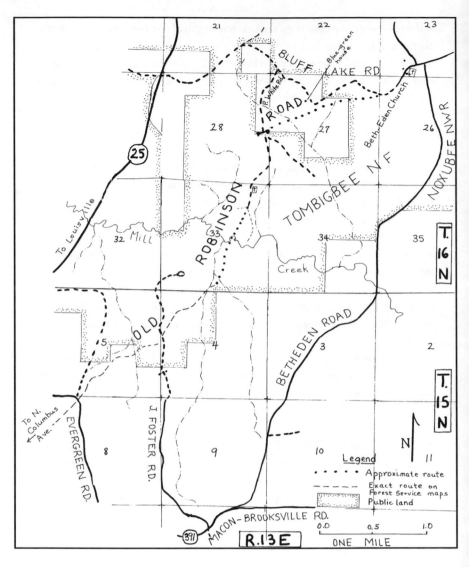

MAP 24. Old Robinson Road, Tombigbee National Forest (Ackerman Management Unit)

gers could buy meals, and horses were changed. The stand was a few hundred yards west of the historic Beth-Eden church, the second Lutheran Church in Mississippi (founded in 1848 or 1853). Beth-Eden has been steadily declining in population since at least the turn of the century. It once had a cannery and, as late as the mid-1970s, a country store.

Robinson Road was still well traveled during the Civil War, but later various segments were abandoned as towns and communities grew and patterns of travel shifted.

Access: The abandoned part of Robinson Road on the Tombigbee NF is not maintained as a trail, and intersections with existing roads are not signed. Since the old road has not been cleared, come prepared to bushwhack.

The easiest place to find the old road is where it crosses J. Foster Rd. (FS 986). From Louisville, take N. Columbus Rd. and turn east on Macon-Brooksville Rd. (State Hwy 391). Foster Road heads north from Hwy 391 about 0.3 mile west of the junction of Betheden Rd. North of the residences along the first mile or so of Foster Rd., the pavement ends and you enter national forest land. You will come to a gate 1.65 miles from Hwy 391. Between March 1 and September 15 the gate is closed, and you must walk the remaining 0.3 miles to the intersection of the old road. It's obvious on the east side of FS 986, angling off to the northeast.

The Forest Service Tombigbee NF map shows part of the road as FS 985, but the road has not been improved in any way. The Service intends to preserve the remaining undisturbed portions. A log landing (place where logs were loaded for transport to a mill) has disrupted the roadbed on the west side, but you could presumably pick up the route beyond the landing, although most of the area west of FS 986 was recently clearcut and has probably been disrupted to some extent.

For more information and references, see the section on Noxubee National Wildlife Refuge. I recommend that you take the Tombigbee NF map and the relevant topographic map with you when you explore (see below). Note that significant portions of the old roadway are on private land. You will need permission from the landowners to explore this land.

As you explore this old road and other historic areas on federal land, remember that picking up or digging up cultural remains, whether prehistoric or historic, is prohibited by federal law.

Maps: Betheden topo map is recommended. Also, the Louisville/Winston County Chamber of Commerce has issued an excellent map of the county and city with all roads named (Park St., P.O. Box 551, Louisville, MS 39339; 601-773-3921).

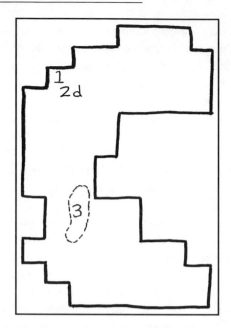

MAP 25. Trace Management Unit, Tombigbee National Forest

TRACE MANAGEMENT UNIT

D 10

• **Chuquatonchee Bluffs Research Natural Area** (proposed), E of New Houlka, Chickasaw County (no designated trails). The bluffs are on the south side of upper Chuquatonchee Creek. The area has been relatively undisturbed for 80 years and includes prairie edge habitat that has never been cleared for agriculture. Most soils in the national forest are acidic; the soils of the bluffs are alkaline and support an unusual assemblage of trees and herbaceous plants, some uncommon.

The area proposed as a research natural area is just north of Davis Lake, on the north side of County Road 903, the paved road that leads to the Davis Lake Recreation Area from the Natchez Trace Parkway. At least two woods roads that are closed to public vehicle entry leave Rt. 903 and enter and/or cross the area.

D 10 • **Davis Lake Recreation Area and Trails,** between Okolona and Houston, Chickasaw County (ca. 1.0-mile trail network). The recreation area is on the north side of 200-acre Davis Lake. It's a popular stopover spot for people driving the Natchez Trace Parkway and also with fishermen. There is a spacious and attractive overflow campground open to primitive campers.

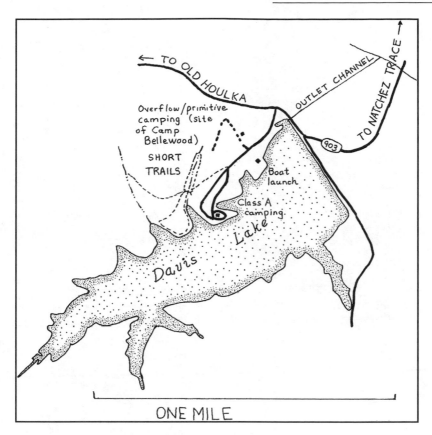

← TO OLD HOULKA

OUTLET CHANNEL

TO NATCHEZ TRACE

Overflow/primitive
camping (site
of Camp
Bellewood)

SHORT
TRAILS

903

Boat
launch

Class A
camping

Davis Lake

ONE MILE

MAP 26. Davis Lake Recreation Area and Trails

A trail marked "Fishing Trail" leaves the paved road at the gate to the developed campground. It leads over a slight rise to a broad footbridge over a small but deeply entrenched stream. On the other side of the stream, three separate trails diverge.

The path to your right as you face away from the campground leads through the bottoms along the entrenched stream, crosses it on a footbridge, and returns to the first bridge on the other side. This is (or was) an interpretive trail. Many of the mature trees en route are or were identified by species, including walnut, water oak, red cedar, yellow poplar, and shortleaf and loblolly pine, but most of the sign placards were missing when I hiked the trail in April 1993. Altogether, the three trails probably total about a mile.

Davis Lake was constructed in 1934 by the Civilian Conservation Corps, which also built "Camp Bellewood" on the north side of the lake where the overflow campground is today. Two lines of cabins met at a pavilion or lodge.

MAP 27. Witch Dance Trail, showing potential campsites for backpackers

In 1961 it was a Girl Scout camp. Today only chimneys of the pavilion/lodge and brick walks buried in the dirt remain. Raymond Rowland of Houston remembers cabins on the opposite side of the lake also. The buildings were torn down in about 1966.

D 10

● **Witch Dance (Tombigbee) Trail,** between Houston and Van Vleet, Chickasaw County (15-mile loop with shorter loops possible). This trail is a long oval loop on the west side of the Natchez Trace. The beginning/end of the loop is within the Natchez Trace Parkway. The eastern part follows high ridges through half-grown pines, while the western segment goes up and down small valleys. You will cross sunken roads, reminders that the area was once settled and farmed. The northern end follows the abandoned grade of a branch of the Mobile & Ohio Railroad. It linked Houston with Okolona before 1940.

The name Witch Dance is perhaps derived from Witch Dance Hill on the other side of the Trace Parkway. In any case, there are said to be bare spots in the vicinity where no vegetation grows. Local folklore says that's because witches dance there.

The area owes its topography to the Ripley Formation and Prairie Bluff Chalk that date from the Upper Cretaceous Period (approximately 70 million years ago). You may find marine fossils in outcrops on the area, including shark teeth, fish vertebrae, and especially the large extinct clam *Exogyra*.

The trailhead is at the Witch Dance Picnic Area on the Natchez Trace, but it is possible to take advantage of the roads and a trail cutoff and make a shorter loop hike or ride.

The route is generally well marked with white painted horseshoes and three-inch-wide white painted rings about 10′ up on trees. The route was originated marked with brown posts with routed horseshoe symbols on top; some of these remain to guide you.

There is a problem at the northern end where the trail meets two recently clearcut areas that have been replanted with pines. It's easy to lose the east part of the loop at the end of the clearcut—be on the lookout for the trail, which turns east from the clearcut area and descends through undisturbed woods to the railroad grade. It is also easy to miss the point where the trail leaves the grade and starts heading back south. It follows the eastern edge of another clearcut/pine plantation at the edge of an unlogged stream valley. (The map of the Tombigbee NF does not show the northwest portion of the trail loop accurately.)

Access: The designated beginning and end are the Witch Dance Picnic Area at Mile 233.2 on the Natchez Trace. You can also access the trail at the two points where it crosses FS 116 (904 on the Forest Service map). Be on the lookout for the paint-blazed trees.

The northern end of the trail comes close to the Forest Service's Trace Work Center/Chickasaw WMA headquarters on State Hwy 32. The access road has been blocked by a mound of earth. You must wade Dicks Creek and climb up to the truncated end of the old railroad grade, which once crossed the creek on a trestle, to reach the marked trail.

Facilities: The only facilities are at the Witch Dance picnic area, where you will find flush toilets, picnic tables, grills, and a parking area. Hitching racks for horses are off to the west of the main trail. Horseback riders as well as bicyclists pedaling the Trace are permitted to camp overnight here, but other camping is prohibited.

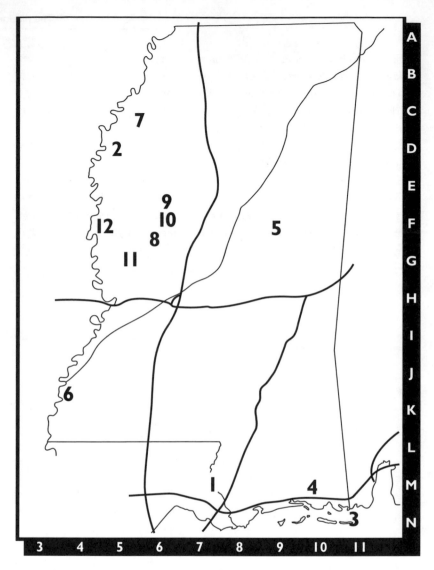

MAP 28. The national wildlife refuges in Mississippi

LEGEND

1	=	Bogue Chitto NWR
2	=	Dahomey NWR
3	=	Grand Bay NWR
4	=	Mississippi Sandhill Crane NWR
5	=	Noxubee NWR
6	=	St. Catherine Creek NWR
7	=	Tallahatchie NWR (planned)

8–12	=	Yazoo NWR Complex
8	=	Hillside NWR
9	=	Mathews Brake NWR
10	=	Morgan Brake NWR
11	=	Panther Swamp NWR
12	=	Yazoo NWR

2. The National Wildlife Refuges

Mississippi's 11 national wildlife refuges (NWRs) are among nearly 500 administered by the U.S. Fish and Wildlife Service, a branch of the U.S. Department of the Interior. NWRs are set up for specific wildlife-related purposes. For Mississippi's NWRs the main goal is the preservation, enhancement, and restoration of wetland wildlife habitat. A particular objective for most is maintaining and creating habitat for wintering waterfowl, mostly ducks. Six of the 11 refuges are on the Delta, which is on the Mississippi Flyway, used by migratory waterfowl that breed in the northern Great Plains and north into Canada. The Mississippi Sandhill Crane and Grand Bay NWRs are on the Gulf Coast in existing and restored coastal savanna wetlands.

Endangered species such as bald eagles also benefit from the NWRs, as does an array of wildlife, fish, and plants that are not endangered. Mississippi Sandhill Crane and Grand Bay NWRs were created to save the endangered nonmigratory subspecies of sandhill crane. As a by-product, an entire vanishing coastal ecosystem is being saved and expanded. The mature pine woods of Noxubee NWR support many colonies of endangered red-cockaded woodpeckers.

Recreation is not a main purpose of NWRs, but it is an important side benefit. Hunting and fishing, probably the most popular recreation on most NWRs in this state, are allowed when they are compatible with or complement the overall goals of the refuge. They are prohibited only in the Mississippi Sandhill Crane, Grand Bay, and St. Catherine NWRs. Except for these three refuges, all have boat ramps. Ramps are about the only recreation facilities most of them have. The only NWR with picnic tables and a campground is Noxubee, and its primitive campground may be phased out within a few years. Otherwise, camping (including backcountry camping) is not allowed in NWRs.

Day use is welcomed at all NWRs. Many refuges have checklists of birds free for the asking. Except in Noxubee NWR, designated hiking trails tend to be short, but many refuges have other "trails" (often dirt roads for administrative use) that are open to ATVs only during the hunting seasons. Hikers can use them year round. More adventurous people can take to the swamps in canoes.

New NWRs are still being created in Mississippi. One, still in the preliminary planning stages and thus not mentioned in this guide, is in Tallahatchie County.

In the future, we can expect to see more opportunities for wildlife viewing under the new Watchable Wildlife Program, including roadside tours and observation platforms overlooking swamps, lakes, and other wildlife habitat. More facilities for the handicapped, including fishing piers and short paved nature trails, are also likely.

M 8 BOGUE CHITTO NATIONAL WILDLIFE REFUGE,

U.S. Fish and Wildlife Service, 1010 Gause Blvd., Bldg. 936, Slidell, LA 70458 (504-646-7555). Refuge is W of Picayune, Pearl River County, Mississippi, and E of Bush, St. Tammany Parish, Louisiana (ca. 37,000 acres)

This is the middle of the three public wildlife areas protecting fish and wildlife habitat in the floodway of the lower Pearl. Approximately 21 miles long, the national wildlife refuge (NWR) is contiguous with the Old River Wildlife Management Area (WMA) on the north and the Pearl River WMA on the south.

The floodway of the lower Pearl River, locally known as Honey Island Swamp (interestingly, no one seems to know where Honey Island is) begins near Bogalusa, Louisiana. Here the floodplain widens to as much as seven miles. It is threaded with accessory river channels, bayous, sloughs, and oxbow lakes and brakes with bald cypress and tupelo. Much of the basin may be under water in the spring. Higher ground is covered with bottomland hardwoods, including water oak, red maple, magnolia, yellow poplar, Carolina ash, loblolly pine, and spruce pine. White sand banks fringed with sycamore and black willow line the Pearl in the upper portion of the basin. Below the I-10 bridge, trees disappear and are supplanted by coastal marsh.

Because of its high fertility, the floodway supports an impressive array of vertebrates. Mammals include deer, river otters, bobcats, and gray squirrels. As many as 166 species of birds have been identified, among them 11 species of herons, egrets, and ibises, including rare white and glossy ibises. Ducks, except for the abundant wood duck, are not common. Swallow-tailed kites, Mississippi kites, and bald eagles can be seen. Expert birders can find up to 33 species of wood warblers, many of them neotropical migrants that pass through the area during their spring and fall migrations. In addition, 131 spe-

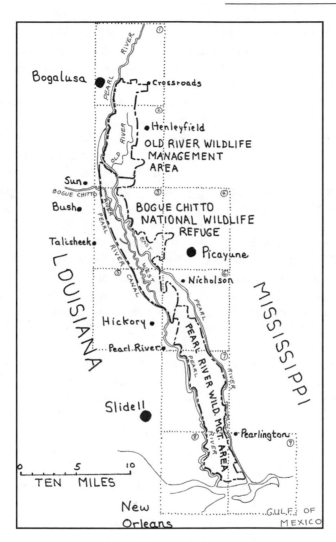

MAP 29. Public wildlife areas on the lower Pearl River (Honey Island Swamp) showing relevant 7 1/2' topographic maps: 1) Bogalusa East, 2) Henleyfield, 3) Industrial, 4) Picayune, 5) Hickory, 6) Nicholson, 7) Haaswood, 8) Rigolets, 9) English Lookout

cies of reptiles and amphibians and 140 species of fish make their homes here.

The NWR is threaded with large and small streams, including the East and West Pearl rivers, the lower end of the Bogue Chitto River, and Wilson Slough. The West Pearl, Bradley Slough, and Holmes Bayou have been designated natural and scenic streams by the state of Louisiana.

The Bogue Chitto NWR was authorized in 1980. The Service has authorization to purchase up to 40,000 acres from willing sellers to assure the preservation of some of the rapidly disappearing bottomland hardwood wildlife habitat in the lower Mississippi Valley.

Most of the area is accessible only by motorboat or canoe. A 1986 Fish and Wildlife Service brochure recommends a canoe trip across the refuge from west to east, beginning at Lock 3, following the Bogue Chitto and West Bogue Chitto rivers south to Wilson Slough, going up the slough to the East Pearl and downstream to Walkiah Bluff Water Park. There may be a strong current to paddle against in Wilson Slough. The trip is recommended when the gauge on the Pearl River at Bogalusa is 12' or higher.

Also recommended is a leisurely canoe trip into the "Tupelo Pond," the largest cypress/tupelo brake in the refuge. It is on the east side of the Pearl River Canal just south of Lock 2. For additional information about canoe trips outlined in this section and in the descriptions of the Old River WMA and Pearl River WMA, as well as other trips that are entirely on the Louisiana side of the state line, consult *Canoe Trails of the Deep South*, by Estes, Almquist, and Carter, and *Trail Guide to the Delta Country*, edited by Sevenair (in the bibliography).

Within the refuge, camping is permitted only along the banks of the following major streams: the Bogue Chitto River, Wilson Slough, the West and East Pearl rivers, and Holmes Bayou. No hiking trails have been developed, and none is planned. The levee along the Pearl River Canal makes an excellent trail, however, especially for birders.

Best Time to Visit: The refuge is open year round except when the gauge on the Pearl River at Bogalusa reaches 16.5' MSL. From late winter to spring, much of the area will be flooded. Most land will be dry in the fall. Hunting seasons roughly coincide with those in the rest of Mississippi and Louisiana.

Facilities: The only developed facility on the Mississippi side is Walkiah Bluff Water Park on the East Pearl River west of Picayune. It has a concrete boat launching ramp, picnic tables, pavilion, playing fields, and a display board set up by the Service. It also has a campground with RV hookups and restrooms with showers, but this part was closed in the fall of 1992. Visitation has fallen off since the park was constructed because the Pearl River seems to be abandoning the sharp bend at the park. A combination of man-made and natural factors is responsible, with much of the remaining flow now heading south through Ice Box Bayou about a half mile upstream. The river usually has too little water to accommodate motorboats from July through the fall. Sometimes it is nearly dry. Mississippi and Louisiana have been involved in a political tug-of-war over the volume of water in the West (Louisiana) and East (Mississippi) side for years.

On the Louisiana side, two public boat launching facilities are on the Pearl River Canal near the north and south ends of the refuge at Locks 3 and 1.

Access: Walkiah Bluff Water Park is on Walkiah Bluff Rd. Follow the signs from State Hwy 43. You can also enter the refuge on the Mississippi side by carrying your canoe or johnboat down to Hobolochitto Creek at the Burnt Bridge Road bridge, about 3.5 miles south of the junction of Hwy 43.

Lock 3 is at the east end of Louisiana Hwy 16 west of Sun. The access road to Lock 1 leaves Hwy 41 3.6 miles north of Hickory at the intersection of Hwy 36.

To reach Lock 2, follow Hwy 41 north about 20 miles from I-59 at the Pearl River exit. A short road leading to the lock leaves Hwy 41 about halfway between Talisheek and Bush. Lock 2 has no boat launch, but canoes can be portaged in. To reach Tupelo Pond mentioned above, carry your canoe from the parking lot across the lower lock and about 100 yards south down the eastern levee. Put in at an open water pond at the base of the levee. Turn right (east) to get into Tupelo Pond.

For information on the current level of the Pearl River at Bogalusa, call the U.S. Army Corps of Engineers in Vicksburg (601-631-5669 or 631-5672) or the National Weather Service at Slidell, Louisiana (504-641-4343). It's also printed daily in the weather section of the *Times-Picayune* (New Orleans). Flood stage is 18'.

Maps and Literature: The U.S. Fish and Wildlife Service has three brochures for visitors: a general description with map, a brochure with current hunting and fishing regulations and seasons with map, and a list of birds by season. Topo maps are recommended. (See Map 29 for area covered by each map.)

Canoe Rental, Shuttles, Instruction, and Guide Service for Honey Island Swamp: Dreamchasers, c/o Dale Polkey, 2516 Belle Chasse Hwy., Gretna, LA 70053 (504-362-9552); Byron Almquist, 6976 Gen. Haig St., New Orleans, LA 70124 (504-283-9400).

DE5

DAHOMEY NATIONAL WILDLIFE REFUGE,

U.S. Fish and Wildlife Service, Mississippi Wetland Management District, P.O. Box 1070, Grenada, MS 38902-1070 (601-226-8286). Refuge is W of Cleveland in Bolivar County (9,500 acres)

Dahomey is the biggest remaining piece of William Faulkner's "big woods." It includes a few large fields, but it's mainly a forest with typical bottomland hardwoods, including Nuttall oak, water oak, cherrybark oak, green ash, shag-bark hickory, elms, and pecans. Among the more unusual plants are pumpkin ash (*Fraxinus prutunda*) and Arkansas manna grass (*Glyceria arkansana*). The woods flood in the winter and early spring and are important wintering grounds for migratory ducks. Year-round residents include deer, bobcats, wading birds, and turkeys.

On topographic maps, the land looks almost flat, but the three named bayous that meander through the refuge—Belman, Stokes, and Stillwater—are in deep trenches that are difficult to cross. During the fall, they are almost empty.

State Hwy 446 runs through the refuge. Only two gravel roads open to the public penetrate it. (Take care in wet weather—your car could get stuck.) The topo maps also show numerous "jeep roads" that are off limits to the motoring public. Some of these are improved logging roads that have not been used recently but are still edged with brush that keeps you away from the woods you may have come to see. Others are narrow trails recently used by off-road vehicles. If you really want to get the feel of the woods, try some cross-country travel with map and compass.

The refuge was open to squirrel, rabbit, and deer hunting during 1992–93. Persons on the refuge during the hunting seasons are urged to wear at least 500 square inches of blaze orange above the waist during the archery season (October 1–November 20). All other public uses are prohibited during the gun deer hunts.

Dahomey is a former plantation founded in 1833 by F. G. Ellis. He named it after the African homeland of his slaves. The Nature Conservancy purchased it in 1990 and turned it over to the Fish and Wildlife Service. Since then the Service has acquired some additional acreage.

Best Time to Visit: Fall is the best time. Large areas may be flooded in the spring; humidity and insects will discourage all but the most dedicated in the summer. The area is closed to visitors except deer hunters during the gun deer hunts (December 2–15 in 1992, but the dates will vary). Find out in advance when these hunts are scheduled.

Access: A good starting point for exploring the refuge on foot is the parking area and hunters' check station at the site of the old Benoit Hunting Club lodge. Eventually the refuge headquarters may be located here. It's on the north side of Highway 446 at the edge of a field (nonrefuge land) 10.6 miles west of Boyle, which is on U.S. Highway 61.

Maps and Literature: The Service issues a brochure for hunters that includes a small map showing public access roads. It is updated annually and gives the planned hunts for the season. You should get one in advance for fall trips. For exploring the area on foot, copies of the Lobdell and Beulah topo maps (the latter shows only the extreme northern portion) are recommended.

GRAND BAY NATIONAL WILDLIFE REFUGE,

Contact Manager, Mississippi Sandhill Crane National Wildlife Refuge, 7200 Crane Lane, Gautier, MS 39553 (601-497-6322) beginning in 1995; no public information will be available before that time. (12,100 acres proposed)

This new refuge straddles the Mississippi-Alabama state line between Pascagoula and Mobile, encompassing one of the largest coastal pine savanna wetlands left on the Gulf Coast of Mississippi and Alabama. The savannas are characterized by widely scattered clumps of longleaf and slash pine and a great variety of grasses, sedges, and herbaceous plants. All are adapted to the coastal climate, with its well-defined wet and dry seasons. Fires set by lightning often burned the savannas during dry periods until they were suppressed by the white man. Closer to the coast, the savanna intergrades with coastal marshes.

The U.S. Fish and Wildlife Service already owns the southernmost 2,649 acres and hopes to acquire the remaining acres by purchasing them from willing sellers and by acquiring development rights. It would like to establish a second breeding population of the endangered Mississippi sandhill crane there. The only surviving wild cranes now are on the Mississippi Sandhill Crane NWR about 24 miles to the west. A second resident population at Grand Bay would help assure the survival of the cranes in case a disaster wiped out the population on the other refuge. The Service would periodically burn the savanna to duplicate lightning fires and maintain habitat for the cranes and the other savanna animals and plants. (For more information on the cranes and pine savanna, see the following section on the Mississippi Sandhill Crane NWR.)

The refuge is also ideal habitat for another notable endangered bird, the southern bald eagle. Breeding eagles would be introduced to the new refuge by rearing young eagles on towers. To keep the eaglets from losing their fear of people, the birds are not permitted to see humans at close range. This technique, known as hacking, has successfully returned eagles to Horn Island.

The coastal marshes are winter grounds for migratory ducks, including the red-breasted merganser, lesser scaup, redhead, ring-necked duck, mallard, and American widgeon. Trees on the coast are also important resting and jumping-off points for many species of neotropical songbirds on their way to and from their winter ranges south of the Gulf of Mexico. The marshes are exceedingly rich in nutrients and are thus important feeding and breeding grounds for more than 80 species of fish.

Potential Facilities: Opportunities for wildlife viewing and photography on land and by boat will be developed when land acquisition is completed. Substantially more public access and use will be permitted than on Mississippi Sandhill Crane NWR.

MN 10 MISSISSIPPI SANDHILL CRANE NATIONAL WILDLIFE REFUGE,

7200 Crane Lane, Gautier, MS 39553 (601-497-6322). The refuge is N of Gautier, Jackson County (19,273 acres, 0.8-mile interpretive trail)

The refuge includes five separate parcels that extend on both sides of Interstate 90 from the Pascagoula River west to Ocean City. It is the locus of an impressive effort to restore a substantial piece of coastal plain piney woods to an approximation of what it was like when the first white men set foot on the coast. The prime beneficiary of this work is the tall, stately bird that occurs only in three scattered groups on the coastal savannas of Alabama, Mississippi, and eastern Texas. The crane cannot be separated from its habitat, so as it is rescued from oblivion, an entire complex of ecosystems is also being restored. The Mississippi sandhill crane is a subspecies of sandhill crane (*Grus canadensis pulla*). It is a long-legged gray bird five feet tall that superficially resembles the great blue heron.

Sandhill cranes are widespread. Most North American sandhills breed in Canada and Alaska. They migrate south across the Great Plains to their wintering grounds on the Gulf Coast, southern Oregon, and California. The Mississippi sandhill cranes and the other two isolated coastal groups find everything they need for breeding and wintering in one place and do not migrate. They closely resemble the migratory sandhills but are somewhat larger and darker in color. Migratory cranes sometimes visit the refuge in the winter, but the two subspecies do not interbreed.

The cranes can easily be distinguished from great blue herons by their red foreheads and—more visible at a distance—their rather long tail feathers that curve down and resemble a Victorian lady's bustle. A crane flies with its neck extended, while a flying heron holds its neck in a tight **S**-curve.

The Mississippi sandhill crane's habitat is the water-logged savannas that once stretched from the Florida panhandle across Alabama, Mississippi, and

Louisiana. Here the cranes search for food on the surface—fruit, insects, and amphibians—and probe for worms and roots just beneath.

These wet meadows, growing on acidic soils, were not suited for agriculture or development, but the white settlers who came to the area in the early 1800s ran great herds of cattle, sheep, and pigs across the savannas. Stock raising remained the only economic use of the area after the scattered patches of virgin longleaf and slash pines had been cut in the early 1900s. The cranes survived the logging and were able to coexist with livestock, but in the 1950s pine plantations became the dominant use. The savannas were ditched and drained, and closely spaced pine seedlings were planted. At the same time, urban and industrial developments on the fringes of the growing communities on the Gulf Coast began to spread into the cranes' habitat.

The Mississippi subspecies was put on the federal endangered species list in 1973. The refuge was established in 1975, and the Fish and Wildlife Service has gradually been acquiring property as it finds willing sellers.

Most of the acquired land had been drained and planted with pine. To restore the land for cranes, the Service cuts and bulldozes most of the pines from the drained savannas and then uses prescribed burning to control shrubby understory vegetation. Drainage ditches are plugged, and road dikes and water control structures are installed to restore the original wetland conditions. Rye grass, chufa, and corn are planted on cleared, plowed strips to supplement the crane's preferred foods during the winter.

Even earlier, in 1975, the Service had embarked on a captive breeding and restocking program. The crane population on the refuge has increased from 30 in 1973 to 120 in early 1992. Some cranes that were hatched in captivity have begun to breed in the wild, but unfortunately the 12 or so wild breeding pairs that inhabit the refuge are having little success in rearing chicks.

Although cranes are the refuge's mission, other wildlife has also benefited. Red-cockaded woodpeckers, which are also on the federal endangered list, had earlier abandoned their nesting and roosting trees on land now in the refuge because they cannot live in forests with a tall, dense understory of young trees. (Before 1900, fires set by lightning maintained open, parklike groves of pines.) As the Service removes much of this understory, the woodpeckers are beginning to return. Bog plants, including sundews, club mosses, pitcher plants, pipeworts, and orchids, are becoming more abundant. In fact, more species of plants have been identified on pine savanna wetlands than in any other ecosystem in North America.

Raccoons, white-tailed deer, foxes, coyotes, and opossums are common on the refuge. So are reptiles and amphibians, including cricket frogs, pig frogs, and four species of poisonous snakes—pygmy rattlers, copperheads, cotton-mouths, and coral snakes.

In addition to cranes, 157 species of birds have been identified on the refuge. Harriers and red-tailed hawks hunt the savannas for rodents, and warblers and other songbirds thrive in brushy areas.

Facilities: The only public facilities are the visitor center, nature trail, and restrooms. Picnic and camping facilities are not provided, and hunting is not permitted, to avoid disturbing the cranes.

The Service does aim to provide environmental education and wildlife-oriented recreation, however. The office/visitor center has mounted cranes and other wildlife species on exhibit and also shows films and slides of the refuge. A nature trail three-quarters of a mile long begins and ends at the center. It leads through a beautiful restored upland savanna with scattered pines and palmettos and descends to the edge of a swamp along Bayou Castelle. Wildflowers stud the savanna in the spring, and the birding is excellent.

Your chances of seeing a crane along the trail are poor. The refuge does offer tours of other parts of the refuge during January and February, however. During the tour, you will probably be taken out to a blind overlooking the acclimation pens for the young cranes reared elsewhere, and you can observe how the land is being restored and managed. Your chances of seeing and/or hearing cranes are good.

The visitor center is open six days a week. At other times, the access road to the center is closed, but you can pick up information brochures just outside the gate.

Access: The visitor center and adjacent nature trail are the only parts of the refuge open to the public. To reach them, turn north on the Gautier-Vancleave Road at Exit 61 on Interstate 10, just north of Gautier, and drive three miles. The access road is clearly marked on the right (east) side. You can also get on the Gautier-Vancleave Road from U.S. Hwy 90 on the north side of Gautier.

F 10 **NOXUBEE NATIONAL WILDLIFE REFUGE,**

Rt. 1, Box 142, Brooksville, MS 39739 (601-323-5548). The refuge is between Starkville and Louisville, Oktibbeha, Winston, and Noxubee counties (47,000 acres, ca. six miles of designated hiking trails)

Noxubee NWR straddles the confluence of the Noxubee River and five lesser streams that meet in a floodplain up to two and one-half miles wide. The uplands are mostly gently rolling to almost flat except for the steeper terrain in

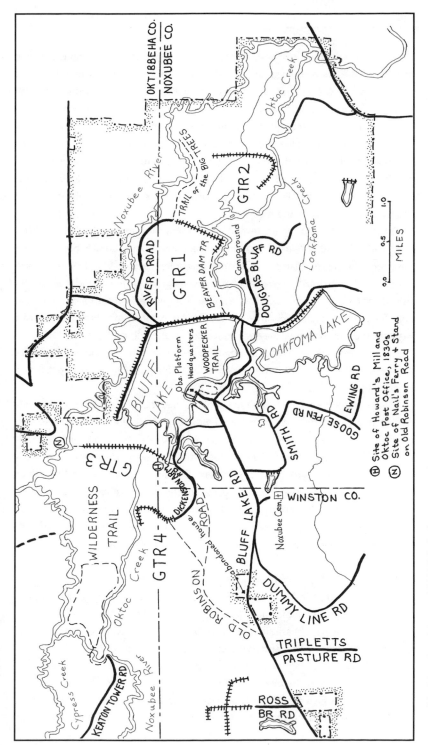

MAP 30. Noxubee National Wildlife Refuge, central portion

the Bevill Hills in the southwest portion. The refuge includes agricultural fields, two large lakes, and at least one smaller one, but most of it is forested. The floodplains are the habitat of an array of bottomland hardwoods, including cherrybark, overcup, willow, water, Nuttall, and swamp chestnut oak, sweetgum, elm, ash, red maple, sycamore, and beech. Higher ground is dominated by loblolly and shortleaf pine, but there are also mixed pine/hardwood forests. The upland forests are actively managed by selective thinning and prescribed burning to control the understory. The fields are used to grow food for waterfowl and other wildlife, including corn, grain sorghum, soybeans, small grains, pasture grasses, and legumes.

Parts of the floodplain are leveed off to form two permanent lakes, 1,200-acre Bluff Lake and 600-acre Loakfoma Lake. It also is exceedingly popular with fishermen during the March 1–October 31 fishing season. Bluff Lake is a good place to paddle a canoe. Groves of bald cypress grow within it, and the rule requiring motorboats to proceed at "no wake" speeds guarantees a peaceful setting. The lakes are partially drawn down in the summer to allow herbaceous vegetation to grow; when they are reflooded in the fall, it's food for ducks.

Other levees on the floodplain back up water in four greentree reservoirs that expand habitat for wintering waterfowl. They are filled in late fall and emptied in the spring.

A full complement of wildlife typical of the area occurs on the Noxubee, including deer, wild turkeys, raccoons, beavers, and alligators. More than 215 species of birds have been recorded since 1940. Among them are approximately 450 introduced giant Canada geese that are permanent and noisy residents. Native wood ducks also breed here. Between November and March as many as 25,000 waterfowl, mostly ducks, winter on the refuge. Most of them are mallards, gadwalls, American widgeons, and green- and blue-winged teals.

Endangered species also live on the refuge. It has several colonies of red-cockaded woodpeckers. Bald eagles sometimes winter there, as does, since 1985, a wood stork.

Noxubee NWR probably attracts more outdoor lovers than any other national wildlife refuge in Mississippi. Hunting is permitted during fall and winter, and there is a spring gobbler hunt that may last until May 1. Some people, many of them from nearby Mississippi State University in Starkville, come to picnic, hike, ride mountain bikes, and conduct various biological studies.

Until 1830, the area was part of the Choctaw Nation. It was cleared, settled, and farmed even before the Indians had been removed. A historical survey done for the Fish and Wildlife Service found six cemeteries on the refuge, and there were once six churches and three schools as well as four water mills and a Choctaw council house. Unfortunately the soil was generally poor and prone to erosion. During the 1930s the Rural Resettlement Administration purchased much of the land that is now in the refuge. The Soil Conservation Service managed it until 1940, when it was transferred to the agency now known as the U.S. Fish and Wildlife Service. The Service takes pride in its role in restoring the land to productive forests and wildlife habitat.

Trails: Noxubee is filled with logging trails/firebreaks that are closed to public use by motorized vehicles but open to foot travel. Hunters are the main users. Four formal trails are open to hikers and mountain bikers. I have also included a description of an abandoned segment of a historic old road in the trail descriptions that follow. During the spring you are likely to encounter some flooding. If the water isn't too deep, you can wade in sneakers, preferably with shallow cleats. Take a staff to keep your balance on slippery surfaces and to probe for unexpectedly deep trenches.

● **Woodpecker Trail** (ca. 0.5 mile). This loop takes you through a stand of pines that includes a colony of red-cockaded woodpeckers. Many birders come here to add one of these endangered birds to their life lists. You can readily identify the trees in which the woodpeckers have constructed cavities for rearing their young and roosting at night because they have been stripped of their bark around the hole. The bare wood is covered with whitish resin flowing from pits that the birds maintain. The favored trees look somewhat like candles. (The birds did not paint the white rings around the trunks of these so-called cavity trees, however.) Other species of woodpeckers can also be seen.

The Service maintains the forest to the red-cockaded woodpecker's liking by removing understory by prescribed burning and by allowing the trees to live at least 80 years. The birds peck cavities only in living pines with red heart disease, which rarely affects trees less than 60 years old.

Directly across the road from the parking area for the trail is an elevated walkway that leads to an observation platform overlooking Loakfoma Lake. Here you can observe the giant Canada geese, wood ducks, and other wildlife.

● **Beaver Dam Trail** (ca. 1.0 mile). This nonlooped trail takes you through the hardwood bottoms along Oktoc Creek. You will pass by some very large old hardwood trees. It comes to a dead end at the south end of the levee enclosing Greentree Reservoir 1. You can follow the levee to its other end and continue your hike on the Trail of the Big Trees. The total distance on the two trails and the levee is about 3.3 miles one way. If the trail is flooded near the start, before you cross the footbridge, come back and do it another day.

- **Trail of the Big Trees** (ca. 1.3 miles). The route is alongside the Noxubee River. You will see many huge hardwoods, many of them water oaks, that are about 100 years old. If the access road to the trail (River Road) is gated and flooded, you should probably come back another day to do this trail.

- **Wilderness Trail** (ca. 3-mile loop). This trail makes a loop in the "Wilderness," so called because the Atlanta office of Fish and Wildlife Service proposed in 1974 that 1,200 acres of bottomlands between the Noxubee River and Oktoc Creek be designated a federal wilderness area. The proposal was not approved at a higher level in the Service, so the U.S. Congress has never voted on it. The Service is managing the area as a wilderness, however.

    A large fallen tree with a cable for a handrail serves as a bridge across the river. A local Sierra Club group proposed and constructed the trail in 1992–94.

- **Old Robinson Road** (4.0 miles). An abandoned segment of this important 19th century road, which connected Jackson with Columbus, makes an interesting trail, although it is not marked as such. Old Robinson Road is now Bluff Lake (Louisville) Road in the southwestern part of the refuge, but it diverges near the abandoned community of Winston.

    The Natchez Trace followed watershed divides most of the way from Natchez to Knoxville, but Robinson Road went more or less in a diagonal line and crossed many slow-moving rivers and streams, each bordered by wide swamps. The swamp on the south side of the Noxubee River within the present refuge was perhaps the worst. An old timer in Betheden recalled that the old road had 16 bridges in one and one-quarter mile. Probably much of it was on a levee or causeway. No description of the Noxubee Swamp causeway has survived, but the Jackson Military Road, built a few years earlier, was probably similar: "The causeways were laid over all marshy spots by placing small timber close together and in a latitudinal direction to the road; ditches, three feet deep and four feet wide, were cut on each side of the causeways and the earth strewed over the timber."[1] Where the roadway crossed Oktoc Creek, Howard's Mill and a post office stood for a time in the 1830s.

    During the 1820s the Noxubee River was crossed by a ferry operated by Daniel Nail, who was probably a half-breed Choctaw. Nail had a "stand" on the north side of the river. By 1832 a toll bridge spanned the river. It was sold and operated by a succession of owners until after the Civil War, when it was sup-

---

[1] "General Jackson's Military Road," *Mississippi Historical Society Publications* 11 (1910):410.

planted by a new, free bridge built by Oktibbeha County. The bridge was still in use in 1909, but in the 1970s all that was left was a single concrete anchor. For more information on Old Robinson Road, see the section on the Ackerman Unit of the Tombigbee National Forest in this guide. Also see Futvoye's "The Robinson Road," Phelps' article with the same title, and Carroll's *Historical Sketches of Oktibbeha County*, all listed in the bibliography.

The abandoned road starts on the north side of Bluff Road about 1.1 miles west of the junction of Dummy Line Road. As you drive west, you will pass an abandoned house on an inholding of private land and then the boundary of refuge land marked by two white-and-blue goose Fish and Wildlife Service signs. The route of the old road can be followed to the north end of the levee impounding Greentree Reservoir 3. Fish and Wildlife Service employees sometimes use the old road, so no bushwhacking is necessary.

An alternative hike takes you to the end of Keaton Tower Rd. Leave the old road at the south end of the levee impounding Greentree Reservoir 4. Walk north on top of the levee to Oktoc Creek. Then turn west and follow an un-official trail along the south side of the creek. Just downstream of the diver-gence of the creek and the Noxubee River, more than one fallen tree spans Oktoc Creek. The Sierra Club hopes to improve one of them as a bridge in the near future.

Best Time to Visit: The refuge is open all year, but the Noxubee River can rise and fall several feet in a day or two. The bottomlands are often flooded in the spring.

Unlike some other Mississippi national wildlife refuges, the refuge is open to hikers during the deer hunting seasons. Be sure to wear blaze orange if you go then.

Facilities: Many picnic tables, with mowed grass and big trees, are spaced along Louisville Road on the south side of Bluff Lake. There's also a boat ramp, a telephone, and a restroom with flush toilets at the southeast corner of Bluff Lake, near the junction of Bluff Lake and Singleton Roads.

Noxubee is the only Mississippi national wildlife refuge with a campground. Along Douglas Bluff Road, it's spacious but without frills—only two old-fash-ioned nonchemical privies and spaces to park, build a campfire, and set up a tent. It's open between October 1 and May 1. Usually the Fish and Wildlife Ser-vice does not provide campgrounds on refuges; this one exists only because hunters have no other camping place nearby. It could be closed altogether within five years. If it is, you could use one of the primitive campsites in the Ack-erman Unit of the Tombigbee National Forest, which is contiguous with the refuge on the west, or camp anywhere else you please on national forest land.

Maps and Literature: The Fish and Wildlife Service distributes three maps of the refuge: (1) a large map with a schedule of seasonal wildlife events on the back; (2) an 8.5" × 11" map showing gravel roads, recreation facilities, lakes and streams, and maintained trails; and (3) another map similar to the second one but also showing temporary logging access trails and firebreaks. In addition, separate brochures on hunting and fishing are available. Often the first map and the brochures are in the information booth at the junction of Bluff Lake and Singleton Rd. at the southeast corner of Bluff Lake. To be sure of getting copies, however, ask the refuge office for them in advance. There is also a checklist of all bird species identified on the refuge, available only from the office. The Bluff Lake topo map is useful.

K 4 ST. CATHERINE CREEK NATIONAL WILDLIFE REFUGE,

P.O. Box 18639, Natchez, MS 39122 (601-442-6696). The refuge is S of Natchez in Adams County (13,478 acres in 1993; approximately 34,256 acres proposed)

This is one of Mississippi's newest national wildlife refuges. It was established in 1990 southwest of Natchez within St. Catherine's Bend on the Mississippi River. It is a complex of low-lying lakes, swamps, old fields, hardwood bottoms, and flat, partially willow-covered sandbars along the Mississippi River. Loess hills and U.S. Hwy 61 border it on the east. Within the refuge, Old St. Catherine Creek flows through a series of lowlands and 400-acre Butler Lake on its way to the river.

The refuge exists to provide duck habitat and to protect the ducks themselves, which are mainly mallards, pintails, blue-winged teals, and wood ducks. Water backs up Old St. Catherine Creek in the spring and on into early summer as the river swells with the melting snows from the Great Lakes region. Much of the refuge floods. Migratory ducks have the greatest need for flooded wetland habitat during the fall and winter, however. Refuge managers will put the ditches and water control structures that farmers erected to keep cleared lands from flooding to good use by altering them to hold water on the land during the fall and winter.

Ducks are by no means the only water birds on the refuge. Wading birds are abundant. Green herons, cattle egrets, snowy egrets, great egrets, little blue herons, great blue herons, anhingas, white ibises, glossy ibises, Louisiana herons, and wood storks (an endangered species) have all been seen. Doves and quail are abundant, and woodcocks winter in the woods and fields. Raptors cruise the fields, and wintering bald eagles (another endangered species) are attracted by carcasses of waterfowl that perish from natural causes. Another endangered bird, the peregrine falcon, sometimes stops by while migrating. Birders will also see shorebirds, a variety of songbirds, and wild turkeys. Mammals are represented by white-tailed deer, feral hogs, squirrels, rabbits, coyotes, beavers, otters, mink, nutria, raccoons, gray foxes, red foxes, bobcats, and opossums.

Magnolia Nature Trail (ca. 0.7 mile, not looped): The trail begins at Bourke Road E of the refuge office. It climbs up to the top of a bluff. Here you can turn either left or right and walk in the shade along the bluff. Benches are provided. Birders and people who like wildflowers will enjoy this trail. Because it's on high ground, it doesn't flood and is open all year.

Best Time to Visit: Waterfowl viewing is best during the winter. Cross-country hikers will encounter the least flooding and fewest bugs in the fall and early winter. Access via canoe or johnboat is best in the spring when water levels are high.

Facilities: As of early 1992, no facilities for visitors were provided at the refuge, and because of budget constraints, none is likely in the near future. The only hunting planned for 1992 was an archery deer hunt in the fall.

Access: The office and visitor center and the nature trail can be reached by turning off U.S. 61 east onto Beltline Hwy in the southern part of Natchez. Follow the road to a T intersection with Bourke Road. Turn south (left) and proceed 1.5 miles through the community of Cloverdale to the office, which is at the end of a short drive on the west side of the road.

The southern end of the refuge, including Butler Lake and the lower end of Old St. Catherine Creek, is accessible via Hutchins Landing Rd., which intersects U.S. Hwy 61 about 8 miles S of the junction of Beltline Hwy. Turn west onto Hutchins Landing Rd. and bear right at a fork in the road about 3 miles west of Hwy 61. From the fork, the road descends the loess bluffs to the floodplain of the Mississippi River in about 0.8 mile. In 1994 the road was not improved. Take care and don't get stuck in the soft deep sand! During the spring you're not likely to get beyond an oil well because the swollen Mississippi usually overflows onto the low lying land. If you are canoeing, keep away from the fast current to the west. Butler Lake is said to be almost devoid of trees and not especially scenic.

Maps and Literature: A brochure with a small map of the entire refuge is available from the refuge office. The Sibley 7.5' topo map is recommended for exploring the southern part of the refuge. The Natchez and Deer Park maps cover the extreme northern and western portions.

YAZOO NATIONAL WILDLIFE REFUGE COMPLEX,

Manager, Rt. 1, Box 286, Hollandale, MS 38748 (601-839-2638)

The complex includes five separate refuges in the southern part of the Delta/Yazoo Basin, all administered by a single refuge manager.

The five refuges provide habitat for ducks that breed in the northern United States and in Canada and fly south along the Mississippi Valley Flyway to spend the winter in the Gulf states. The most abundant species is the mallard. Other abundant ducks include widgeon, green-winged teal, gadwall, and wood ducks. Thousands of geese winter in the Yazoo NWR. You may also see large flocks of white pelicans and cormorants as well as many species of songbirds, raptors, and marsh birds.

Alligators live in all five refuges. Large mammals include white-tailed deer, fox and gray squirrel, swamp and cottontail rabbit, red and gray fox, flying squirrel, coyote, and armadillo. Beaver, muskrat, nutria, spotted and striped skunk, mink, otter, weasel, raccoon, opossum, and bobcat are also present. Small mammals include common mole, shrew, eastern chipmunk, bats, cotton rat, eastern wood rat, meadow mouse, and house mouse. Numerous species of warm water fish inhabit the brakes, ponds, and bayous.

All five refuges include cypress/tupelo brakes, oxbow lakes, and bottomland hardwood forests. Three—Hillside, Panther Swamp, and Yazoo—also include fields that had been cleared and converted to agriculture before the Fish and Wildlife Service acquired them. These are wholly or partially used to grow food for wintering waterfowl and other wildlife.

The only trail constructed specifically for hiking is the half-mile-long Alligator Slough Nature Trail in Hillside NWR. All but Mathews Brake have field and woods roads designated as ATV trails, however, or abandoned roads usable as hiking trails. The ATV trails are open to ATVs only during the hunting seasons; joyriding is prohibited at all times. Hikers can use them all year except during the firearm deer season. More ambitious people can explore the brakes and oxbow lakes by canoe.

Best Time to Visit: Migratory ducks begin to arrive on the refuges in late September, with peak numbers from November through February. Geese begin to arrive in late December; they are most abundant in January and February.

The best time for hiking is October through November. Flooding peaks in late winter and spring, the best time to try some exploring by canoe. Summers are typical of the Delta—hot and humid.

Hunting is permitted on all refuges in the complex. During the firearm deer season, other uses such as hiking and bird watching are prohibited for public safety. You can ask the refuge complex headquarters office when the season occurs.

Facilities: No picnicking or camping facilities or restrooms are provided, and overnight camping is prohibited. Leroy Percy State Park is nearby. It has a campground and rental cabins and is a good base for exploring the refuges.

Maps and Literature: Maps are available from the refuge headquarters. In addition, the Fish and Wildlife Service has published a checklist of birds identified on the refuges.

HILLSIDE NATIONAL WILDLIFE REFUGE,   F 6–7
E of Thornton in Holmes County (15,383 acres)

Hillside NWR is an elongate rectangle of wetlands at the foot of the loess hills. The western and northern boundary of the refuge is a levee with a gravel road on top. Watch for alligators in the ponds alongside.

• **Alligator Slough Nature Trail:** The trail is marked by a prominent sign along the levee road about one mile E of U.S. Hwy 49E. Alligator Slough, actually a brake, is filled with lovely bald cypress hung with Spanish moss. During the winter, you may frighten hundreds of ducks into flight. The trail follows relatively high ground on the east side of the brake, crosses the brake and a tributary on a boardwalk, and returns to the levee road on the west side of the brake. Many nest boxes for wood ducks have been erected alongside. The trail is a cooperative venture between the Service and the Tchula Garden Club. When funding is available, interpretive signs and benches will be installed, and the trail will be paved, making it accessible to people in wheelchairs.

At the extreme northern end of the NWR a gravel road leaves the paved road near the town of Howard, following the top of a levee that begins on the east side of the bridge over Fannegusha Creek. This road is excellent for viewing waterfowl, shorebirds, beaver, and nutria and is suitable for the handicapped.

At the southern end of the refuge are open fields planted with food for waterfowl. Levees and water control structures enable refuge managers to flood the fields while migratory waterfowl are in the region. Public use maps distributed to hunters indicate that this portion of the refuge is closed to the public except during October-December deer hunts. Hiker/birders may be allowed to enter at other times, however, if they get written permission from the refuge manager in advance.

Those looking for a more rugged experience could put their canoes into Bear Lake from the levee road or into the deepest part of the brake, which is accessible from Thornton Road.

Maps and Literature: The Tchula, Howard and Thornton topo maps are useful for swamp explorations.

EF7 MATHEWS BRAKE NATIONAL WILDLIFE REFUGE,
Between Cruger and Sidon in Holmes and Leflore counties (about 2,600 acres)

This refuge is essentially a lake fringed with trees. A boat launch provides access. Most people come to fish, but Mathews Brake is also a great place for birding and paddling a canoe. The Service acquired the area in 1980.

The northern part of the brake may be closed to public access between December 1 and March 15. Check with the refuge complex office before you go.

Maps and Literature: The Cruger, Itta Bena, Sidon, and Montgomery topo maps are useful.

F7 MORGAN BRAKE NATIONAL WILDLIFE REFUGE,
N and S of Tchula, Holmes County (7,300 acres)

The Service is still adding land to this refuge, which included four separate areas in 1993. For an overview of the refuge area, follow Providence Road approximately 6.2 miles east from U.S. Hwy 49E to a fire lookout tower on the loess bluffs. (Providence Road begins at the Scottane Gas Company office on Hwy 49E about one mile north of Tchula. It is designated "Oswego" on the Tchula 7.5' topo map.)

The refuge encompasses several intermittently flooded brakes. The two large southern parcels are designated waterfowl sanctuaries and may be closed to all public use except deer hunting between December 1 and March 15. You may be able to enter during that time of the year, however, if you have written permission from the refuge complex headquarters. The Tchula 7.5' topo map shows a dirt road beginning at the hunter permit station at the southern edge of the easternmost parcel that may make a good trail for hiking.

This parcel was once part of Providence Plantation. Just to the north, mostly on the other side of Providence Road, is the square mile of land that

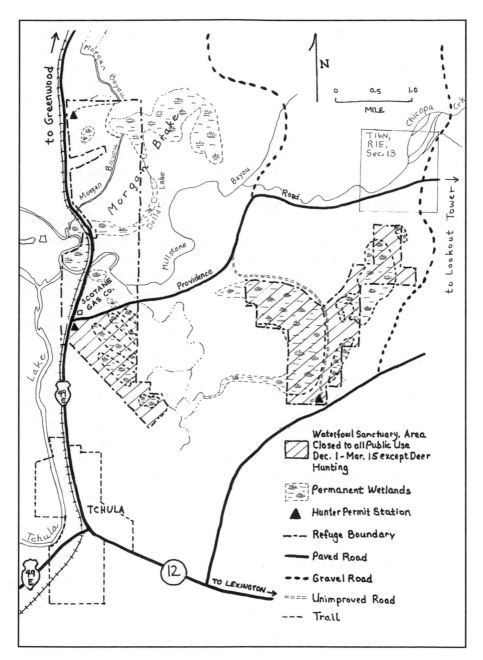

MAP 31. Morgan Brake National Wildlife Refuge

surveyors designated T. 16N, R. 1E, Sec. 13 in 1830. During that year, the Choctaw Indians ceded the land to the United States by the Treaty of Dancing Rabbit. The land passed through 16 different owners until 1989, when part of the former plantation was sold to the Nature Conservancy for transfer to the Fish and Wildlife Service. (See Campbell's book *Providence*, in the bibliography, for more information on the former plantation.)

The northernmost portion, some 1,330 acres, includes part of Morgan Brake itself. It is a complex of bottomland hardwoods, bald cypress/tupelo swamps, and shallow depressions filled with buttonbush, water elm, swamp privet, and willow. The Nature Conservancy purchased the land in 1979 and sold it to the Service the following year.

Five old roads closed to all motorized public use make good hiking trails. To gain access, park at the visitor information kiosk along Hwy 49E about 3.9 miles north of the built-up part of Tchula. Look for a metal gate at the edge of the woods at the northeast edge of the clearing. The old road behind the gate will take you past impressive cypress swamps; some are likely to be dry in the fall.

Maps and Literature: The Tchula and Cruger topo maps are recommended.

G6 PANTHER SWAMP NATIONAL WILDLIFE REFUGE,
Between Yazoo City and Holly Bluff, Yazoo County (28,200 acres)

Panther Swamp is a complex of bottomland hardwood forests and brakes. Much of the northwestern portion was cleared for agricultural use before the Service acquired it. Some of the open fields are planted with food for ducks and geese, while natural herbaceous vegetation is allowed to grow in other periodically flooded fields. Low levees and water control structures allow the refuge managers to flood the fields when migratory waterfowl are present.

The refuge gets its name from Panther Creek, which flows into Lake George, an elongated oxbow lake that connects the Yazoo and Big Sunflower rivers. Several smaller bayous flow into Panther Creek. Equally important is a man-made structure that cuts through the refuge—the Will M. Whittington Auxiliary Channel. Built by the U.S. Army Corps of Engineers, it connects the Yazoo River with the Big Sunflower River to the south. Its purpose is to move floodwaters more quickly from the Yazoo Basin.

Gravel roads run along both the levees that confine the auxiliary channel. When waterfowl are present, you are likely to see many in the flooded fields along the west levee. Several ATV trails branch from these two roads and River

Road, which borders the east side of the refuge. Many of these trails follow pipeline and power line corridors or go through open fields. They can be used for hiking although they aren't particularly scenic. If they are or were recently muddy, however, you can see tracks of many resident mammals on them. The roads that run through forested portions of the refuge are more interesting but are likely to be flooded in late winter and spring.

You may also canoe through the western part of the refuge. Start at Lower Twist Access point, and follow the slough west to Panther Creek. Paddle down Panther Creek (you will have to portage over a couple of barriers on the way) to Lake George. Turn left and proceed to the west levee along the Whittington Auxiliary Channel, where your trip ends.

The first 12,000 acres of what is now Panther Swamp NWR were purchased by the Nature Conservancy in 1977 and transferred to the Service the following year. An additional 10,000 acres have been acquired since then.

Maps and Literature: The Service has a separate map of this large area. The Bayland SE and Holly Bluff topo maps are useful for the canoe trips.

YAZOO NATIONAL WILDLIFE REFUGE, F 5
NE of Glen Allan, Washington County (ca. 13,000 acres)

This refuge encompasses Swan Lake, a long-abandoned loop of the Mississippi River. (Lake Washington, which is just to the west, is a more recently abandoned channel.) In addition, Yazoo NWR includes several other natural water-filled depressions and sloughs as well as man-made impoundments and greentree reservoirs.

Agricultural fields occupy a substantial portion of the refuge. The land is farmed under a cooperative agreement with the Fish and Wildlife Service. Farmers grow soybeans, corn, milo, and wheat. One-fourth of the crop is left in designated fields for waterfowl, deer, and nongame wildlife.

No hiking trails have been designated, but field roads and roads for administrative use are open to ATVs during the hunting season and to foot travel all year. Alligator Pond in the southern part of the refuge is particularly recommended to hikers and nature lovers. Here you may see marsh birds, wood ducks, turtles, and alligators plus lots of ducks in season. A gravel road between the pond and an adjacent slough that is closed to public vehicles follows a levee about 1.4 miles. It ends at Yazoo Refuge Road. Those wanting more exercise can walk in a loop around Alligator Pond on nearby field roads. Parts of these roads will be flooded in the winter, however.

Adventuresome people seeking a wilder setting could put their canoes into

Swan Lake. More properly a brake, it contains large cypress, tupelo gum, and water hyacinths. You may encounter otter, beaver, mink, and nutria and lots of waterfowl in season. The undergrowth is quite thick in places, so you will also have to be prepared for lots of bushwhacking and dodging. The water level can get low in late summer, but generally there should be enough water for a canoe or pirogue.

Yazoo NWR is Mississippi's first national wildlife refuge. Land acquisition began in 1936.

Maps and Literature: The Service issues a separate map of the area. The Percy, Glen Allan, and Swan Lake NW topo maps are useful.

3. The National Park System

Mississippi has 3 of the more than 350 areas in the National Park System. A branch of the U.S. Department of the Interior, the National Park Service has the dual and often challenging mission of protecting the biological, geological, historic, and prehistoric features of the parks and making them available for public recreation and education.

GULF ISLANDS NATIONAL SEASHORE,

3500 Park Rd., Ocean Springs, MS 39564 (601-875-0821)

Established by an act of Congress in 1971, the national seashore stretches from West Ship Island south of Biloxi, Mississippi, eastward to Santa Rosa Island south of Fort Walton Beach, Florida. It encompasses 16,759 acres of coast and offshore islands plus a two-mile-wide margin of the Gulf of Mexico around each. Mississippi's share includes five units: the Davis Bayou portion on the coast and four of the state's five barrier islands offshore. From west to east, the islands are West Ship, East Ship, Horn, and Petit Bois islands. The barrier islands are separated from the mainland by the Mississippi Sound, a shallow passage about six miles wide.

Your starting point for your first visit to Gulf Islands will be the visitor center in the Davis Bayou Unit near Ocean Springs (see below).

Maps and Literature: Ask for the brochure, which has excellent color maps of the coastal units but not the barrier islands.

DAVIS BAYOU UNIT (401 ACRES) N 10

The coastal portion of the national seashore is surrounded on three sides by the town of Ocean Springs, but because of dense trees and undergrowth, you will hardly be aware of it. Davis Bayou is a short stream beginning only a few miles to the east. Several thousand years ago during the Ice Age, when more of the earth's water was bound up in glaciers, the ocean was much lower. Davis

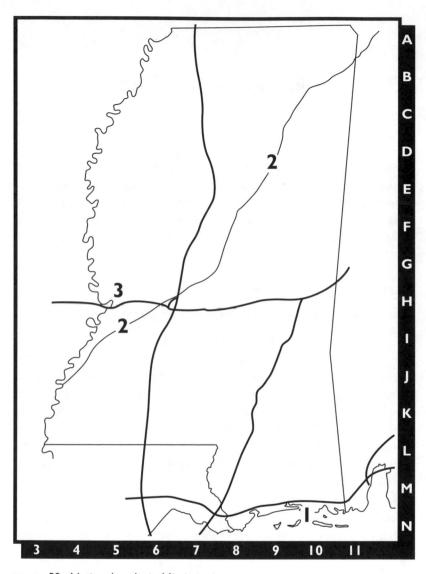

M A P 32. National parks in Mississippi

LEGEND

1 = Gulf Islands National Seashore

2 = Natchez Trace Parkway

3 = Vicksburg National Military Park and Cemetery

Bayou would have been much narrower then, but now its lower valley is inundated by the Gulf of Mexico.

The area was originally set aside in 1937 as Magnolia State Park. Even then it was recognized as one of the last unspoiled sections of the Mississippi Gulf Coast.

Three lesser bayous meander through the park. All are fringed with wide expanses of coastal marshes, dominated by shoal grass, manatee grass, turtle grass, widgeon grass, and many species of red, brown, and green algae. Here the salt water of the Gulf mixes with fresh water from the land. These coastal grasslands are extremely fertile and are a vital component of the Mississippi Sound ecosystem. Many invertebrates, including commercial varieties of shrimp and more than 200 species of fish, breed and/or grow to maturity here. Many species of duck winter in these estuaries, and shore and marsh birds live there all year.

Barely above high tide are lowland hardwood swamps. Maples, cypress, sweetgum, bay, and ash border the marshes and inland ponds. They are supplanted by other hardwoods on higher ground, with beech, magnolia, oaks, hickories, and pine on the highest ridges. Farther inland the pine-palmetto flatwoods take over, dominated by longleaf, loblolly, and slash pine, wax myrtle, and saw palmetto.

The Nature's Way Trail (0.5-mile loop) leads through marshes and past an observation platform. Points of interest are marked with numbered posts; brochures are available at the visitor center. Another unmarked trail well known to birders follows the fence line marking the west border of the park, paralleling Hanley Road on the west side of the unit. A shorter loop on boardwalks, suitable for the handicapped, begins behind the visitor center.

Best Time to Visit: The park is open all year. Best time for seeing migratory birds in transit between Central America and North America is April and October.

Facilities: The William M. Colmer Visitor Center and Park Headquarters offers a 30-minute orientation film, a display of artwork by Walter Anderson, and other exhibits. Go there to ask questions and learn about boat tours to the barrier islands. During the summer, ranger naturalists conduct tours of the marshes in flat-bottomed johnboats. It also has an excellent selection of books for sale on the history and natural history of the Gulf Coast. As of 1991–92, the Park Service offered Saturday evening campfire programs about the Gulf Island's history and natural history.

Fishing piers are a short walk from the visitor center. No license is required to try your hand at fishing or crabbing. There is also a boat launching ramp.

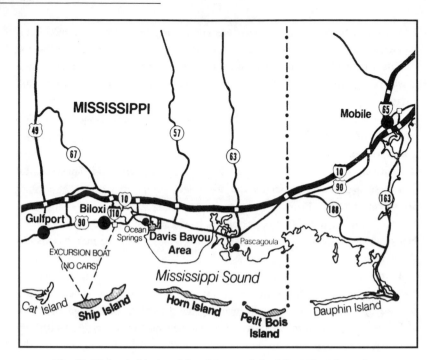

MAP 33. Gulf Islands National Seashore and the Mississippi Sound

One facility you won't find here is a sandy beach or a place to swim. The national seashore's beaches are out on the barrier islands.

The Davis Bayou Unit also has a 51-unit campground, each unit with electrical and water hookups; a tent camping area for groups and small parties; and a large picnic ground with pavilions. Check in early; the 51-unit campground is likely to be filled by late in the day year round.

Access: The way to the park entrance is well marked from Interstate 10 and U.S. 90 at Ocean Springs.

Maps and Literature: The Park Service brochure with maps (see above) should be adequate for your visit. Also useful is the topo map for Ocean Springs.

THE BARRIER ISLANDS AND MISSISSIPPI SOUND

Mississippi's barrier islands are unique among the places described in this guide. Most people who know them find them special.

Most of North America's Atlantic and Gulf coasts are protected from the open ocean by long, narrow sandy islands up to 30 miles offshore. Those in the

Gulf Coast National Seashore are part of a chain that begins with Dauphin Island south of Mobile and continues west off the Mississippi coast with Petit Bois (pronounced "petty boy"), Horn, East Ship, West Ship, and Cat islands. On the average, they are 10 miles off the coast. Between the islands and the coast is the Mississippi Sound. The Sound is generally less than 20' deep and less saline than the Gulf of Mexico because rivers bring in fresh water and nutrients. Beyond the islands the floor of the Gulf slopes gently south to the edge of the continental shelf, about 90 miles out.

Indians frequently visited the islands, and they are rich in recorded history. Because of their instability—they may be completely under water during hurricanes—few man-made structures have persisted, and it has proven impractical to put the islands to commercial use. For example, in the 1920s a dance hall and casino were built on the Isle of Caprice, which had emerged between Horn Island and Ship Island in about 1900. The sea oats that anchored the dunes on the island were commercially harvested. The sea began to reclaim the island, and in the 1947 hurricane it disappeared entirely. The consensus now is that the barrier islands should remain undeveloped—available for recreation and allowed to serve their natural function as barriers protecting the Gulf Coast from the full force of storms.

The barrier islands are made of white sand. Beaches rim the islands, wider on the Gulf side and thrown up into dunes inland. The extensive root systems of sea oats, a grass that can withstand the salt, great heat, and dryness of the dunes, are largely responsible for stabilizing the dunes. Among the islands now in the national seashore, all but West Ship have slash pines and sometimes scrub oaks on higher, more stable ground. Beaches are narrower on the protected north sides of the islands and have inlets leading into protected salt marshes. Toward the middle of the islands are brackish ponds lined with cattails and other marsh plants.

The barrier islands have moved west and changed shape since they were first mapped by the French in 1699. They move by losing sand from their eastern ends and adding sand to the west. Petit Bois Island, for example, was once attached to Dauphin Island. Part of it was still within the Alabama state line as late as 1950. Today it's entirely within Mississippi. As the islands erode, black lines of peat derived from former marshes are exposed. Carbon 14 dating indicates that the marshes existed only a few hundred years ago.

Taking a boat out to the barrier islands is a memorable part of any trip to the islands, at least for those of us who live inland. Bottle-nosed dolphins are likely to accompany you, and gulls and pelicans may fly overhead. The Sound is busy with ships. Double-rigged shrimp trawlers may be the most numerous, but you may also encounter oceangoing freighters and intercoastal tugs pushing barges.

Most visitors to the barrier islands will do some beachcombing. Be sure to wear sneakers to protect your feet. Mole crabs, southern coquina clams, and ghost crabs are among the most common residents of the beaches. Ghost crabs dig burrows up to about an inch in diameter well above the high tide line. They are out mainly at night, but you may see their linear tracks all over the beach. All kinds of dead sea creatures wash up—among them jellyfish and Portuguese man-o'-war. Beware of their tentacles, which can inflict painful stings. You are permitted to collect seashells but not live animals. To avoid stepping on stingrays—which create an extremely painful wound that may require medical attention—shuffle your feet in the water. Never swim alone; powerful offshore currents can sweep you into deep water.

Two large islands—Cat Island and Deer Island—are not described because they are privately owned. Cat Island is the westernmost of the Mississippi barrier islands. Deer Island, less than a mile south of Biloxi, is not a barrier island but an extension of the coast. Several thousand years ago, during the Ice Age, it was connected with the mainland when the sea level was lower.

Access: Ferries make regular round trips between Gulfport and Biloxi to West Ship Island between March and October. The only company that can legally charter trips to East and West Ship islands is Pan Isles, Inc. (see below). The other barrier islands are accessible only by private or charter boat. It is not safe to take rowboats or canoes across the Sound. Sea kayaks are an option for those experienced in their use on open water (see Sevenair, *Trail Guide to the Delta Country*, in the bibliography).

Only a few boat companies are legally chartered to take passengers to Horn and Petit Bois islands. Contact the park office for an up-to-date list.

What to Bring on a Trip to the Barrier Islands: Most of the places described in this guide are in deep forest. The barrier islands are a different world, with intense light reflected from the white sand beaches and open sea. For a day trip at any time of the year, you should take sunblock lotion, a hat with a brim, insect repellent (mosquitoes, no-see-ums, and gnats can be terrible in warm weather), a long-sleeved shirt and long pants for further protection from insects and sunburn, sunglasses, and eyeglass holders (a strap or cord) so that you won't lose your glasses in the water. You will also need sneakers for beachcombing, and one gallon of water per person per day. Add meat tenderizer to your first aid kit for treating jellyfish stings. Options include binoculars and a canoe or inflatable boat for exploring lagoons and ponds. During cold periods of the year, bring a warm jacket, warm socks, and boots.

For camping, bring rope so that you can string your food between two trees at night and while you are away from camp during the day, to protect it from raccoons. A tarp with poles and sand stakes that will do double duty as a sunshade and rain protector is a good addition. Your tent should be equipped with no-see-um netting. Sand stakes or oversized tent stakes for your tent are a good idea; small, slender stakes do not hold well in loose sand when the wind is strong.

In cold, windy weather a campsite on the lee side of dunes or woods will give you protection. In warm, still conditions, the tips of the islands are better, because constant breezes and lack of vegetation discourage biting insects.

The barrier islands are becoming increasingly popular with campers. Do your part to minimize your impact. Never camp on top of dunes; the vegetation that holds them in place is fragile. Your campfire (if any) should be near the edge of the water, not in the woods. The islands are often dry, and it's easy to start a forest fire. Use only driftwood. Your tent should be sited so that you don't trample ground vegetation as you come and go. The same number of people does less damage in small parties than in one large party.

Literature: The National Park Service has an excellent free brochure entitled *Camping on a Wilderness Island.* More detailed information on navigating to the barrier islands is in Toups and Jackson's *Birds and Birding* and Sevenair's *Trail Guide* (see the bibliography).

● **Petit Bois Island** (1,466 acres). This is the second largest Mississippi N 11 barrier island. It is about seven and one-half miles long and up to three-quarters of a mile wide. All of it is a national wilderness area. The name is French for "little forest." The island has only ten acres of woods—a strip of slash pine on the widest part. It is difficult to walk across the island because of the large marshes in the interior. Many species of birds live on and around the island— plovers, reddish egrets, many kinds of shorebirds, marsh birds, gulls, terns, and, in the winter, diving ducks and common loons.

The best anchoring points for small boats are near the tips of the islands and just west of the trees on the north shore. Boaters should watch out for a sunken barge near the west tip within 100 yards of the north shore. It may or may not be marked by a buoy.

During warm weather the ends of the island are best for camping because the constant winds keep insects in check. In cold weather the woods offer some protection.

● **Horn Island** (3,650 acres). More than 13 miles long and up to three- N 10

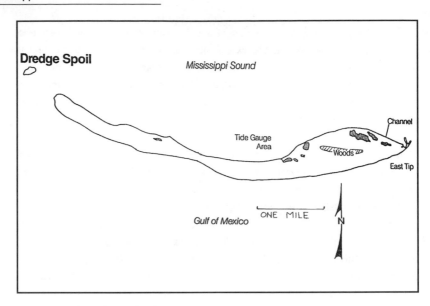

MAP 34. Petit Bois Island

 quarters of a mile wide, Horn Island is the largest of Mississippi's barrier islands. Except for a strip across the middle that accommodates a Park Service ranger station, it is a federally designated wilderness area.

Commensurate with its size, Horn Island has the greatest diversity of habitat of the National Seashore's barrier islands. It is surrounded by white sand beaches. Inland are sand dunes 25' to 35' high. High ground in the interior is forested with mature slash pines, in some places free of understory, in others with dense understories dominated by palmettos. Both fresh- and saltwater marshes spread across low ground in the interior, and there are two sizable tidal lagoons. The largest, Big Lagoon, has extensive mud flats at low tide that are attractive to shore birds. Ranger Pond (formerly known as Oyster Pond because of abundant oysters) is ringed with salt marshes inhabited by marsh-dwelling birds. Both these lagoons are great to explore by water, with lots of opportunity for wildlife viewing. They are off limits to motorboats, but you could bring a canoe or other small boat with you.

Many ospreys nest on Horn Island. Their bulky nests of sticks in dead pines are one of the trademarks of the island.

Wildlife biologists have selected this large isolated island for projects designed to restore two southern species threatened with extinction—the southern bald eagle and the red wolf. Bald eagles were once widespread in

Mississippi but became nearly extinct after World War II because of indiscriminate use of DDT. Eggs were taken from the nests of wild eagles in Florida and flown to the George Mikoch Sutton Avian Research Center in Oklahoma. Here they were incubated and the newly hatched chicks reared until they were eight weeks old. The chicks were then flown to a hacking tower 30' high on Horn Island, where they were fed but kept from close contact with humans. Some 40 chicks were fledged between 1986 and 1989. As expected, the young eagles left the island, but biologists hoped that at least some would eventually return to breed. This hope was fulfilled in 1990-91, when a mated pair returned to the island and reared a chick. They fledged another the following year and, in 1992-93, successfully reared two chicks.

The red wolf once occurred throughout the southeastern United States, but by the early 1970s it had nearly vanished. The survivors were on Louisiana's Gulf shore and were interbreeding with coyotes. They were captured and bred in captivity to build up their numbers. The U.S. Fish and Wildlife Service then began introducing them to relatively safe places within their former range.

A pair of red wolves was put on Horn Island in 1989. The plan was to keep them there five years. The pups they reared in the wild would be used in reintroduction projects elsewhere. The pair ranged over the entire island; their large, doglike tracks could be seen almost anywhere, but the wolves themselves were rarely glimpsed. They lived mainly on rabbits and raccoons. The pair was removed before the five years were up because they had no offspring. The Service may resume the experiment later, however.

Arrowheads and pottery shards show that Indians visited Horn Island before Europeans arrived. The island was first called Isle à Corne, the French version of its present name, on a map dating from 1732. Apparently it referred to a powder horn that an early visitor lost on the island. Between 1845 and 1920 the Waters family lived on the island, raising livestock and crops. In the late 1800s and early 20th century, the Gulf side of the island was used as a loading area for logs rafted out from the coast. Here they were loaded on ships bound for the northeastern states and foreign countries.

The island was closed to all public use between 1943 and 1945, when the U.S. Army took it over and built a station for research in biological warfare. You can still see the foundations of some of the buildings in the pine woods at the end of an old road leading west from the ranger station. At the site now known as The Chimney was an incinerator with a tall brick chimney. The chimney fell over during Hurricane Frederick, but its remains were still visible in the late 1980s.

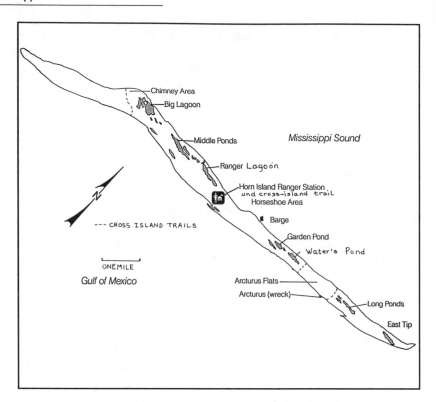

MAP 35. Horn Island. Broken lines indicate cross-island trails.

In 1958 a portion of the island became a national wildlife refuge managed by the U.S. Fish and Wildlife Service. It became part of the national seashore in 1971 and a wilderness area in 1978.

Horn Island is still not safe from environmental damage. In 1992, for example, Sea Pride Industries announced its plan to install a fish farm in the Gulf about two miles south of Horn Island. Millions of fish would be raised in nets hanging 30' down from huge barges. Many environmentalists are concerned that the rain of feces and uneaten fish food will pollute the Gulf near the island. The Gulf Islands Conservancy has been organized to address this issue and others that may threaten the ecosystems of the islands and Mississippi Sound.

Visiting Horn Island: Next to Ship Island, Horn Island is the most popular destination of visitors. Most come between April and September. Still, the island is long enough to allow parties to space themselves out. March, October, and November are good times to avoid crowds, but it is sometimes quite cold. Few people camp on the island in the middle of winter, between December and February.

Four trails cross the island. You can work your way across elsewhere, but more likely, you will be stopped by lagoons and marshes. The trail ends are good destinations for day trips because you can quickly get from one side of the island to the other. Arcturus Flats on the east end (named after a wrecked ship, the *Arcturus*, on the south side) and the Horseshoe Area on the west end are particularly recommended for day trippers, especially birders.

You have many potential camping places on the island. The time of year will affect your selection of a campsite. In warm periods of the year the ends of the island are favored because the strong winds and distance from vegetation diminish the hordes of mosquitoes and other biting insects. During cool periods of the year the north-facing beaches afford protection from the wind.

Walter Anderson (1903–65): This Ocean Springs artist is an integral part of the lore of Horn Island. His style has been compared to that of Van Gogh and Picasso. Between 1946 and his death, the island and its flora and fauna were the principal subjects of his watercolors and drawings. He used a rowboat or skiff to cover the 12 miles between his studio/cottage at Shearwater Pottery and the island. (This type of craft is not recommended for the purpose—Anderson, a powerful man, capsized and almost drowned at least three times.) His favorite campsite was on the east curve of the Horseshoe. He would haul the boat ashore, turn it upside down to create a shelter, and work in isolation for as much as three weeks at a time. He was a keen—or, more accurately, ecstatic—observer of nature and strove to record fleeting images (see Agnes Anderson's *Approaching the Magic Hour*, in the bibliography). He also kept detailed journals, or "logs," of his daily observations (see Sugg, ed., *The Horn Island Logs*, in the bibliography).

During his lifetime, some people thought he was a kook, but since his death his powerful art has attained national attention. If you like art or just want to experience more of the natural world of Horn Island, you will want to see some of his works. A few of his wood carvings are displayed at the visitor center. The Walter Anderson Museum of Art in Ocean Springs features other works, including a famous mural he painted on the walls of the adjacent Ocean Springs Community Center (Walter Anderson Museum of Art, 510 Washington Ave., Ocean Springs, MS 39564; 601-872-3164. Open Mon.-Sat. 10–5, Sun. 1–5, closed New Year's Day and Christmas; admission fee).

● **West and East Ship Islands.** Before 1969 these islands were a single ⃝ 10 island that the French named Isle aux Vaisseaux because it had a natural protected harbor on the north side. The island was in a key position during the days of sailing ships because all vessels bound for New Orleans and the mouth

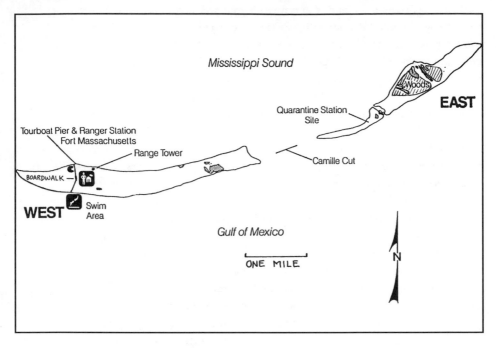

Mississippi Sound

Quarantine Station
Site

EAST

Tourboat Pier & Ranger Station
Fort Massachusetts
Range Tower

BOARDWALK

Camille Cut

WEST

Swim
Area

Gulf of Mexico

ONE MILE

N

MAP 36. West and East Ship Islands

of the Mississippi River as well as the Mississippi Gulf Coast had to pass near its western end. It has been owned in turn by France, England, Spain, and the United States. The French installed a magazine and barracks there in 1717.

Prior to Hurricane Camille, Ship Island had a narrow flat area in the middle known as Ship Island Flats. Camille's 200-m.p.h. winds and 30′ tides cut through the Flats, replacing them with a stretch of open water between West and East Ship islands known as the Camille Cut.

West Ship Island (555 acres), 3.7 miles long and up to 0.34 mile wide, is the least varied in terms of habitat of the five Mississippi barrier islands. It is, however, of considerable historic interest. It is the only one that is easily accessible to people who don't have their own boats, being linked to the coast by regularly scheduled ferries between March and October.

The principal attraction for many visitors is Fort Massachusetts, dating from Civil War times. One of the last masonry coastal forts to be built in the United States, the horseshoe-shaped structure is built of concrete and red brick, slate and granite shipped from the New England states. The Army Corps of Engineers began construction in 1859. Early In the Civil War the Confederates seized the island. Federal forces took it back within a few months and used the island as a staging area for the capture of New Orleans. After the war, construction resumed.

The fort was finally finished in 1866, but it was obsolete before it was completed, because rifled cannons were put into use during the Civil War. These cannons had spiral grooves on the surface of the bore that caused projectiles to rotate around their long axes. Masonry forts could not withstand the impact of these spinning projectiles. Troops withdrew from the island in 1875, and in 1901 the army sold the cannons for scrap metal.

When the fort was completed, it was 500' from the west end of the island. Now it's more than a mile from the end. It is also being undercut. To prevent it from collapsing into the Sound, sand from dredging operations is periodically deposited against it.

National Park rangers conduct tours of Fort Massachusetts between Memorial Day and Labor Day. Tours may be taken at other times by special arrangement.

A boardwalk runs across the island from the dock and fort to a swimming beach on the Gulf side of the island. It leads over a salt marsh and goes past a pond. Marsh birds and alligators dwell here, and in the winter, migratory ducks may be in the pond.

You can walk around the entire island on the beaches in a few hours, taking time out to swim, picnic, and bird-watch. You may see a variety of gulls, terns, black skimmers, and marsh birds. No trees grow on the island, but there are lots of graceful sea oats.

Facilities: Restrooms, snack bar, swimming beach, bathhouse with showers, picnic shelters, umbrellas for rent.

Access: Ferry service to West Ship Island from Gulfport begins on the first Saturday in March and continues to the last Sunday in October.

For Further Information on Ferry Service: Pan Isles, Inc., P.O. Box 1467, Gulfport, MS 39502. Boat Docks and Ticket Offices: Gulfport Yacht Harbor, Hwy 90 at Hwy 49 (601-436-6010; recording 864-1014). Departure from Point Cadet Marina, Biloxi, by charter only (601-864-3797).

East Ship Island (362 acres) is 2.6 miles long and up to a half mile wide. It's the smallest of the Mississippi barrier islands but is second only to Horn Island in diversity of habitat. It has 75 acres of woods—mostly mature slash pine but also a small stand of live oaks in the center near the south beach. Inland are salt marshes and a freshwater lagoon fringed with woods that provide good campsites with shelter from the sun and wind. Ospreys breed on East Ship, and great egrets and great blue herons have a rookery in the interior. Two artesian wells flowed near the west end of the island, but they no longer exist. As the east end of the island erodes away, several acres of peat have been exposed, marking the sites of former marshes.

Between 1878 and about 1910, the U.S. government and later the state maintained a yellow fever quarantine station on the northwest side. All incoming vessels were inspected and fumigated here. The buildings were later used as a recreation retreat by Keesler Air Force Base personnel and for informal camping by other parties until they were destroyed by Hurricane Camille in 1969.

It is difficult to walk across the island, but you can walk around it in a couple of hours. You can swim on the Gulf side. East Ship is an undeveloped paradise for campers. For solitude, go in the off seasons or during the week.

Access: The island is accessible only by private or charter boat. It is best approached near the middle on the north side. No real channel goes to the shore, but an old abandoned channel leads to the former site of the quarantine station, marked by a pile of black rocks on shore. Only dinghies or small crafts can go all the way to the shore. Deep draft vessels should anchor well offshore in at least 10′ of water.

NATCHEZ TRACE PARKWAY,

Superintendent, R.R. 1, NT-143, Tupelo, MS 38801 (601-680-4025 or 680-4027). The Parkway is a 450-mile-long controlled access highway through Mississippi, Alabama, and Tennessee (309 miles in Mississippi)

The Natchez Trace is actually two different roads: the Old Natchez Trace and the Natchez Trace Parkway. The Old Natchez Trace coalesced from Indian trails in the 1700s. Between 1780 and 1820 it was vital to commerce in the frontier area then known as the Old Southwest, which included Mississippi. Settlers in the Ohio River Valley, Kentucky, and Tennessee could get higher prices for their agricultural produce, flour, tobacco, millstones, iron, whiskey, and other goods in Natchez and New Orleans than they could around their homes. The easiest way to transport the goods was to float them down the Ohio, Tennessee, and Mississippi rivers in flatboats. Rowing, poling, or towing the boats back upstream hundreds of miles was hardly feasible, so the boatmen sold them for lumber and walked or rode horseback overland back to the Cumberland River at Nashville.

Until 1820, most of the Trace in Mississippi ran through the Choctaw and

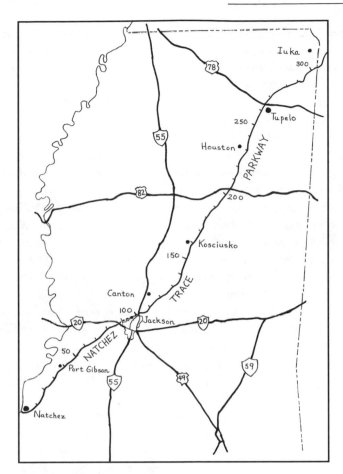

MAP 37. Natchez Trace Parkway, showing every tenth milepost.

Chickasaw Indian nations. It was what we would call a trail today but not as good as the horseback trails described in this guide, because travelers had to ford streams and rivers and slog across swamps. The Trace became a national road in 1801. Improvements were made, but it was still impassable for wagons.

The Old Trace as a unit was largely abandoned in the early 1820s. By then, steamboats were chugging up the Mississippi and other major rivers. It was quicker and easier for boatmen to go by steamboat than trek overland on the Trace.

The Natchez Trace Parkway roughly follows the Old Trace. In many portions, in fact, it was built right over the old road. Its purposes, however, are different. The Parkway is a product of the 1930s. The parkway concept originated in New York City in the late 1920s. Parkways are landscaped, elongated parks, that allow car owners to glide along in comfort, temporarily escaping the bustle and confusion of urban living. To maintain tranquillity, commercial vehicles are prohibited. Parkway construction also provided jobs to young men out of work in the Great Depression and then brought tourists and their dollars into the state.

U.S. congressman Jeff Busby, a native of Tishomingo County, introduced a bill to study the concept of a parkway in 1932. Actual construction began in the late 1930s and is still proceeding at a leisurely pace. Only three sections remained to be completed as of 1992. The segment that will parallel Interstate 220 west of Jackson and Clinton should be completed by the year 2000.

As you drive the Parkway today, stopping to read interpretive signs, hiking short nature trails, and visiting historic sites, your mind will be suspended in a strange world, somewhere between the pre-1830 frontier and modern times.

Facilities: Within Mississippi, the Park Service provides 15 picnic areas, some with restrooms and others without. Within Mississippi, the Parkway itself has only two campgrounds, at Jeff Busby and at Rocky Springs. Both have flush toilets but no showers or hookups for RVs. Other public campgrounds with RV hookups are within a few miles of the Trace in nearby state parks and national forests. Nearby towns have additional, privately owned campgrounds and motels.

Maps: The Park Service has an excellent map and guide to the Parkway. You can pick it up at facilities along the Trace or order a copy by phone or mail.

The visitor center at Tupelo has a small exhibit on the history of the Old Trace and sells books on its history and natural history. Two interesting historical accounts are Crutchfield's *Natchez Trace* and Daniels' *Devil's Backbone* (see bibliography). Park rangers are on hand to answer questions.

PARKWAY TRAILS AT LEAST ONE MILE LONG

Eight hiking and horseback trails between 1 mile and more than 20 miles long parallel various segments of the Parkway. Designated hiking trails are for hikers only, while horse trails are open to both equestrians and hikers. Wheeled vehicles of all kinds, including bicycles, are prohibited on trails. As of late 1993, backpacking is officially permitted only if you camp on the berm of the paved road. However, the policy is likely to change as more of the Natchez Trace National Scenic Trail is completed. The Park Service may give you permission to camp along the trail if you tell them approximately where you intend to stop and don't build fires.

- **The Natchez Trace National Scenic Trail.** This trail will follow the entire 450-mile length of the Parkway from Knoxville to Natchez, including the 309 miles in Mississippi. It was authorized by an act of Congress on March 28, 1983. It is to be available for bicycling, hiking, and horseback riding. Bicycling is already allowed on the paved Parkway, and an additional paved bicycle trail may be constructed near Jackson. It is likely that the Scenic Trail itself will be exclusively for horseback riders and hikers.

Because no funds were appropriated for the trail, the Park Service is depending on volunteers to build it. A few segments have been built, but the entire trail may not be completed until after the year 2000. For an update on completed and partially completed sections, contact the Natchez Trace Trail Conference, P. O. Box 1236, Jackson, MS 39215; 601-956-0045.

These segments are a preview of the completed trail. Most of the terrain is gentle or rolling, but there will be some rugged hilly sections. Commercial logging does not occur along the Trace, so you will ride or walk through some stands of beautiful large trees. Open cultivated fields and pastures are interspersed with the forests. Often you will be in sight of farm buildings, and occasionally, subdivisions. Mileposts along the trail will be opposite the corresponding mileposts on the Parkway, making it easy to locate precisely your position. They will not indicate the actual trail miles.

Don't expect a wilderness setting when you hike or ride the trail. Most of the Parkway runs down the middle of a strip of land only 600′ to 1,000′ wide, so the trail will usually be no more than 300′–500′ from the paved road. With the exception of a few segments where the strip of federal land widens, you will always hear traffic on the Parkway. You will also see the vehicles much of the time, especially where you cross fields.

With the exception of the Tupelo Horse Trail and the Witch Dance Trail, none of the trails are looped in late 1993. If you are a one-car party and would like to take a circuit trip without retracing your steps, consider bringing a bicycle and chaining it to a tree where you plan to end your walk. Be sure it is out of sight of any roads.

- **Old Trace Trail:** Mile 16.8–20.0 (near Fayette). This 3.5-mile segment is the longest fragment of the old abandoned Trace. Few people know about this trail because it's not shown on the Parkway map distributed to visitors and is not marked along the paved Parkway. It is the wildest trail along the Parkway—crossed by no roads and out of sight and sound of vehicles. The spell is broken only at the northern end, where the sunken Trace passes along the edge of a large recent clearcut on private land. J4

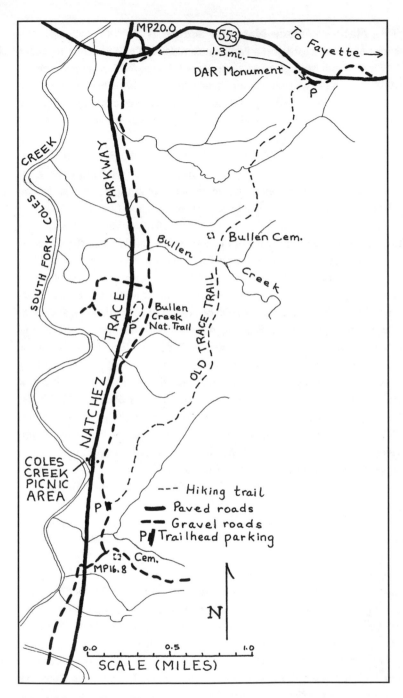

MAP 38. Old Trace Trail

Much of the trail is deeply sunken into the loess hills. Sometimes it's more like a fern-filled ravine than a trail, joined occasionally by other old roads almost as deeply sunken. Other parts are not sunken and follow ridgetops. (Old Indian trails and frontier roads stayed on ridges as much as possible to avoid poorly drained spots that would turn into mud holes in wet weather.)

The trail crosses two creeks, Bullen Creek and another to the north of it. It is just as travelers on the Old Trace found it: there are no bridges. When the water is high, you may have to wade. Here and in other spots about halfway along it's easy to lose the route. Watch for can lids painted red and nailed in trees and orange surveyors tape marking the route. If you are going north, avoid the deeply rutted recent logging road going uphill on your left after you cross the second creek. Instead, keep alongside the stream valley to your right.

Access: To reach the southern end, turn off on a gravel road at Mile 16.8, just northeast of the bridge over Coles Creek. In 0.2 mile, turn left onto another gravel road. The parking area for the trail is on the right after another 0.2 mile.

The northern end is on State Hwy 553. Leave the Parkway at Mile 20.0 and proceed 1.3 mile toward Fayette. Watch for a gravel road on the right and a stone monument erected by the Daughters of the American Revolution marking the route of the old Trace. Turn onto this road, and in a short distance you will come upon a sign marking the trail and space to park.

If you want to make a circuit hike, you could start at the southern end of the Old Trace, turn left on Hwy 553, and then turn left on a gravel road just before 553 goes under the Trace overpass. Return to your car on this gravel road, which is little used and in deep woods.

- **Rocky Springs/Old Trace Trail/Owens Creek Trail:** Mile 52.4– I5
54.8 (near Port Gibson). Site of a vanished town and a lesson in land abuse, one of the longest surving segments of the Old Trace, and a hiking trail through rugged terrain to two waterfalls.

Between Mileposts 54.2 and 55.9, the Natchez Trace Parkway, normally a narrrow corridor, widens to encompass part of the extinct town of Rocky Springs, a segment of the original Natchez Trace, and a half mile of a delightful, sandy-bottomed creek appropriately named Little Sand Creek. The area is shaded by large pines and hardwoods and is one of the most pleasant and interesting portions of the Trace.

The Vanished Town of Rocky Springs (1792–1930): A 0.2-mile interpretive looped trail leads through the heart of a town that had 2,616 inhabitants in 1860. During its heyday just before the Civil War, Rocky Springs had at least a dozen large houses, including an elegant mansion on the highest hill, a brick Methodist church, at least two stores, a bakery, a post office, a Masonic lodge, schools, carpenters, a wheelwright, a well digger, a cabinetmaker, a cotton gin, and blacksmiths. It also provided higher education—Rocky Springs Academy and Southern Female College.

Most notorious in its early days was the Red House Tavern, built in 1796 to serve travelers on the Old Natchez Trace. Until 1802, it was also the place where local highwaymen and bandits assessed visitors and decided which ones would be worth accosting and murdering later in remote spots along the Trace. In 1802, territorial governor William C. C. Claiborne sent troops to the village to ferret out the bandits and hang them.

In May 1863 General Ulysses S. Grant marched into town. He set up temporary headquarters in the Methodist Church and appropriated the mansion as his sleeping quarters. His troops looted the stores but left the buildings intact.

Today only the church, constructed in 1837, remains, along with a couple of old safes that were too heavy to carry away and some old cisterns. Yellow fever epidemics in 1878 and 1888 killed many people. They are buried in the old cemetery beside the church. The Great Depression was the final blow to the community, which saw its last store close in 1930.

An old photograph taken in 1900 on display at the site tells the real story of the demise of the town. The remaining buildings are perched precariously on the edges of steep-walled gullies testifying to more than a century of land abuse. The first settlers around Rocky Springs were subsistence farmers. Soil erosion wasn't much of a concern to them because everyone knew that when the land wore out, there would always be more virgin land to clear and cultivate. During the 1820s large plantations became the economic base. All the land was cleared and planted with cotton—even steep slopes. By the 1850s the value of contour plowing in preventing erosion was well known, but still furrows were plowed up and down hills. Gullies grew deeper and wider as the topsoil vanished, and eventually the land was useless for farming.

 Trail to Rocky Springs (0.2-mile loop): The trail takes you to the site of Rocky Springs, from which the town derived its name. Deforestation and erosion lowered the water table, and the spring dried up long ago, but some elderly former residents showed the Park Service where it used to be.

 Old Natchez Trace (1.5 mile, not looped): The old Trace went right through the middle of the town of Rocky Springs. The 0.7-mile segment from the parking area near the town site to Little Sand Creek is a delightful walk through a mature forest of pine and oak. East of the creek, the old Trace continues another 0.8 mile. Part of it is deeply sunken with old trees struggling to stay upright on the banks. It ends at the Raymond–Port Gibson Road in a patch of kudzu.

Trail to Owens Creek (2.5 miles): The trail runs from the edge of the turn- around loop road in the picnic area to the falls of Owens Creek along the Parkway. Except for the first quarter mile or so, it more or less follows the northwestern edge of park land, which is about 0.1 mile from the paved Park- way. Even though it's close to the Parkway, it's usually out of sight and sound of traffic. The terrain is often exceedingly rugged, and the trail makes consider- able detours around steep-walled ravines. Today it's in deep forest of beech and oak. Probably it was once a gentler landscape before it was cleared, farmed, eroded, and turned back to nature for healing.

There are two falls on Owens Creek, one close to the Parkway and one back in the woods, out of sight to all but hikers. Old-timers say the falls used to have more water, but past land abuses have reduced the flow. Shaded picnic tables (but no drinking water) make this a good stopping place for your hike.

Picnic Area Loop Trail (ca. 0.5 mile): This unmarked but well built gravelly path leads through the deep woods between the looped turnaround at the end of the road leading to the picnic tables and the Parkway. It is not marked at either end, but you can find it easily by taking the gravel path to the se- cluded picnic tables at the upper (north) end of the loop and continuing be- yond them. The trail ends by more picnic tables at the lower (south) end of the loop.

Proposed 25-Mile-Long Horse/Hiking Trail from Rocky Springs south to State Hwy *553:* The Natchez Trail Conference, composed mainly of horseback riders, has signed a contract with the National Park Service to construct a trail on the southeast side of the Parkway. It should be completed by 1997. The northern end, with a staging area for riders, will be about 0.3 mile south of the turnoff to Rocky Springs, at the point where a gravel road presently goes under the Parkway. This trail will become a component of the trail proposed to run the entire length of the parkway.

Facilities at Rocky Springs: Campground with tables, grills, and flush toilets but no showers or RV hookups; amphitheater; separate picnic ground; visitor information center (no exhibits).

Maps: The Park Service's color map and brochure give the layout of part of the Rocky Springs area. The route of the Old Trace is shown on signboards. The entire area is shown on the Carlisle topo map, although none of the trails is depicted.

H 7

● **Lonesome Pine Horse Trail:** Mile 110.4–130.9 (near Jackson and Canton). The route passes through maturing loblolly pines and oaks and across small streams on the northwest side of Ross Barnett Reservoir. Sometimes you are close to pastures just outside the park boundary. You rarely see the reservoir.

The trail is being constructed by volunteers, mainly horseback riders. As of the fall of 1992, the trail had been completed on the south to a small arm of the reservoir extending outside the Parkway boundary at Parkway Mile 110.4. The trail crosses State Hwy 43 on a piece of the original old Trace (marked by a stone monument erected by the Daughters of the American Revolution) and continues north at least two miles. The unimproved route, marked with orange surveyors tape, extended to the Yockanookany Picnic Area.

The Parkway runs through rather low ground between Hwy 43 and the Yockanookany Picnic Area. Be prepared for mud and wet feet from late winter through spring.

Facilities: A parking lot and staging area are provided just south of Hwy 43 off Yarnell Road. There are no restrooms or other amenities. You can also access the trail from the River Bend Picnic Area, which has a parking lot, flush toilets, water, and a picnic table.

Access: You can park your vehicle on the grass on the reservoir side of the Parkway at the southern end of the trail at Mile 110.4. It was marked with a modest brown sign reading "Motorized Vehicles Prohibited on Horse Trail" in 1992. As mentioned above, the designated entrance point is near Hwy 43.

River Bend Picnic Area is at Parkway Mile 122.6. Park in the area north of the restrooms, walk across the Parkway, and follow a gravel road to a water tower. The future route of the trail, marked with orange tape, crossed the clearing around the tower in the fall of 1992.

E 9

● **Little Mountain Trail:** Mile 193.1 (near Ackerman). This one-mile trail winds up the north side of Little Mountain in the Jeff Busby Site off Mile 193.1 on the Parkway. The slope becomes progressively steeper near the top but the trail is well constructed. A loop interpretive trail along the way features plants used for food by Indians and early settlers. Your reward at the top (604' above sea level) is an outstanding view of the forested hills to the south.

Facilities: The Jeff Busby Site is a major stopover site along the Parkway, with a picnic area, gas station, convenience store, telephone, resident ranger, and campground with flush toilets but no showers or RV hookups. There is a restroom and parking area on top of Little Mountain. Exhibit panels explore changing uses of the land since the Indians first arrived.

Access: The hiking trail begins in the campground across the road from the restrooms.

- **Witch Dance (Tombigbee) Trail:** Mile 233.2 (near Houston). A 15-mile loop, mostly in the Tombigbee National Forest. See Tombigbee NF for description.

D 10

- **Tupelo Horse Trail:** Mile 260.2–261.8 (Tupelo). A 3.5-mile loop on the west side of Tupelo. The southern part of the loop is through an early succession forest with cedar, osage orange, and heavy undergrowth between the Parkway and suburban backyards. The trail meets a gravel road, now closed to the public, and makes a wide loop in a large field. At its northeastern extremity it is near the Chickasaw Village exhibit and parking area. It doesn't seem to have much horse traffic and would probably make a nice jogging trail. It is also an extension of the Old Town Hiking Trail, making possible a one-way hike of 6.4 miles.

C 10

The bulge in the federal property line more than accommodates the Chickasaw Village exhibit. This wide spot was once a national monument created by a proclamation of President Franklin D. Roosevelt in 1938. At that time archaeologists believed the Chickasaw village site was Ackia (Akia), the fortified town that Jean Baptiste le Moyne, Sieur de Bienville, governor of Louisiana, unsuccessfully attacked on May 26, 1736. Later historians established that Ackia was actually located in what is now the built-up part of Tupelo. The national monument was dismantled in 1961, and the property was incorporated into the Parkway.

Facilities: The West Jackson Street trailhead has a parking area and hitching rack. At the Chickasaw Village is a parking area and a place to sit protected from sun or rain. No toilets or water are available at either site.

Access: The W. Jackson St. trailhead is within the strip of land along the Parkway, and you can see it from the Parkway, but you can't drive to it from the Parkway. To reach it, you must drive a roundabout route through Tupelo. Leave the Parkway at State Hwy 6 (Mile 259.7 or 260.0), go east on Hwy 6 to Thomas St. (second red light), turn north (left) on Thomas St., and drive to Jackson St. Turn west (left) on Jackson St., and drive under the Parkway overpass. The paved parking area at the trailhead is on the right.

To avoid driving through Tupelo, you could start at the Chickasaw Village Exhibit. An unmarked spur path leads about 50' from the outline of the round

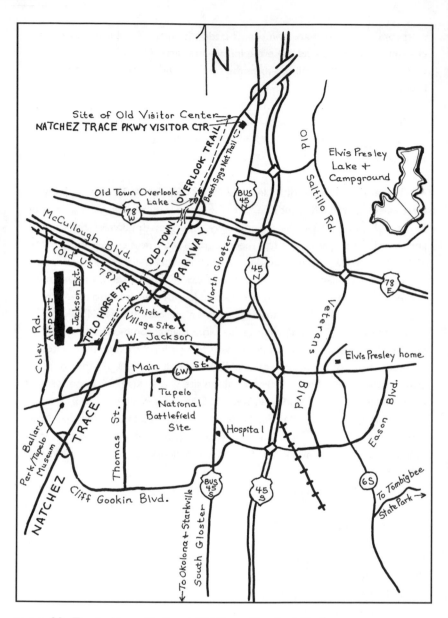

MAP 39. Tupelo Horse Trail and Old Town Overlook Trail

(winter) house at the far left of the village site. Look for a metal horse-and-rider sign marking the mowed pathway of the Tupelo Horse Trail. Horseback riders are not allowed to use this parking lot as a staging area.

Maps: Sherman and Tupelo 7.5′ topo maps (not necessary but interesting).

● **Old Town Overlook Trail:** Mile 261.8-266.0 (Tupelo). This trail, restricted to hikers, runs 4.6 miles from the Chickasaw Village Site to the park headquarters/visitor center. It gets its name from an overlook about halfway along the trail. Here you can see over the gently rolling and flat terrain of the Black Prairie Belt and the flat farmland along Old Town Creek. Until their removal to Oklahoma in 1832, the Chickasaw had several villages here, and much of the fertile land had been cleared for their fields.

C 10

The trail crosses creeks on well constructed bridges and boardwalks. Part of the time you are in extensive open fields, with Parkway traffic not far away. Other times you are in the woods with big oaks and pines. North of the crossing of old U.S. Hwy 78, the trail parallels a road in a low income rural neighborhood. South of the Old Town Overlook you pass a borrow pit pond that is popular with local fishermen. Borrow pits are created when earth and rock are removed for construction projects, especially highways. The route is easy to follow except possibly where the trail crosses major roads and highways (there are at least three). You have your very own minilane over new Hwy 78, a four-lane highway.

The trail has nothing to do with the Old Natchez Trace, which was farther to the west. It was constructed by the Youth Conservation Corps in the 1970s.

Access: The south end of the trail is easy to find at the Chickasaw Village Site. Roughly halfway to the park visitor center, it runs right behind the signboard at the Old Town Creek Overlook (Mile 263.9). The northern end is in a shaded parking area across the Parkway from the visitor center. The parking area is adjacent to the site of the original visitor center and park headquarters, used between 1941 and 1961.

Map: The Tupelo topo map is useful.

PARKWAY INTERPRETIVE TRAILS

Twelve interpretive trails dealing with natural history have been constructed along the Parkway in Mississippi. They take between 10 and 20 minutes to walk and feature various plant communities, the common species that live there, and human uses of these plants. (If you have trouble finding the plants singled out by the signs, they may have died since the trail was marked.)

J 4 • **Bullen Creek Nature Trail:** Mile 18.4 (near Fayette). A 15-minute walk through a mature forest of loblolly pine that is being supplanted by hardwoods. The original hardwood forest was cleancut, farmed (most likely cotton—faint furrows are still visible), and then abandoned and claimed by pines, which matured to old age and are now dying out. A beautiful area.

H 7 • **Cypress/Tupelo Swamp Nature Trail:** Mile 122.0 (near Canton). This trail is a favorite with nature lovers. A boardwalk takes you across the swamp, studded with the swollen buttresses of bald cypress and tupelo, and on to a view of wetlands along the upper end of the Ross Barnett Reservoir and the Pearl River.

G 8 • **Southern Pines Nature Trail:** Mile 128.4 (near Canton, adjacent to the Choctaw Boundary historical sign). Features the ecology and uses of pines, especially the two species found along the Trace—loblolly and shortleaf. A 10-minute walk.

G 8 • **Myrick Creek Nature Trail:** Mile 145.1 (near Carthage). The trail highlights abandoned beaver ponds and dams, a canal that the beavers used to transport food to their lodge, and scars caused by beavers' gnawing at the bases of trees. It also covers the ecologic succession of plant species in former beaver ponds. Display panels at the parking lot feature the beaver. This is a level trail, probably usable by the handicapped.

F 8 • **Hurricane Creek Nature Trail:** Mile 164.3 (near Kosciusko). The tour compares the trees found in moist bottomlands along Hurricane Creek with those found on slopes and on ridgetops. The pine on the ridgetop will gradually be supplanted by hardwood trees, because pine seedlings can't grow in the shade.

F 8 • **Cole Creek Nature Trail:** Mile 175.6 (near Ackerman). This 15-minute walk takes you across slow-moving Cole Creek and a small cypress-tupelo swamp and into the adjacent mixed hardwood bottomland forest. A mound left by the roots of a fallen tree that has decayed and disappeared, decaying dead trees, and the buildup of soil from the accumulation of sediment during high water are featured.

E 9 • **Jeff Busby Nature Trail:** Mile 193.1 (near Ackerman). The trail is cut into the steep side of Little Mountain. It features plants used for food by early white settlers and Indians.

- **Chickasaw Village Nature Trail:** Mile 261.8 (near Tupelo). The loop starts at the site of a Chickasaw Indian village. The foundations of two circular winter homes, a rectangular summer home, and a log fortress are outlined in concrete. The trail features plants that the Chickasaws used.

C 10

- **Beech Springs Nature Trail:** Mile 266.0 (near Tupelo). A paved loop through a forest that is reclaiming worn-out abandoned farmland along the Parkway. People in wheelchairs could probably negotiate the trail with someone to help them.

C 10

- **Dogwood Valley Nature Trail:** Mile 275.2 (near Tupelo). The walk follows part of the Old Trace. The small valley has an unusual number of flowering dogwoods, some very large and probably more than 100 years old.

C 10

- **Donivan Slough Nature Trail:** Mile 283.3 (near Marietta). The trail follows a slough and goes through its associated backwater. Characteristic trees and understory plants are featured.

VICKSBURG NATIONAL MILITARY PARK AND CEMETERY,

Superintendent, 3201 Clay St., Vicksburg, MS 39180 (601-636-0583). The park is in Vicksburg, Warren County (1,324 acres)

This park commemorates the Siege of Vicksburg, a key event in the Civil War—the men who died there and the citizens of Vicksburg who persisted for 47 days before lack of food and water forced them to surrender to the Union forces. The park is shaped like a partial crescent, following the crests of loess hills and partially encircling the city of Vicksburg on the east and north. Here outnumbered Confederate troops retreated to trenches on May 18, 1863, and prepared to resist advancing Federal troops. In the past two days the Feds had decisively defeated them at the Battle of Champion Hill and on the east side of the Big Black River.

The Union soldiers, led by General Ulysses S. Grant, were unable to dislodge the Rebels and dug a second series of trenches paralleling those of the Confederates. The stalemate ended on July 4, when Confederate general John C. Pemberton surrendered to Grant. It's not surprising that only black people celebrated the Fourth of July in Vicksburg until a few years ago.

For many years after the war, people mainly wanted to forget the whole tragic experience. In 1887 Louisiana was the first state to erect a monument to its veterans in Vicksburg. A group of Union and Confederate veterans formed an association in 1895 to lobby for the establishment of a military park. Their efforts were successful, and on February 21, 1899, President William McKinley signed the bill establishing the national military park. Today almost 1,300 monuments, plaques, equestrian statues, and busts line a 16-mile paved circuit route through the park. The tour roughly follows the trenches of the Union and Confederate divisions.

Near the northwest end of the park rests the partially restored ironclad gunboat U.S.S. *Cairo*, protected under a great iron canopy. It was sunk in the Yazoo River on December 12, 1862, by a crude electronically detonated mine—the first vessel in history to suffer such a fate. An underground museum adjacent to the *Cairo* displays artifacts recovered from the vessel when it was removed from the river in the early 1960s.

Park roads are favorites for jogging, walking, and bicycling. No formal hiking trails have been built, but there are at least two little known attractions for hikers and naturalists—the Al Scheller Scout Trail and a waterfall and springs on lower Mint Bayou.

Best Time to Visit: The park is open daily except Christmas. Special activities, including reenactments of the Siege, occur, especially around July 4.

Facilities: Camping is not permitted in the park, but a private campground is adjacent to the park boundary north of the Clay St. exit on I-20. There are also several motels close to the park. Picnicking is permitted only at the Cairo Museum and at Tour Stop 12. Bring water.

Access: The usual beginning and ending point for visitors is the park visitor center, which is about a half mile from the intersection of Clay Street and Interstate 20 on the eastern edge of Vicksburg.

Maps and Literature: The park gives out a brochure with an excellent map. You can pick a copy up at the visitor center or ask the Park Service to mail one to you. The visitor center sells several books on the Civil War and has exhibits and an 18-minute orientation film.

 • **Al Scheller Scout Trail,** contact: Steve Elwart, 143 Woodstone Dr., Vicksburg, MS 39180 (601-636-9788) (approximately 12 miles long). This trail, unique among those described in this guide, is an orienteering route requiring a compass. History is the main feature, but the route takes you through a variety of landscapes, from mowed lawns around monuments to undisturbed woods in steep-walled minivalleys in the loess hills.

If you take this hike, you will find it an adventure, and you will get lost at least once. Before you commit yourself—especially if you are leading a group—call Steve for an update.

You will find no worn or maintained path on this route, which was laid out by Al Scheller in 1975 or 1976. You must have a copy of the booklet printed and distributed by the Vicksburg Trail Committee, which is affiliated with the Andrew Jackson Council of the Boy Scouts of America in Vicksburg. You should be able to get copies at the park visitor center. Don't forget to bring a compass, drinking water, and toilet paper. And be forewarned that there is lots of poison ivy in the woods.

The circuit route begins and ends at the visitor center. Plan on 8 hours of hiking, not counting a break for lunch and perhaps a visit to the Cairo Museum. With your compass, you will be proceeding by azimuths, the number of degrees (clockwise) from due north. On your way to the national cemetery and the Cairo Museum, you'll see the different types of scenery that the park has to offer. The only water and restroom facilities en route are at the Cairo Museum.

White-tipped posts mark the points where the route enters the woods. You can't count on the posts entirely. Sometimes people remove them or move them from their proper places, sometimes they get bent over, and sometimes the vegetation is so overgrown that they are invisible. The route is within the perimeter roads, however, and if you get lost you will soon hit one of them.

The guide booklet is filled with historical notes on the markers, monuments, and trenches you will pass. Boy Scouts who want an award for doing the route will fill out an answer sheet in response to questions in the booklet.

Best Time to Visit: In late fall, winter, and early spring, when the leaves have fallen and visibility is good. Also, the leaves will be off the poison ivy.

Maps and Literature: To do the trail, you need the brochure and map of the park distributed by the Park Service plus the guide booklet to the Al Scheller Scout Trail. Both are available at the visitor center, but call in advance to make sure the Scheller guide is available.

- **Falls of Mint Spring Bayou.** Vicksburg's 30′ waterfall is one of its best-kept secrets. Even though it is not far from busy Washington Street, it's a remarkably secluded beauty spot.

The falls are at the bottom of the small, steep-walled valley of the bayou, which drains the northern third of the park. Here the bayou has eroded through the wind-blown loess deposits that blanketed the Vicksburg area less than 30,000 years ago and cuts into 25- to 15-million-year-old marine deposits (Miocene and Upper Oligocene). A 12.8′ layer of solid gray rock, known to geologists as the Glendon limestone, forms the lip of the falls. It lies on top of 17′ to 20′ of relatively unconsolidated gray marl—the Byram

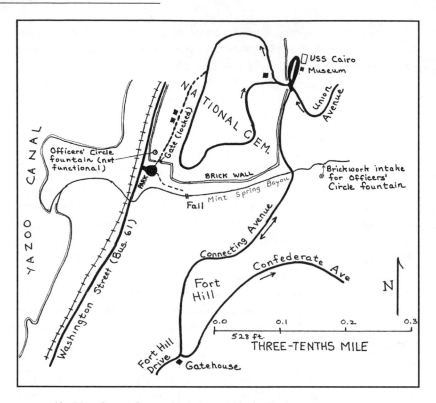

M A P 40. Mint Spring Bayou, Vicksburg Military Park

marl—that is loaded with shells of marine animals. The falling water has deeply undercut the soft marl.

Below the falls, the bayou meanders a bit, disappears under the highway, and then empties into the Yazoo Diversion Canal. Until 1876, the diversion canal was part of a very sharp bend on the Mississippi River. The force of the water deeply undercut the river's outer banks. The bayou couldn't erode its valley quickly enough to keep pace, especially through the resistant Glendon limestone, and so it was left hanging, descending to the river in a series of steps in the limestone that culminate in the lower falls.

Flatboaters who used to float raw materials down the Mississippi River often stopped at the mouth of the bayou, named after the wild mint plants that grew there. Vicksburgers claim that the mint julep—bourbon whiskey with ice, sugar, water, and a fresh sprig of mint—originated here. Some inventive boatman tried adding mint to his whiskey and liked the result. Vicksburg, however, is not the only area in the Old South claiming to be the source of the julep.

The falls and surrounding valley are too steep to climb out of, but you can walk through the cemetery or drive around through Vicksburg to the spring. In dry periods, water bubbles out on top of the Glendon limestone in the flat-bottomed streambed. During the 1890s, the spring was lined with brick, and some was diverted into a pipe that ran into a fountain made of an upended cannon barrel in the officers' circle at the bottom of the cemetery. Water gushed out of the cannon strictly through gravity. The pipe was severed when the present bridge on Connecting Ave. in the park was constructed.

The bayou and its spring were important during the Siege of Vicksburg. The steep valley formed a natural barrier between Confederate trenches on the south side and Union trenches on the north. Water was scarce for both sides. The spring was an important source of water for troops on both sides, and blue- and gray-coated soldiers must have declared a temporary truce there.

Best Time to Visit: The best time to see the falls is after a heavy rainfall, but you will have to wade or perhaps forgo a visit to the spring when the falls are at their best.

Access: To reach the falls, park outside the locked gate at the lower end of the national cemetery along Washington St. north of Vicksburg (Business U.S. Hwy 61). Note officers' circle with the upright cannon in the cemetery. Turn about 90° from the gate and head for some unmowed grass and shrubs, and you should see a faint footpath. Continue on into the woods and the footpath will become more obvious. The falls are about 100 yards from the parking area. The trail is not maintained, so poison ivy is abundant. The last part of the trail is very steep. (Note: A curb was recently installed across the parking area, closing it to vehicles. Park on the west side of Washington St. N of the locked cemetery gate and walk back along the highway.)

You can walk from the parking area on Washington St. to the spring by climbing over the low brick wall around the cemetery and walking up to Connecting Ave. on the paved roads through the cemetery. Or you can drive back into Vicksburg and turn left at the first stoplight (First East St.). Go uphill three blocks and turn left on Cherry St., which becomes Fort Hill Rd. and leads to the military park. Turn left onto Connecting Ave. at the booth at the park boundary, crossing the bridge over Mint Spring Bayou. Park at the parking lot next to the U.S.S. *Cairo* and walk back to the near side of the bridge and climb down to the top of the waterfall. Walk up the stream bottom about 200' to the spring, which is lined with large bricks with circular and rectangular basins. When the water is low you'll hardly get your feet wet. When it's higher, you'll be wading in up to a foot of water. When the bayou is really high, you may not be able to go in at all.

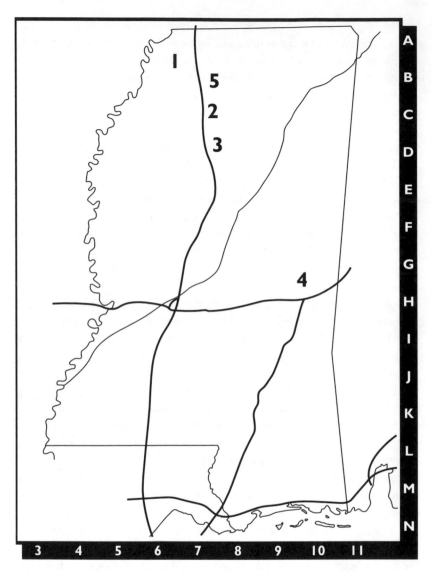

MAP 41. U.S. Army Corps of Engineers Reservoirs in Mississippi

LEGEND

1	=	Arkabutla Lake
2	=	Enid Lake/George Payne Cossar State Park
3	=	Grenada Lake/Hugh White State Park
4	=	Okatibbee Lake/Okatibbee Water Park
5	=	Sardis Lake/John W. Kyle State Park

4. U.S. Army Corps of Engineers Reservoirs

Five of Mississippi's six large reservoirs are projects of the Corps of Engineers, and the Corps is responsible for their operation and maintenance. These huge lakes were built principally for flood control, but recreation is an important side benefit. The four largest are components of the Yazoo Basin Flood Control System. They are built across four of the principal tributaries of the Yazoo River in northwestern Mississippi to control flooding in residential, industrial, and agricultural areas in the Yazoo Basin (also known as "The Delta"). Authorized by an act of Congress in 1936, they were completed between 1940 (Sardis Lake) and 1954 (Grenada Lake).

The smallest and most recent of the major Corps impoundments, Okatibbee Lake, was finished in 1968. It impounds tributaries of the upper Pascagoula River basin north of Meridian.

The sixth large reservoir, Ross Barnett, was built solely for water supply and recreation. It is owned and operated by the Pearl River Water Supply District. Ross Barnett's water level and surface area remain essentially constant all year, in contrast to Corps reservoirs, which fluctuate widely with the seasons. They are partially emptied in the fall and early winter to maximize flood storage capacity in late winter through late spring, when the level is highest. In late spring, the water level is gradually reduced to an intermediate level that is better for water-related recreation during the peak visitor use in the summer.

Facilities: All five Corps of Engineers reservoirs have numerous recreation sites on their shores, ranging from simple boat ramps to elaborate Class A campgrounds with beaches for swimming and sunbathing, RV hookups, hot showers, and trails for hiking, bicycling, off-road vehicles, and fitness. The campgrounds are the finest and best maintained in Mississippi. At least two of the reservoirs have amphitheaters near one of their larger campgrounds. Evening programs on local natural and cultural history are presented here during the peak summer season.

Water-related activities such as fishing, boating, water skiing, and swimming are the main attractions of these big reservoirs. Except for Okatibbee, however, each has an interpretive trail. These trails, part of the total recreation package offered by the larger areas, are short (usually a half-mile loop) and have been constructed to meet a very high standard, with wide sturdy bridges. They will not satisfy someone looking for a wild and rugged outdoor experience.

In addition, the Corps has installed two trail networks that are more than four miles long. More trails and longer trails are possible in the future, although some would have to cross areas flooded for various periods from late winter to late spring.

B 7   ARKABUTLA LAKE,

Field Office, Rt. 1, Box 572, Coldwater, MS 38618 (601-562-6261). The lake is NE of Arkabutla and SW of Hernando in Tate and DeSoto counties; Coldwater River Nature Trail System, a 6-mile network for hikers and cyclists, including the 0.3-mile Big Oak Interpretive Trail; Swinging Bridge (Beaver Pond) Nature Trail (ca. 0.5-mile loop)

The northernmost of the large impoundments in the Yazoo Basin, Arkabutla Lake was completed in 1943. The dam extends across the Coldwater River. When it is full, the reservoir occupies 33,400 acres (52 square miles). In the summer, it is closer to 11,240 acres (18 square miles).

Access: To reach the dam and the trails from the north, take State Hwy 301 from Eudora (not shown on the state highway map, it is at the crossroads of Hwys 301 and 304 west of Hernando). From the south, follow Hwy 301 north from Arkabutla.

General Maps and Literature: The Vicksburg District Corps of Engineers has published two excellent free guides to the lake, each with color maps. *Arkabutla Lake*, for general use, emphasizes recreational facilities. *Arkabutla Lake: Hunting & Fishing Map* is a color topographic map, with enlarged maps of areas of particular interest to hunters. It does not show the hiking trails, but it is worth having if you want to explore other areas of the lake.

● **Coldwater River Nature Trail System,** including the Big Oak Nature Trail. This is the most extensive and scenic trail network in northeast Mississippi. It is open to hikers and mountain bicycles. The Mississippi Natural Heritage Commission has designated approximately 450 acres of river bottom forest between the Outlet Channel and Pratt Rd. as a natural area. This area will not be logged.

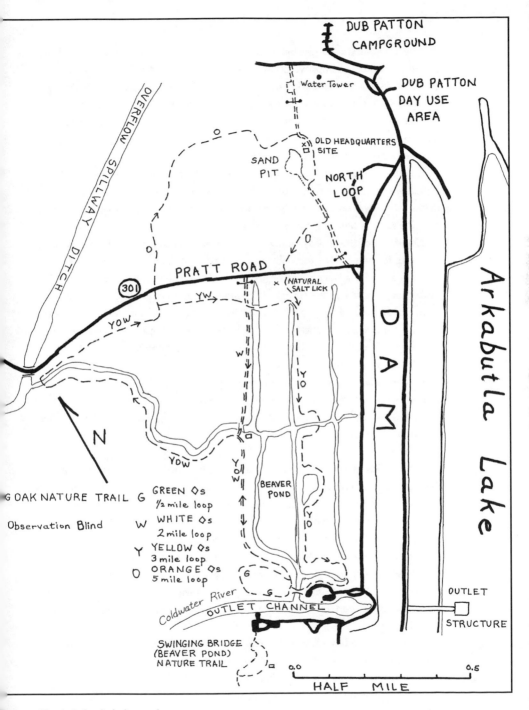

DUB PATTON
CAMPGROUND

Water Tower

DUB PATTON
DAY USE
AREA

OLD HEADQUARTERS
SITE

SAND
PIT

NORTH
LOOP

OVERFLOW SPILLWAY DITCH

PRATT ROAD

(301)

YW→

YOW→

(NATURAL
SALT LICK

W

Y
O

YOW

D A M

Arkabutla Lake

YOW→

YOW

GOAK NATURE TRAIL G   GREEN Os
                       ½ mile loop

Observation Blind   W   WHITE Os
                          2 mile loop

BEAVER
POND

Y
O

Y   YELLOW Os
     3 mile loop

O   ORANGE Os
     5 mile loop

N

G

G

Coldwater River   OUTLET CHANNEL

OUTLET

STRUCTURE

SWINGING BRIDGE
(BEAVER POND)
NATURE TRAIL

0.0

0.5

HALF   MILE

MAP 42. Arkabutla Lake outlet area

The trail system lies just below the dam impounding Arkabutla Lake. Three straight channels to improve drainage were constructed at least 50 years ago. Another naturally meandering stream remains. Today river bottom forest covers the whole area. Some large bald cypress, oaks, beech, and honey locust are more than 100 years old. More than 125 growth rings were counted on one huge old cypress stump along the meandering stream. Other common trees include hickories, river birch, and sweetgum.

Deer are abundant; chances of seeing some on your hike are excellent. Bobcats, foxes, fox squirrels, turkeys, and raccoons are also common. Wood ducks take advantage of nest boxes. In the quiet streams you may see turtles and fish such as bluegills, sunfish, gar, and bass.

One loop of the trail system goes north of Pratt Road onto higher ground that was farmed before the dam was constructed. When the Corps of Engineers acquired the land, it was planted in loblolly pine that is now managed for timber. Here also was the Corps of Engineers headquarters while the dam was being constructed, between 1940 and 1943. You can see the old concrete safe and the concrete foundations of the old laboratory, which has been converted into a wildlife observation blind. (Another blind has been installed in the middle of the natural area.)

Four overlapping loops of one-third, two, three, and five miles have been marked with colored diamonds on posts. The principal starting point for all the loops begins with a staircase that descends to a bridge across a deep ravine that drains the natural area. Watch for water birds and turtles sunning on the logs below.

The Big Oak Nature Trail, marked in green, is about 0.3 miles long. It leaves the main trail on your left. Numbered points of interest in 1992 were: (1) wildlife (common species include opossums, raccoons, gray and fox squirrels, deer, and woodpeckers); (2) hackberry tree; (3) slippery elm tree; (4) water oak; (5) shellbark hickory; (6) flowering dogwood; (7) mockernut hickory; (8) American hornbeam; (9) American beech; (10) touch-me-not (orange and yellow flower); (11) southern red oak; (12) pawpaw (a small tree); (12) swamp chestnut oak; (13) red mulberry tree; (14) honeylocust tree; (15) red maple; (16) channel of the Coldwater River; (17) boxelder tree; (18) sycamore; and (19) river birch.

Two-, Three-, and Five-Mile Loops: The two-mile loop is marked with white diamonds, the three-mile loop with yellow, and the five-mile loop with orange. All three loops pass near a wildlife observation blind in deep woods in the middle of the area. The most interesting trail segment is the portion that follows the natural meanders of a stream on the three- and five-mile loops. Here you will see giant cypress and lots of evidence of beavers—dams, lodges, and the gnawed stems of shrubs and small trees that they have cut down for food and construction materials. If you sit and watch quietly, especially near dusk, you may see the beavers themselves.

Points of interest on the five-mile loop and their distances from the beginning of the loop include: rest area and fish/wildlife observation site (0.40); rest area and beaver observation island (0.85); 120-year-old cypress tree (1.2); original construction headquarters building site and wildlife observation platform (2.5); wildlife food plot (3.0); and beaver pond and rest area (4.0).

The trail system was designed with mountain bicycles in mind. The two-mile loop is mostly level, with only a few inclines. The three- and five-mile loops have more bumps, steeper inclines, and sharp turns to challenge more advanced cyclists.

Best Time to Visit: The trail system is open all year except for one week in early December. At this time a special deer hunt for handicapped hunters is conducted, and other uses are suspended. Call the field office before planning a hike at this time.

Access: The principal access point, with a generous parking area, is at the end of the road on the north side of the outlet channel below the dam. It leads past picnic tables to a pavilion.

You can also start at the north end of the five-mile loop at the Dub Patton Recreation Area at the north end of the dam. Drive past the entrance to the camping area on your right and the recreation area water tower on your left, and turn left on a gravel road in a field. Park at the gate and walk about 0.1 mile to the old headquarters site and picnic table in a clearing.

Maps and Literature: The Corps of Engineers offers an excellent booklet, *Coldwater River Nature Trail System*. Request a copy from the Arkabutla Lake field office.

- **Swinging Bridge Nature Trail** (Beaver Pond Nature Trail). This trail is about a half mile long and is for hikers only. It is not an interpretive trail, but it has many points of interest. It first crosses an old channel of the Coldwater River and climbs up to a flower garden set in deep woods. Azaleas, which bloom in May, are the centerpiece. Benches are spaced around the edge of a circle.

The looped part of the trail begins here. Take the right fork. On your right is a bald cypress swamp in the old channel. You will be on an old road part of the time; the swinging bridge crosses a gap once spanned by a bridge. At the farthest south point of the loop trail, a one-way trail continues on the old

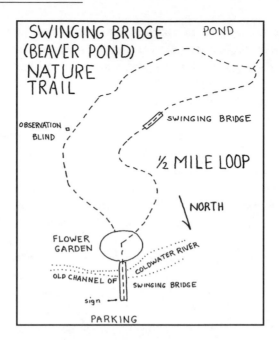

SWINGING BRIDGE
(BEAVER POND)
NATURE
TRAIL

POND

OBSERVATION
BLIND

SWINGING BRIDGE

½ MILE LOOP

NORTH

FLOWER
GARDEN

COLDWATER RIVER

OLD CHANNEL OF
SWINGING BRIDGE

sign →

PARKING

MAP 43. Swinging Bridge (Beaver Pond) Nature Trail

road, dead-ending at a once and future beaver pond (not filled in 1992). (Beaver ponds are temporary; the beavers abandon them when they exhaust nearby food sources). The way back is through pines. You will pass a wildlife observation blind in a clearing.

Access: The trail begins near the end of the paved road on the south side of the outlet channel. The nearby restroom is for hikers as well as campers in the primitive campsites along the channel.

C 7–8 **ENID LAKE/GEORGE PAYNE COSSAR STATE PARK,**

Park Manager, Enid Lake Field Office, P.O. Box 10, Enid, MS 38927 (601-563-4571). George Payne Cossar State Park, Rt. 1, Box 67, Oakland, MS 38948; (601-623-7356). The reservoir and park are NE of Enid in Yalobusha and Panola counties (4.5-mile partially looped Rocky Point National Recreation Trail for hikers, horseback riders, and four-wheelers; 2.0-mile partially looped Quail Run Trail for hikers; 0.5-mile Beech Hollow Nature Trail loop for hikers only; and 0.5-mile Water Valley Recreation Area loop hiking trail)

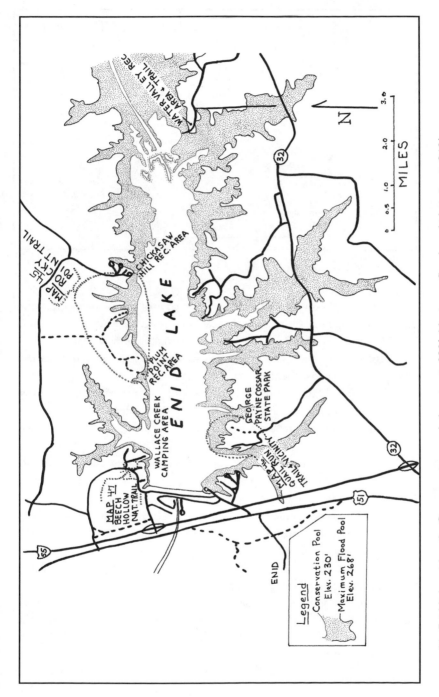

MAP 44. Enid Lake and trails. Conservation pool elevation is 230'. Maximum flood pool elevation is 268'.

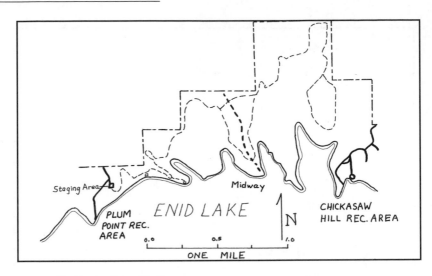

MAP 45. Rocky Point Trail

Enid Lake is the smallest of the four flood control reservoirs In the Yazoo Basin. Built across the Yocona (pronounced YAK-co-na) River, it was completed in 1952 and covers 28,000 acres (44 square miles) at maximum capacity.

Access: The dam and visitor center are accessible from Interstate 55 at Exit 233 (Enid exit). Follow the signs.

Maps: The Vicksburg District of the U.S. Army Corps of Engineers has issued an excellent free color map and guide to the reservoir. The state park also has a brochure and separate map.

• **Rocky Point Trail** (4.5 miles, partially looped). This trail network begins and ends at the Plum Point Recreation area on the north side of the lake. A round trip to the farthest point and back is about 8 miles.

The trail takes an exceedingly crooked route toward the Chickasaw Hill Recreation Area and turns back on itself before actually reaching that area. It stays on higher ground to avoid low-lying areas that flood when the reservoir is full. Along the way you'll descend to the sandy edge of the reservoir and pass by some impressive gullies now in deep woods.

The trail is a designated national recreation trail. It is open to horseback riders, hikers, four-wheelers, and mountain bicycles but not to motorcyclists. It was constructed in 1984 with horseback riding in mind but seems to be little used by equestrians.

Facilities: Plum Point Recreation Area has a primitive campground and swimming beach. The trailhead has a large parking area and a restroom, but

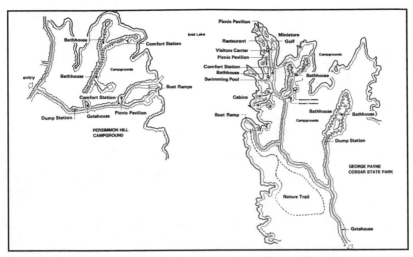

MAP 46. Quail Run Nature Trail, George Payne Cossar State Park

no hitching racks. No overnight camping facilities for parties with horses are provided.

- **Quail Run Nature Trail** in George Payne Cossar State Park (2.5 mile loop). This trail is a pleasant stroll through mostly oak and hickory woods with some nice groves of loblolly pines. Some old oaks with large side branches are a sure sign that the land was once cleared pasture. Much of the route follows woods roads abandoned when the reservoir was built or before. At the south end of the loop is a deeply sunken old road that dead-ends at the lake.

    Access: The trailhead is at the parking lot for the boat ramp. Follow the signs to the boat ramp.

- **Beech Hollow Nature Trail** (0.5-mile loop). The first half of the trail follows a deep ravine that empties into the lake. Along the way is a giant old beech and a covered bridge/minipavilion spanning the ravine.

    Numbered posts are keyed to a guide booklet to the trail. If you don't see any on the trailhead signboard, ask at the Enid Lake visitor center. The items of interest are likely to change from year to year because trees, etc., die. As of 1992, the numbered points were: (1) box for squirrels, (2) erosion gully, (3) American beech, (4) southern red oak, (5) American holly, (6) loblolly pine, (7) white oak, (8) mockernut hickory, (9) flowering dogwood, (10) influence of sunlight exposure on tree species, (11) American hornbeam, and (12) yellow poplar.

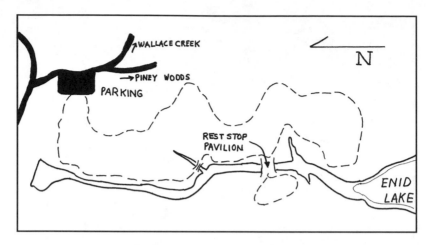

MAP 47. Beech Hollow Nature Trail

Access: The trailhead is marked by a large signboard and parking area on the paved road to the Wallace Creek Recreation Area. (A trail for mountain bicycles begins on the opposite side of the road.)

• **Water Valley Recreation Area Hiking Trail** (0.5 mile loop). It takes only about 15 minutes to walk this trail through an abandoned farm, but the scenery is attractive and varied. You will pass through a dense grove of red cedars and past a lakeside marsh (good birding potential), an old silo, a plowed field, and a big old catalpa tree.

Access: The trailhead is along the access road to the Water Valley Landing Recreation Area on the southeast side of the lake. See map of Enid Lake.

D 8 **GRENADA LAKE/HUGH WHITE STATE PARK,**

Resource Manager, Grenada Lake, Box 903, Grenada, MS 38901 (601-226-5911). Manager, Hugh White State Park, PO Box 725, Grenada, MS 38902-0725 (601-226-4934). The reservoir and park are NE of Grenada in Grenada County (Haserway Wetland Demonstration Area with one mile trail network, 2.2-mile Lost Bluff Hiking Trail, 0.7-mile Old River Trail loop, 3.3-mile nature trail network in state park)

Grenada Lake is one of the largest reservoirs in Mississippi. It was constructed across the Yalobusha River and began operating in January 1954. The depth of the lake can fluctuate 38', and the surface area of the impoundment

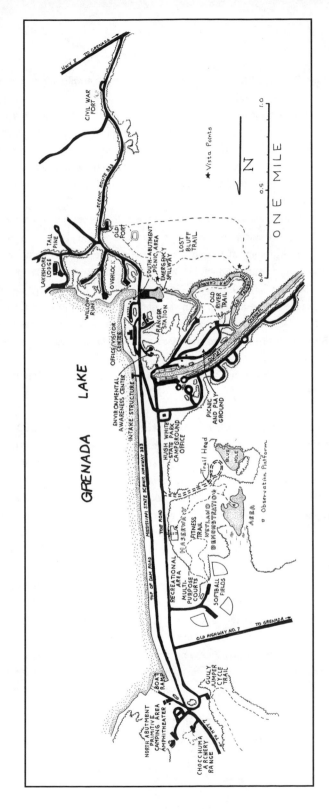

MAP 48. Grenada Lake outlet area. A star indicates vista points on the Lost Bluff Trail.

can vary from 9,800 acres to 64,600 acres (15–101 square miles). At minimum depth it has a 54-mile shoreline.

Although the reservoir was built for flood control, recreation is an important side benefit. Water is the principal attraction for the 2.5 million visitors who come every year—to boat, water ski, fish, and swim. There are also trails and interpretive facilities for those interested in natural history and human history. These facilities are concentrated just below the dam and on the southeastern side of the lake.

In addition to the trails described below, there is a motorcycle trail and a fitness trail. During the summer, the Corps sponsors evening programs on the cultural and natural history of the region. Your first stop at Grenada Lake is likely to be the visitor center, which has a small museum and an aquarium.

Maps and Literature: The U.S. Army Corps of Engineers, Vicksburg District, publishes an excellent free brochure on recreational opportunities at Grenada Lake. It includes a large map of the lake. You can pick up a guide booklet to the Old River Trail and a brochure on the Haserway Wetland Area at the visitor center.

A map of Hugh White State Park showing the nature trails is available at the park lodge/office.

- **Haserway Wetland Demonstration Area.** This is a 330-acre complex of natural wetlands, old borrow areas excavated for fill for the dam that have collected water and have revegetated with natural wetland plants, moist soil areas (open areas with herbaceous plants producing seeds that ducks like to eat), and artificially planted food plots for ducks. A greentree reservoir will also be installed. A trail network about a mile long leads to two observation platforms, one overlooking a natural-looking borrow pit wetland and the other a moist soil area. The trails lead through bottomland hardwood forests with bridges over sloughs.

Despite its size and broad shallow edges, the Grenada Lake does not protect wetlands or waterfowl habitat. The water is left high well into the spring growing season, then withdrawn until the follow winter. Plants cannot adapt to this flooding regime, so the lake normally has a wide, bare drawdown zone. Various state waterfowl areas, including the Malmaison Waterfowl Management Area, have been provided to compensate for the waterfowl habitat destroyed by Grenada Lake and by other subprojects of the Yazoo Basin Plan.

- **Old River Interpretive Trail.** This a 0.6-loop that follows the edge of a meander of the original Yalobusha River channel, which was severed when the outlet channel from the dam was constructed. It also crosses both arms of a U-shaped oxbow lake. The trail begins and ends near the picnic area and playground near the south end of the dam.

The Corps has printed an 18-page booklet to the trail that describes and illustrates the 22 species of trees that are labeled around the trail (plus a rattan vine). The path is covered with fine gravel. Two covered small pavilions with benches along the way—one built right over the oxbow lake—invite you to sit and watch for wood ducks, turtles, and wading birds or just contemplate. Except for a stairway in the middle of the loop, the trail is probably suitable for wheelchair-bound people if someone assists them over the rough spots.

- **Lost Bluff Hiking Trail.** This is a 2.2-mile loop in the rugged terrain just southwest of the dam. It includes overlooks of the dam, outlet channel, and original channel of the Yalobusha River and passes across deep hollows with ferns and virgin timber. It's only a 700' walk from the parking area to a redoubt built by the Confederates in 1862 to keep General Grant from crossing the river and away from Grenada. It is one of eight earthen forts built for this purpose; another, about a mile further south on Scenic Rt. 333, has been restored.

- **White State Park Nature Trail System.** Starting near the lodge, it's 3.7 miles to Little Mountain and back. Little Mountain is 486' high, the highest point near Grenada Lake.

OKATIBBEE LAKE/OKATIBBEE WATER PARK,

H 8

Resource Manager, Okatibbee Lake, P.O. Box 98, Collinsville, MS 39325 (601-626-8431). Okatibbee Water Park, 9283 Pine Spring Rd., Meridian, MS 39305 (601-737-2370). The lake and park are NW of Meridian in Lauderdale County.

As of June 1993, Okatibbee Lake has no trails within the scope of this guide. The manager of the water park is hoping to build a horseback/hiking trail, however, that would include an all-day loop in addition to two-hour and four-hour loops. The addition would create about 25 miles of trail, a welcome addition to this trail-poor area of the state. A nature trail might be incorporated into the two-hour loop. It is not certain whether the trail will be constructed; inquire about its status.

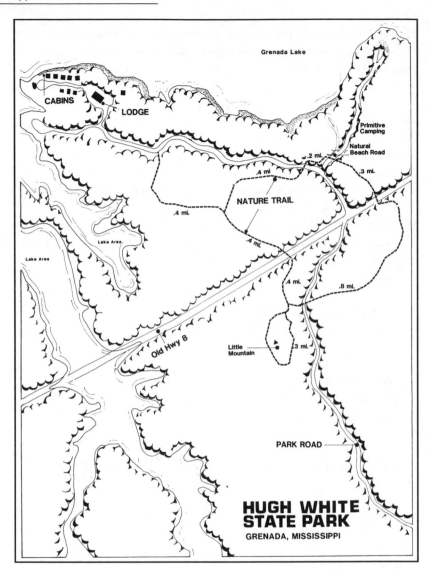

MAP 49. Hugh White State Park

C 8 SARDIS LAKE / JOHN W. KYLE STATE PARK,

Sardis Lake Field Office, P.O. Drawer 186, Sardis, MS 38666 (601-563-4531); John W. Kyle State Park, Rt. 1, Box 115, Sardis, MS 38666 (601-487-1345). The lake and park are E of Sardis and NW of Oxford in Panola and Lafayette counties (1.5-mile Sandstone Nature Trail; ca. 0.7-mile Clear Springs Nature Trail; ca. 0.5-mile state park nature trail)

The dam across the Tallahatchie River that is responsible for this reservoir was completed in 1940. It was the first of the four giant reservoirs on the tributaries of the Yazoo River. Filled to capacity, it covers 58,500 acres (91 square miles). In the summer, it usually occupies 32,100 acres (50 square miles).

Facilities: Including the state park, Sardis Reservoir has 18 public recreation areas. During the summer, park rangers present programs on the area's wildlife, natural features, and cultural history. In addition to the trails described below, Sardis has a two-mile fitness trail.

Access: The dam, field office, and state park and most of the recreation areas are along or near State Scenic Hwy 315, which crosses Interstate 55 at Exit 252 (Sardis exit). If you are coming from the south, turn east at Exit 243A (Batesville exit) and then north (left) on Hwy 315 in eight miles.

Maps and Literature: The Vicksburg District Corps of Engineers free guide to Sardis Lake, which has a map, is excellent. The state park has a map of its facilities and nature trail.

• **Clear Springs Nature Trail.** If awards were handed out for the best-constructed and most scenic boardwalks through Mississippi's swamps, this trail would likely win first prize. It's a loop about 0.7 miles long, but it is split in half by a gravel access road. The boardwalk is south of the road. Gently curved, it goes through a beautiful cypress/tupelo swamp. Benches set in a widened part invite you to linger and look. Nearby, in 1992, was a large, well-constructed beaver lodge. Perhaps the beavers were inspired to excellence by the Corps of Engineer work nearby. Most of this half of the trail is accessible to people in wheelchairs.

The trail then crosses River Road and climbs the ridge on the north side of the road. Here it's a narrow path through pine/oak/hickory forest. As you descend back to the road and your starting point, you pass Clear Springs itself, which emerges under a bluff.

Facilities: Chemical toilets and parking area at the trail head.

Access: The trail is more than a mile below the dam. To get there, drive past the Sleepy Bend Camping Area on Hwy 315 and on over a bridge. Turn left about 0.2 mile after the bridge onto River Rd. Proceed about 1.0 mile to the trailhead parking area, which will be on your left.

• **Sandstone Interpretive Trail.** This 1.5-mile interpretive loop trail shares a parking area and restrooms with the 2.0-mile loop Sandstone Fitness

Trail and an amphitheater. Plaques along the way call your attention to interesting features. The route takes you past the "bonsai forest" growing in a colorful borrow area. This was a source of dirt for the dam, which was constructed in the late 1930s. The topsoil was removed from the white and red underlying sandstone layers. Later pines were planted at the site. More than 50 years later, they are still small because of the low fertility of the site. A bit farther on, outside the borrow area, tall loblolly pines are the same age but are much larger because of better growing conditions.

Access: The trailhead is near the Sardis Lake field office at the south end of the dam, at the intersection of State Hwy 35 and Scenic Loop Hwy 315.

 • **State Park Nature Trail.** This trail is about half a mile long and runs through maturing pine/hardwood forest, starting at the lakeside picnic area on the south, passing through the group camp, and ending at the tennis courts and swimming pool.

5. The State Parks

Mississippi's 28 state parks offer an array of outdoor recreation opportunities, with more amenities than you'll find in the national forests. Complete information is available from the Public Information Office, Division of State Parks, Department of Wildlife, Fisheries, and Parks, P.O. Box 451, Jackson, MS 39205-0451 (601-364-2120).

A typical state park includes an artificial lake or fronts on a large reservoir maintained by the U.S. Army Corps of Engineers or the Tennessee Valley Authority. Those without lakes are alongside the Gulf of Mexico. Fishing is a main attraction. Boat launch ramps are provided, and most have fishing boats for rent. Several also rent canoes and paddleboats. Many have swimming beaches. If swimming in the lake isn't feasible, a pool is often available.

For day users, the parks provide picnic areas, including large pavilions that can be reserved in advance for groups. The typical state park recreation package also includes playing fields and playground equipment for the kids. A few parks have miniature golf courses and tennis courts.

For overnight stays, you usually have a choice between a cabin or camping. Campgrounds are equipped with restrooms with hot showers and flush toilets and sometimes a laundromat. The regular campgrounds have hookups for RVs and trailers. For tent campers and others who don't want hookups, separate primitive camping areas have been set up. They tend to be more primitive than national forest campsites. Don't count on having a table in a primitive state park campground.

Cabins have heat, air conditioning, and kitchenettes and are stocked with bed linens and basic cooking utensils. Pets are not permitted in cabins. Capacity ranges from 2 to 12 people. Cabins are classified by age and architectural style as deluxe, standard, or rustic. Deluxe cabins are the newest and most modern. Standard cabins were built during the 1950s and 1960s and are generally of brick or wood. Rustic cabins were constructed by the Civilian Conservation Corps in the 1930s and early 1940s and are made of stone or rough-hewn wood. Reservations are not required but are highly recommended.

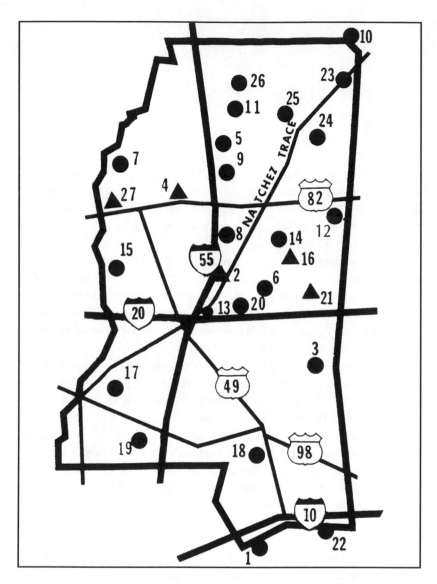

MAP 50. Mississippi state parks (See Table 2 for key to numbers.)

● State park

▲ Historial interest park

Minimum length of stay for reserved cabins is three nights during the spring/summer season (Memorial Day to Labor Day) and two nights during the rest of the year.

A typical state park also has a lodge with an activity room with computer games and pinball machines. Catered meals are provided to groups. Few have restaurants, but most have a snack bar open during the summer and a store with a few basic supplies for campers.

Ten state parks have group camps that are popular with youth and religious groups and for family reunions. Between Memorial Day Weekend and Labor Day weekend, a group must have at least 40 campers. During the rest of the year, the minimum number is 25. All have air conditioned dormitories or air conditioned cabins with separate rooms for counselors. There are playing fields for softball, football, and soccer and separate docks and swimming areas. With one exception, meals are served in a cafeteria or restaurant. (Hugh White State Park has four kitchenettes in which groups can prepare their own meals.)

Nineteen state parks are described in detail in this guide. Among those omitted are several that are interesting historically but too small to have trails more than a half mile long. Among them is Casey Jones Railroad Museum at Vaughan, featuring late 19th-century railroad artifacts and a full-sized steam engine; Florewood River Plantation State Park outside Greenwood, a reconstructed plantation with "living" exhibits; and Winterville Mound State Park near Greenville, an impressive set of Indian ceremonial mounds and a small museum. Two others are simply too small to be included: Sam Dale Historical Site, north of Meridian, and Golden Memorial State Park, outside Walnut Grove.

Trails: Many state parks manage to pack an amazing network of trails into an areas of only a few hundred acres. Generally trails are well marked with paint blazes. The Youth Conservation Corps did a lot of work on these trails in the 1970s. It built charming little rustic archways, each different, to mark the beginnings of trail systems in many parks.

Tishomingo State Park is the traditional favorite of hikers. Other parks with good trail networks include Clarkco, Hugh White, LeFleur's Bluff, Legion, Percy Quin, Roosevelt, Trace, Shepard, and Wall Doxey. Percy Quin and Wall Doxey get high marks from birders and other naturalists.

Managers of the individual parks decide whether mountain bicycles are permitted on hiking trails. Bicycles are allowed in Trace and Lake Lowndes parks. Ask the appropriate park office before planning to ride in other state parks.

Table 2. Facilities at State Parks

Numbers on Map 50	Facility or activity available	DEVELOPED CAMPING	TENT CAMPING	VACATION CABINS	GROUP CAMP	RESTAURANT	SWIMMING: BEACH (B) POOL (P)	CAMPSTORE (C) SNACK BAR (S)	LODGE/ACTIVITY BUILDING	PICNIC AREA/SHELTER	NATURE TRAIL	PLAYGROUND	PLAYING FIELDS	TENNIS	MINIATURE GOLF	GOLF	BOAT LAUNCHING	WATER SKIING	FISHING	FISHING BOAT RENTAL	CANOE RENTAL	PEDAL BOAT RENTAL	BICYCLE RENTAL	LAUNDRY FACILITIES	MUSEUM/INTERPRETIVE CENTER
1	BUCCANEER	●	●				BP	CS	●	●	●	●	●	●					●						●
2*	CASEY JONES							S																	●
3	CLARKCO	●	●	●			B	CS	●	●	●	●	●	●			●	●	●	●	●	●		●	
4*	FLOREWOOD							S	●	●		●													●
5	GEORGE P. COSSAR	●		●		●	P	S	●	●	●				●		●	●	●	●		●		●	
6*	GOLDEN MEMORIAL						B		●	●	●								●	●	●	●			
7	GREAT RIVER ROAD	●	●			●		CS	●	●	●	●							●					●	
8	HOLMES COUNTY	●	●	●	●		B			●	●	●	●				●	●	●	●				●	
9	HUGH WHITE	●	●	●	●	●	B	S	●	●	●	●			●		●	●	●	●			●	●	
10	J. P. COLEMAN	●	●	●			P	CS	●	●	●	●				●	●	●	●	●					
11	JOHN W. KYLE	●		●	●		P	B	●	●	●	●	●	●			●	●	●	●			●	●	
12	LAKE LOWNDES	●	●	●			B	S	●	●	●	●	●	●			●	●	●	●		●		●	
13	LeFLEUR'S BLUFF	●	●				P	CS	●	●	●	●	●	●	●	●		●	●	●					
14	LEGION		●	●			B		●	●	●								●	●					
15	LEROY PERCY	●	●	●	●	●	P	S	●	●	●	●	●				●		●	●		●		●	
16	NANIH WAIYA								●	●	●														
17	NATCHEZ	●	●	●						●							●		●	●		●			
18	PAUL B. JOHNSON	●	●	●	●		B	S	●	●	●	●	●				●	●	●	●	●	●		●	
19	PERCY QUIN	●	●	●	●		B	CS	●	●	●	●			●		●	●	●	●	●	●			
20	ROOSEVELT	●	●	●	●		B	C	●	●	●	●	●		●	●	●	●	●	●	●				
21*	SAM DALE									●															
22	SHEPARD		●						●	●	●	●					●		●	●					
23	TISHOMINGO	●	●	●	●		P	S	●	●	●	●	●				●		●	●	●	●		●	●
24	TOMBIGBEE	●	●	●	●		B		●	●	●	●	●	●			●		●	●	●	●			
25	TRACE	●	●	●			B			●							●	●	●			●			
26	WALL DOXEY	●	●	●	●		B	S	●	●	●	●					●		●	●	●	●		●	
27*	WINTERVILLE MOUNDS									●	●	●	●												●

TABLE 2. Facilities at State Parks

* Park is too small to be included in this guide.

Only the two largest state parks, Natchez and Trace, allow horseback riding and backpacking. Both have large "backcountry" areas that are less civilized than you'd expect in a state park. Both also have many traces of past occupation and abuse by the white man—abandoned sunken roads, cemeteries, cisterns in the middle of nowhere, or collapsing buildings. These remnants may impart more of a feeling of past history than do elaborately restored buildings. Unfortunately, park managers seem to regard the backcountry as semiwasteland, too large to fill with cabins, campgrounds, fishing piers, etc. Still, these areas provide valuable opportunities for primitive, dispersed recreation.

The mission of the state parks "is to provide safe and quality family recreational opportunities for visitors of all ages in unique and scenic areas by acquiring, developing, protecting, and efficiently managing park lands, water, and facilities in a way that the economy of the state will be stimulated and the quality of life will be enriched" (Mission Statement for Mississippi State Parks). A more recent, unstated goal is that state parks should be self-supporting or even profitable. As of 1992, Percy Quin was the only self-supporting state park. To make a park profitable, more luxurious resort-type facilities are necessary—golf courses, motels, convention centers, and tennis courts, for example. The more elaborate the facilities, the more park visitors are removed from nature, and the more land in a natural condition must be cleared and perhaps paved. People who know and like the state parks as they are should track—and combat—efforts to turn them into resorts for the affluent.

Facilities: See table 2.

Fees: Apart from entrance fees, there are charges for camping (varied, depending on facilities desired); boat launch; boat rental; swimming; picnic pavilions; lodge and recreational facilities; cabins; and other items. For the latest schedule of fees, contact the Public Information Office, Division of State Parks or the office of the park you want to visit.

Maps and Literature: Separate leaflets without maps are available for each state park. Most park offices have trail maps of their individual parks.

BUCCANEER STATE PARK,

1150 S. Beach Blvd., Waveland, MS 39576 (601-467-3822). The park is W of Waveland in Hancock County (365 acres; ca. 1.5 miles of trail)

Buccaneer is the most highly developed of Mississippi's three Gulf Coast public parks. It is only 27 miles from New Orleans and is thus within easy striking distance for tourists dodging the inflated lodging expenses in that city. A

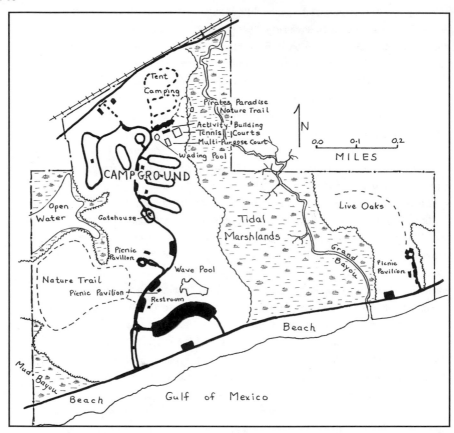

MAP 51. Buccaneer State Park

substantial portion of the park's acreage is given over to a huge RV camp-ground that is inhabited by a mobile community of snowbirds in the winter. An artificial wave-making machine attracts crowds in the summer. Even so, Bucca-neer still has a peaceful nature trail for the hiker.

Just north of the recreation room and on the east edge of the primitive camping area, you will find an observation platform. Just follow the sign pointing out Pirate's Paradise Nature Trail. Only 0.18 mile long, it's hardly long enough to qualify as a trail. You should see a variety of bird life on the tidal marshland along Grand Bayou and in the fringe of woods and brush that borders it.

A longer circuit nature trail (ca. 1.0 mile) begins and ends opposite the first picnic pavilion north of the park entrance. It leads through a dense stand of young pine to the edge of Mud Bayou, then follows the edge of the marsh under large pines and oaks covered with Spanish moss. Allow 45 minutes for the trail, without stops on the way.

The Old Hickory Nature Trail makes a circuit at the picnic area off Beach Drive at the eastern end of the park. In early 1992 the boardwalks across the marsh of Grand Bayou had disintegrated and were unusable. Still, take a short walk through the magnificent giant live oaks that shade the picnic tables and high ground beyond the playing field.

Buccaneer fronts on the Gulf of Mexico. Most of it is protected from hurricanes by a low, stepped seawall. Two small artificial beaches have been constructed. You can see gulls and other seabirds here, at least when the tourists are sparse.

Buccaneer's recorded history extends back to the early 1700s. The famous pirate Jean Lafitte ranged through the area in the late 1700s and lived for a time in the old Pirate's House not far from the park. The campground is on Jackson's Ridge, so named because Andrew Jackson used it as a base of military action during the Battle of New Orleans in 1812. Developed recreation, not history, is Buccaneer's focus, however.

Access: South of U.S. Hwy 90 on Beach Dr. at the southern edge of Waveland. Follow the signs to the park from Interstate 90 or U.S. 90.

CLARKCO STATE PARK, I 10

386 Clarkco Rd., Quitman, MS 39355 (601-776-6651). The park is N of Quitman, Clarke County (815 acres, ca. five miles of designated hiking trail)

Clarkco is one of Mississippi's eight original state parks. It was constructed in 1938 by Civilian Conservation Corps Company 1437, which, with other CCC companies, stayed in barracks in a camp along U.S. Hwy 45 within the park. Four of the original cabins and two large picnic shelters built by the CCC men are still in use. Unfortunately the original water tower and lookout tower fell into ruins and were removed.

Clarkco is a typical state park in layout, but its large size and mature timber make it an especially good place for hikers and naturalists. The 3.5-mile loop trail around the lake is well planned and mostly out of sight of the lake and developments. An observation platform for birders and anyone else wanting an overview of the lake is situated at the upper end of the lake about 0.2 mile east of the primitive camping area.

Beyond the platform you will pass through a remote portion of the park that has large pines and a dense understory dominated by yaupon and young

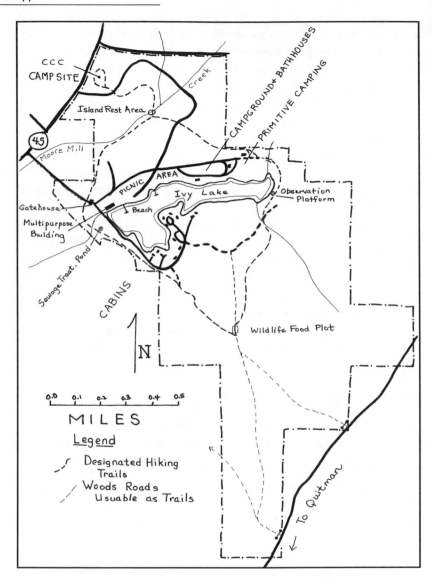

CCC
CAMP SITE

Creek

Island Rest Area

45

Moore Mill

PICNIC AREA

Ivy Lake

Beach

Gatehouse

Multipurpose
Building

Sewage Treat. Pond

CABINS

CAMPGROUND + BATHHOUSES

PRIMITIVE CAMPING

Observation
Platform

Wildlife Food Plot

To Quitman

N

0.0 0.1 0.2 0.3 0.4 0.5

MILES

Legend

Designated Hiking
Trails
Woods Roads
Usuable as Trails

MAP 52. Clarkco State Park

pines. Contrast this with a national forest trail such as the Longleaf or Tuxachanie trails, where the U.S. Forest Service suppresses understory by prescribed burning. Dirt roads rarely used by vehicles lead into the southern part
of the park.

A highlight of the trail is the delightful Island Rest Area, a tiny island in the middle of Moore Mill Creek. On the circuit you will pass through extensive pine forests and flat-bottom creek valleys with dense growths of cane.

A side trail branches off from the lake circuit trail at the Island Rest Area, leading in 0.8 mile to the site of the CCC camp, which was used between June 1934 and the late 1940s. After the camp was abandoned, the buildings were removed. Today you see a well-preserved elevated goldfish pond with rock and mortar walls—once the centerpiece of the camp—and some concrete foundations. If you haven't already done so, stop by the park office in the multipurpose building before you leave and look at the display of photos and information on the CCC in general and on this camp in particular.

Clarkco boasted three state champion trees as of February 1989: bluejack oak (*Quercus incana*), sand post oak (*Q. stellata* var. *margaretta*) and turkey oak (*Q. laevis*).

GEORGE PAYNE COSSAR STATE PARK.　　C 7

See Enid Lake, Corps of Engineers Reservoirs.

GREAT RIVER ROAD STATE PARK,　　D 5

P.O. Box 292, Rosedale, MS 38769 (601-759-6762). The park is adjacent to Rosedale in Bolivar County (756 acres, ca. 1.5 miles of trail)

This is the only developed natural area that brings you right to the edge of the Mississippi River, inside the levee that runs from Memphis south almost to Vicksburg. The purpose of the levee is to protect the Mississippi Delta from flooding, so it's not surprising that the park is flooded from time to time. (Note that all the buildings are on piers.) When you first arrive at the park, you'll probably want to climb up the observation tower for a view of the Mississippi River and the barges slowly being pushed upriver.

The "Deer Meadow Nature Trail" officially begins on the south side of the access road leading into the park, but you can also get to it from the corner of the campground. It more or less makes a loop in the woods between the campground and Perry Martin Lake. The route of the trail may vary from year to year, depending on the swath that has been cleared of undergrowth. Some of the trees between the campground and the main loop are identified.

The forests in the park are adapted to extremes of wetness and dryness. Occasionally the park is flooded. The trees, which are rooted mainly in well-drained

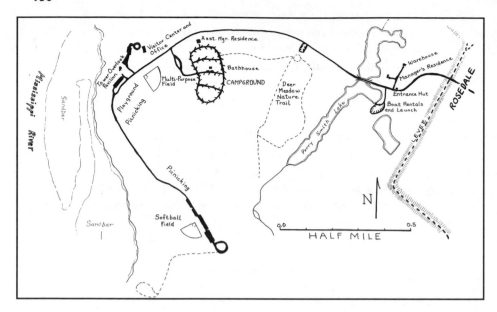

MAP 53. Great River Road State Park

sand, are fast growing and short-lived, ready to take advantage of the shifting course of the river (at least before it was confined within the levee). Typical trees of this riparian forest include willows, box elder, and sycamores.

Access: Turn west off State Hwy 1 and drive through the town of Rosedale and on over the levee to the park.

F 7 HOLMES COUNTY STATE PARK,

Rt. 1, Box 153, Durant, MS 39063 (601-653-3351). The park is SW of Durant, Holmes County (444 acres, ca. four miles of trail)

The park is in rolling hills forested with loblolly pine, shortleaf pine, white and red oaks, cedars, and dogwoods. It is especially beautiful in the spring when the dogwoods are blooming and in the fall when their leaves turn red. The smaller, upper lake has a bathing beach and paddleboats for rent. The lower lake is open to limited water skiing.

The park was constructed by the Civilian Conservation Corps Company No. 4429 between 1935 and 1939. The original six rustic cabins remain, complemented by three more modern duplexes.

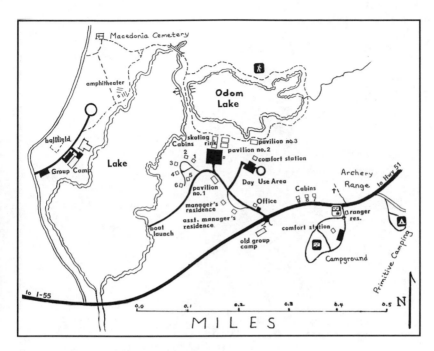

MAP 54. Holmes County State Park

Facilities: In addition to the facilities found at most state parks, the park has a roller skating rink.

Access: Exit 150 on Interstate 55, four miles south of the Durant exit. It's about one mile to the park.

HUGH WHITE STATE PARK. D 8

See Grenada Lake, Corps of Engineers Reservoirs.

J. P. COLEMAN STATE PARK,

613 CR 321`65, Iuka, MS 38852 (601-423-6515). The park is N of Iuka, Tishomingo County (1,420 acres).

This park has more resort-type facilities than most state parks. Most of the land, however, is undeveloped. There is much to attract naturalists.

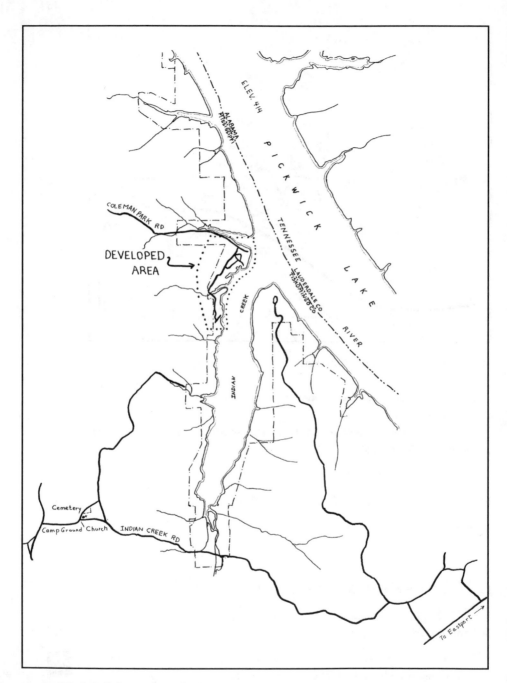

MAP 55. J. P. Coleman State Park

The setting is beautiful, with cool green forests in the summer, and—rare for Mississippi—lots of rocks. Springs flow out of the hillsides. The park's single nature trail had to be abandoned because, when the park boundaries were marked, park personnel found out that the trail went outside the park onto private land. From late summer through early winter, however, the narrow drawdown zone around the edge of Pickwick Lake is good for hiking. The shoreline is partially gravelly, interspersed with ledges of limestone and chert. The shoreline rocks are in the Pride Hill Formation, the same formation as the layers under the sandstone cliffs in Tishomingo State Park.

The lower end of Indian Creek, a half-mile wide, is a major arm of Pickwick Lake. It divides the park in two. All developments are on the west side. The east side has been left an undeveloped trailless nature area to protect rare plants and their habitats. You can drive into this isolated section of the park via a road leading north from Indian Creek Rd.

The Tennessee Valley Authority built the dam that impounds Pickwick Lake during the late 1930s. In 1958 TVA gave the land to the state Park Commission to develop for recreation. It is named after the man who was Mississippi's governor between 1956 and 1960.

Maps: A map of the developed portion of the park is available from the park office. The Yellow Creek topo map is useful if you visit the nature area.

JOHN W. KYLE STATE PARK.   B C 8

See Sardis Lake, Corps of Engineers Reservoirs.

LAKE LOWNDES STATE PARK,   E 11

3319 Lake Lowndes Rd., Columbus, MS 39702 (601-328-2110). The park is SE of Columbus, Lowndes County (710 acres, 3.5-mile interpretive trail)

This park is on the fringe of the Tennessee Hills near the Alabama state line. It opened in 1972. The developed portion has the neat, clean-shaven look typical of more recently constructed parks. It has the full complement of park recreation facilities plus a unique sports complex with a gymnasium, all clustered on the west side of 150-acre Lake Lowndes.

Opossum Nature Trail: The Youth Conservation Corps built this interpretive trail in 1980. It begins at the edge of the dam beyond the campground. The off-road part of the trail is 3.5 miles long; it's a 5-mile round trip if you continue back to your starting point on the paved road. Before starting your hike, stop

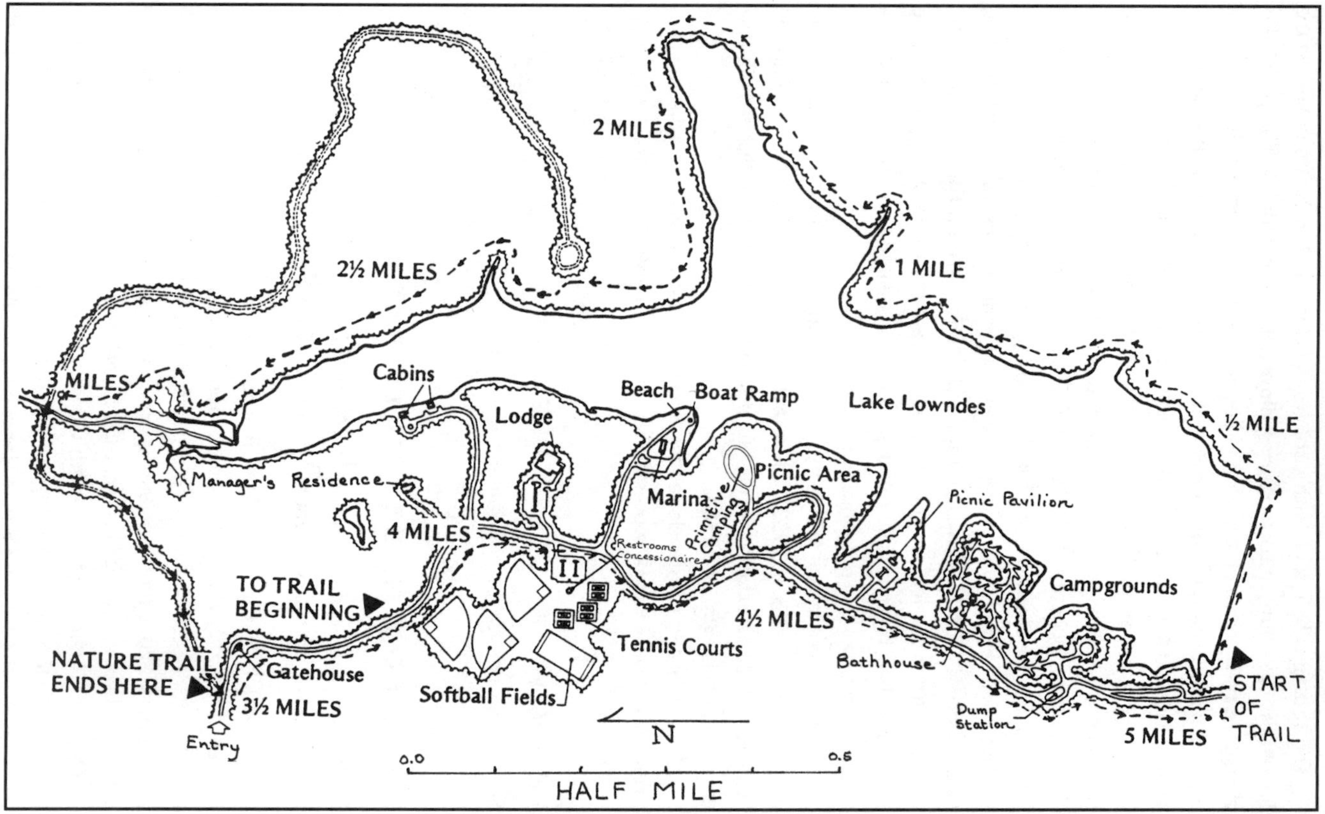

MAP 56. Lake Lowndes State Park

STRINGED INSTRUMENT QUALITY CHECK

- ☑ Truss Rod
- ☑ Neck/Fretboard
- ☑ Peghead/Nut
- ☑ Binding **N/A**
- ☑ Tuning Keys/Hardware
- ☑ Action
- ☑ Bridge/Saddle/Tremolo
- ☑ Finish
- ☑ Body, Bracing, Structural
- ☑ Pickups, Electronics
- ☑ Intonation
- ☑ Case (if applicable)
- ☑ Final Cleaning
- ☐ Accessories
- ☐ Warranty Card (if applicable)
- ☐ Other _____

_____

Date _____

Checked By _____

MUSICIAN'S FRIEND QUALITY CHECK

Every instrument undergoes our special Stringed Instrument Quality Check and complete adjustment before we ship it to you. Changes in temperature and humidity during shipping can alter these adjustments, so your instrument may require some fine tuning. We set your instrument for standard action, and you may want to reset the action to suit your own playing style.

Your guitar/bass comes from the factory with the following gauge/string type:

- ❏ Electric: .009 – .42/Nickel Round Wound
- ❏ Classical: .028 – .43/Normal Tension
- ❏ Acoustic: .012 – .54/Phosphor Bronze Round Wound
- ❏ Bass: .045 – .100/Long Scale
- ❏ 12-String: .010 – .48/Phosphor Bronze Round Wound
- ❏ Other _____

Although we have inspected your instrument before shipping, some "settling" may have occurred. Your instrument was set up with medium action. If the action is too high or too low, we recommend you consult a qualified repair person to set up your instrument to match your personal preference.

If you want to change the string gauge, remember that changing the string gauge will change the tension on the neck and may require a truss rod adjustment.

If your guitar has a Floyd Rose-type Locking Tremolo, tune and change strings as follows:

To Tune Strings:
1. Unclamp locking nut at top of neck.
2. Tune guitar.
3. Reclamp locking nut.
4. Fine tune guitar using the thumbwheels provided at back of tremolo unit.

To Change Strings:
1. Unclamp locking nut at top of neck.
2. Using Allen key provided, unclamp bridge saddle lock (insert Allen key at rear of bridge).
3. Clip ball ends from new strings. Change strings one at a time.
4. To install new strings, simply reverse the above procedure.
5. Follow tuning procedures listed above.
6. Note: If you change string gauges, the tremolo system will need to be adjusted.

INSTRUMENT MAINTENANCE TIPS

1. Keep your instrument in its case when not in use.
2. Keep your instrument away from extreme heat, cold or humidity changes.
3. Use only quality care products such as guitar polish, not furniture polish.
4. Change your strings on a regular schedule.
5. Never remove all the strings at once. This puts added stress on the neck. Change one string at a time.
6. Keep your instrument tuned to proper pitch and adjusted. You may consider purchasing an electronic tuner.
7. Find a reputable instrument repairman and take your instrument in for an annual checkup coinciding with weather changes.

Martin Guitar Strings

Phosphor Bronze Round Wound

10-0001	M530	Extra Light	10-47	**$3.39**
10-0002	M540	Light	12-52	**$3.39**
10-0003	M550	Medium	13-56	**$3.39**
10-0004	M500	12 String Light	10-47	**$7.69**

Marquis 80/20 Bronze Round Wound

10-0010	M1000	Extra Light	10-47	**$3.59**
10-0011	M1100	Light	12-52	**$3.59**
10-0012	M1200	Medium	13-56	**$3.59**
10-0013	M1600	12 String Light	10-47	**$5.79**

80/20 Bronze Round Wound

10-0020	M170	Extra Light	10-47	**$2.99**
10-0021	M140	Light	12-52	**$2.99**
10-0022	M240	Bluegrass	12-56	**$2.99**
10-0023	M150	Medium	13-56	**$2.99**

Dunlop Tortex Standard Picks

Choose .50mm, .60mm, .73mm,
.88mm, 1.0mm, or 1.14mm.

11-0040	**$2.50 Dz.**

Fender Flat Standard Picks

11-0500	Thin	**$2.29 Dz.**
	Medium	**$2.99 Dz.**
	Heavy	**$3.59 Dz.**
	Extra Heavy	**$3.99 Dz.**

D'Addario Guitar & Bass Strings

XL Series Nickel Round Wound

10-0235	XL130	X Super Light	08-38	**$4.59**
10-0236	XL130+	Half Step	085-39	**$4.59**
10-0237	XL120	Super Light	09-42	**$3.39**
10-0238	XL120+	Half Step	095-44	**$3.39**
10-0239	XL125	L.T.H.B.	09-46	**$3.39**
10-0240	XL110	Regular Light	10-46	**$3.39**
10-0241	XL110w	Lt Wound 3rd	10-46	**$3.79**
10-0242	XL115	Jazz/Rock	11-49	**$3.39**
10-0243	XL115w	Wound 3rd	11-49	**$3.79**
10-0244	XL140	L.T.H.B.	10-52	**$3.79**

Nickel for Floyd Rose Tremolo Round Wound

10-0256	FRXL120	Super Light	09-42	**$3.79**

Bass XL Nickel Round Wound

10-0350	XL220	S-Soft/Long	40-95	**$14.99**
10-0351	XL170	Soft/Long	45-100	**$14.99**
10-0352	XL160	Reg/Long	50-105	**$14.99**

Dunlop GuitarTrigger Capo
CHOOSE NICKEL, BLACK OR GOLD.

36-1505	List $14.95	**$9.99**

CALL
7 DAYS
1-800 776-5173

Cleaning Supplies

Martin Guitar Polish		**Fender Polish**	
42-0111	**$5.50**	42-0050	**$6.10**
Fast Fret		**Gibson Pump Polish**	
42-0451	**$5.39**	42-0150	**$4.25**
Fingerease			
42-0450	**$3.95**		

Musician's Friend Polishing Cloth

42-0400 **$2.99**

Musician's Friend String Saver Cloth

42-0399 **$2.99**

D'Andrea Locking Nylon Straps
Patented built-in positive tab-locking system. Eliminates the need for strap locks. Choose black, blue, gold, rainbow, red, or silver. 2" polyweb.

36-4750 List $6.95 **$4.99**

Horizon Neon Guitar Cables
Custom neon-colored 24-gauge cable. Hand-soldered 1/4" plugs. Choose blue, pink, yellow, orange or green.

33-6030	10'	**$6.99**
	15'	**$8.59**
	20'	**$9.99**

The Guitool All-In-One-Guitar Tool
Equipped with seven hex keys (standard and metric), two slot-head and one Phillips-head screwdrivers, and a string cutter to trim guitar and bass strings.

42-0501 List $24.95 **$17.99**

AXman Tubular Folding Guitar Stands
45-2000 List $29.95 **$12⁹⁹**

5 Deluxe Tubular Stands
List $149.75 **$9⁹⁹ea**

AXman Double Guitar Stand

45-2005
List $39.95 **$19⁹⁹**

5 Double Guitar Stands
List $199.75 **$14⁹⁹ea**

CALL 7 DAYS
1-800 776-5173
VISA MasterCard AMERICAN EXPRESS

A SPECIAL OFFER FOR RECENT PURCHASERS:
FREE SHIPPING & HANDLING FOR ANY ORDER YOU PLACE FROM THIS BROCHURE WITHIN THE NEXT 45 DAYS.*

*Just give our customer service representative this source code: 79451003 by the sports center/lodge for a copy of the brochure on the trail, which includes a key to the plants singled out by numbered posts along the first 1.5 miles.

The trail follows the eastern side of Lake Lowndes through hilly terrain with pines and many species of hardwoods. Sometimes it descends to the margin of the lake, and it crosses two small wetlands where streams enter the lake. Your chances of seeing wildlife such as wood ducks and beavers are excellent here. Rustic benches are supplied at good vantage points. The route is marked by vertical white paint blazes and wooden signs. Be careful not to get sidetracked on side routes coming in from the east.

LeFLEUR'S BLUFF STATE PARK, H 7

2140 Riverside Dr., Jackson, MS 39202 (601-364-2344). The park is in Jackson, Hinds County (331 acres, at least 2.5 miles of formal and informal trails)

Even though this park is in the middle of the Jackson metropolitan area, it's easy to feel you are in a remote place merely by walking a short distance. The park is a single block of land on the west side of the Pearl River, but by auto, it appears to be divided into two separate portions: the Mayes Lakes and associated swamps and hardwood bottoms, which you reach from Lakeland Drive; and the nature trail on a bluff, which is at the end of the park road that turns off Riverside Drive.

The Mayes Lakes are at least three oxbow lakes that are former channels of the Pearl River and recall the time before the white settlement, Ross Barnett Dam, channelization, and levees, when the Pearl frequently changed course within its floodplain. The lakes themselves are permanent bodies of water, but alongside are low-lying swamps with large cypress and tupelo gum trees that flood when the Pearl is high and dry up when it's low. The campground and picnic areas, with several shelters large and small, are on oak-shaded higher ground between the lakes.

Old roads and informal foot trails invite hiking and birding. If you walk south through the picnic grounds between the two largest lakes, you will reach a gravel road used only for park maintenance. Keep watch for an old road that turns off to the right just after you cross a short intermittent stream that connects the lake on your right with the one on your left. Turn onto this old road, and soon you'll be in a mature bottomland forest along the Pearl River. Unless the river is high, you'll want to take a side trail to the bank of the river, with its white sand bottom.

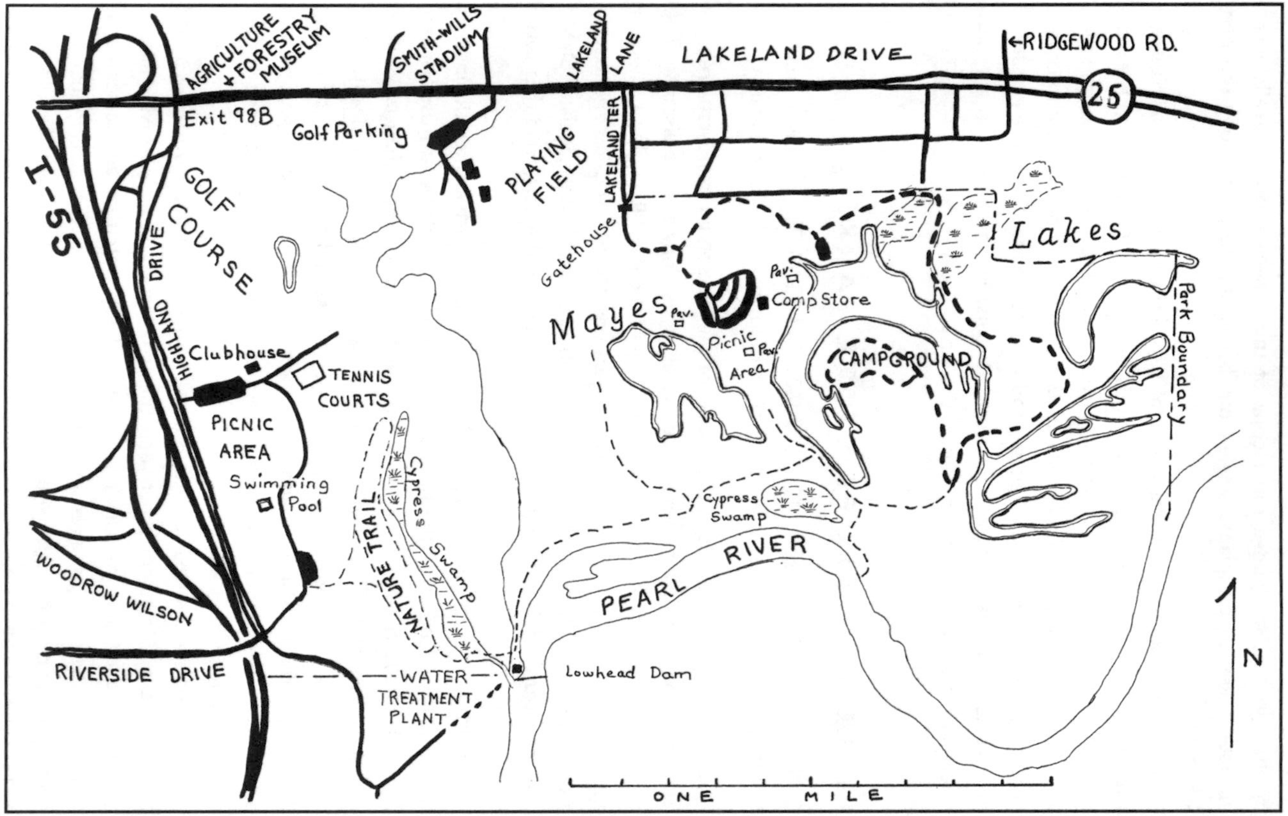

MAP 57. LeFleur's Bluff State Park

About 0.6 mile from the Mayes Lakes picnic grounds, you will arrive at a water treatment plant owned and operated by the city of Jackson and a low dam on the river. Keep away from the plant and the river. Instead, follow a vague footpath to your right. It will lead to a boardwalk across a swamp to the main nature trail on the bluff.

Nature Trails on the Bluff: You can hike to the trails from the Mayes Lakes as described above, or you can drive to the top of the trail through the more developed uplands of the park. Turn east on Riverside Drive, go through the formal gates of the park and proceed past the clubhouse, tennis courts, playground, and swimming pool to a parking lot on your left and the elaborate entrance to the trail.

Below is an updated guide to the nature trails. Not described but as noteworthy as the natural features is the trail itself. It traverses steep sections of the bluff on elevated boardwalks and stairways. Observation decks and benches invite you to pause.

Points of Interest on the Main Nature Trail: (1) Honeysuckle Nook, a cavelike opening made almost exclusively of honeysuckle; (2) Meditation Point, atop a steep bluff, overlooking a backwater of the Pearl River. The main trail turns to the left. Straight ahead, a side trail descends to the backwater and crosses it on a long boardwalk. On the other side is the water treatment plant. Stay away from the river here. Over the years, several fishermen have lost their footing near the dam and drowned. At one time two primitive loop trails, the red loop and the green loop, branched near the boardwalk over the backwater. These loops have not been maintained recently but will, with luck, eventually be restored. (3) May Apple Hill, to the left, which in early spring is covered with may apples, trillium, violets, and phlox; to the right, the bluff is lined with oakleaf hydrangea. (4) First exit: you must walk about one-third of the way; if you do not wish to go down the stairs, turn left and return to the trail entrance. (5) The Pearl River Backwater Swamp: the steps here take you 75' down to the swamp floor. This area is 6' to 8' deep in water when the spring rains come. The swamp is home to the bald cypress, tupelo gum, silver bell, etc. Coons, mink, swamp rabbit, and opossum are at home here. Birds found in the area include the fish crow, barred owl, wood duck, egret, herons, woodpeckers, and many songbirds. (6) Shumard Red Oak: the mighty tree, over 4' in diameter and about 75' tall, is probably more than 100 years old. (7) Fossil Gulch: about halfway up the walls is a layer of greenish gray marl known as the Moodys Branch formation. About 45 million years ago, the site of Jackson was on the edge of a shallow tropical or subtropical sea. A huge variety of molluscs and other marine animals thrived here. (See Dockery, *Mollusca of the Moodys*

Branch Formation, in the bibliography.) (8) White Oak Log, nearly 150 years old when it fell, has been lying on this hillside for almost 30 years. Each ring indicates a year of growth. (9) Beech Grove: beech trees produce food called "mast" for birds and squirrels. The carving in the bark of the tree will remain for years. The oldest date found was 1913. Please don't add your initials. (10) Memorial Marker: a petrified log with a marker in memorial to R. M. Callaway, Sr., who started promoting the nature trail in 1949. (11) Amphitheater.

History of the Park: What is now LeFleur's Bluff State Park came into being in March 1944 when the city of Jackson purchased 331 acres of land at what was then the northeastern corner of the city. It was named Riverside Park and formally opened to the public in 1949. The park was turned over to the state and was renamed in April 1989.

The name LeFleur comes from Louis LeFleur, a French Canadian who had a trading post along the Natchez Trace at French Camp in the late 1700s and early 1800s. He was married, in turn, to two half-breed Choctaw Indian sisters, who bore him many children. One, born in 1800, was the famous quarter-breed Choctaw chieftain Greenwood Leflore. Legend has it that Louis had a trading post on a bluff on the Pearl River near the present intersection of Jefferson and Silas Brown streets and that Greenwood was born there, but there is no evidence to support the idea. The bluff was named by the commissioners who recommended the site for Mississippi's state capitol. Apparently their decision was an arbitrary one. (See McDonald, "Latest Research about LeFleur's Bluff," in the bibliography.)

Access: Take Exit 98B (Lakeland Dr.) in Jackson. To reach the Mayes Lakes, campground, and picnic ground, go east on Lakeland Dr., and turn right on a paved road at the first traffic light. To reach the main nature trail, make a sharp right onto Riverside Dr. and take the first left. Drive through the park entrance gates and past the tollhouse.

F 9   LEGION STATE PARK,

635 Legion State Park Rd., Louisville, MS 39339 (601-773-8323). The park is in Louisville, Winston County (440 acres, at least 1.8 mile of hiking trail)

This little-known state park is in the hills just northeast of Louisville. Time has stood still here since the 1930s. If you are looking for a quiet semiwilderness setting, you will love Legion.

The park is almost entirely forested with a mixture of pines and hardwoods kept free of understory by prescribed burning. It has two small lakes: Lake Toppasha (12 acres) and Lakelet Palila (4 acres). Both are popular with local fisher-

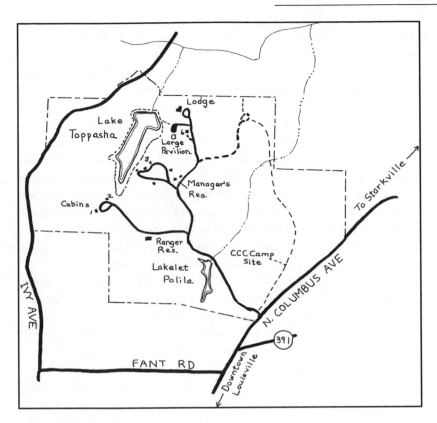

M A P 58. Legion State Park

men but are too small for motorboats and water skiing.

Lake Toppasha is bordered by shelves that look like road cuts but are really natural geologic features that are unusual for the North American coastal plain. Under the park hills there is a layer of slippery clay and clay shales known as the Ackerman Formation. It originated about 58 million years ago when the region was under a shallow embayment of the Gulf of Mexico. Much more recently, streams cut deep little valleys through overlying deposits of sand and clay into Ackerman Formation. Apparently the Ackerman clay could not withstand the stress and permitted the overburden to slip. The hill on which the lodge stands was once a single eminence that split to form subsidiary hills and terraces on the east and west sides. (See Morse's *The Geologic History of Legion State Park*, in the bibliography.)

This park is also unusual because of its recent history. It is one of the 10 original state parks and was constructed by the Civilian Conservation Corps Company No. 480 between 1934 and 1937. It is named after Allen Post No. 62

of the American Legion, which offered the initial 72 acres of the park to the state.

The CCC built a lodge and ten cabins. The lodge, now a designated Mississippi Landmark, is an outstanding example of the rustic architecture for which the CCC is famous, with massive stonework and huge, hand-adzed timbers. (The CCC built lodges for most of the original state parks, but many have since burned down.) Six of the ten cabins survive. They are built entirely of wood, and each has a distinctive stone chimney. The other four cabins have burned down; only the chimneys remain.

Legion State Park was leased to the Pushmataha Area Council of the Boy Scouts in 1954 and lost its status as a state park. It was operated for 25 years as Camp Palila and reverted to the state in 1979. During the 25 years when it wasn't a park, funds for updating and further developing the other state parks were freely available. Legion remained as it was in the 1930s.

Trails: A trail about 0.8 mile long encircles Lake Toppasha. It goes through forests and around two quiet streams that empty into the lake. On the east side, stray from the edge of the lake if you want to see the ruin of a quaint small wood and stone pavilion, an extant minichapel overlooking the lake, and chimneys of former cabins. Parts of the trail may be flooded when the lake level is up.

Another trail begins near the entrance gate. It joins an old gravel road (a predecessor of Business Hwy 25 and the present State Hwy 25) and winds through widely spaced pines. A side trail to your left leads to the stone foundation of a CCC barrack. (A photograph displayed in the Lodge shows what the CCC camp looked like in the 1930s.) The road descends and crosses the creek coming down from Lakelet Palila, and climbs the other side. On top, you will reach a turnaround. The main route turns left and follows the ridgetop, joining the main park road near a small circular flower garden and a sign for the picnic area. Along the way you'll pass two outhouses with covered picnic tables. You can camp here if you like. (The circuit, including a walk back on the road to the entrance, is about 1.8 miles.)

Henry the Hermit: At the turnaround mentioned above, you'll see a narrow trail/fire lane heading north, which leads toward the site of Henry's cabin on private land. Henry McCully, who was shell-shocked in World War I, felt ill at ease around people, and so he retreated to the woods and lived by himself in a log cabin. Children from Louisville often came down to the old road to visit him. He was an excellent shot. Kids loved to toss pennies in the air; he'd get them every time. He lived with his chickens and his garden until he was quite old. Today only a tree full of bullets and the rocks that were the foundation of his cabin remain. The park manager can direct you.

Facilities: Fishing boats for rent. The lodge can be reserved for meetings, banquets, and parties. Legion has one large picnic pavilion and five small ones. Primitive camping is permitted anywhere in the park (campers can even sleep under the large pavilion). Two places have been specially designated for primitive camping, and a flush toilet and hot showers are available. When the state legislature is willing, $850,000 will be allotted to Legion to pave the roads, renovate and reopen three cabins, and install a 20-unit campground with RV hookups.

LEROY PERCY STATE PARK AND WILDLIFE MANAGEMENT AREA

F 5

LeRoy Percy State Park, P.O. Box 176, Hollandale, MS 38748 (601-827-5436). LeRoy Percy Wildlife Management Area, Supervisor, Jackie Fleeman, P.O. Box 261, Cary, MS 39051 (601-873-2413). The park and WMA are W of Hollandale, Washington County (2,442 acres total, ca. three miles of designated trails)

My memory of my first sight of this park is an idealized Old South dream landscape: widely spaced big oaks loaded with thick growths of Spanish moss, a moss-covered picnic shelter made of heavy timbers, log cabins screened by more Spanish moss, and—in a lake beyond massive bald cypress trunks—placid tourists gliding by in paddleboats. It's Mississippi's oldest state park and the only one in the bottomlands of the Delta. LeRoy Percy, Great River Road, and LeFleur's Bluff are the only state parks with natural (oxbow) lakes.

LeRoy Percy is also the only park to have an alligator pond. The reptiles are in an enclosure supplied by an artesian well that maintains a year-round temperature of 78°F. It's one of two such wells in the park. Originally the water from the wells was closer to 100°F, and the cabins built by the Civilian Conservation Corps were kept warm in the winter by artesian water flowing through pipes in the walls.

The lakes are former channels of Black Bayou, which runs through the middle of the park. Most of the park and the wildlife management area are covered with bottomland hardwoods, which are characteristic of Delta land that used to flood every winter and spring.

The wildlife management area, which is mainly south of State Hwy 12, has no maintained trails—only three parking areas that are shown on the map. The park, however, has three trails. The longest and most interesting runs along the west side of the larger lake, Brushy Lake. Narrow one-plank boardwalks cross swamps at both ends of the lake. Be on the lookout for a side trail

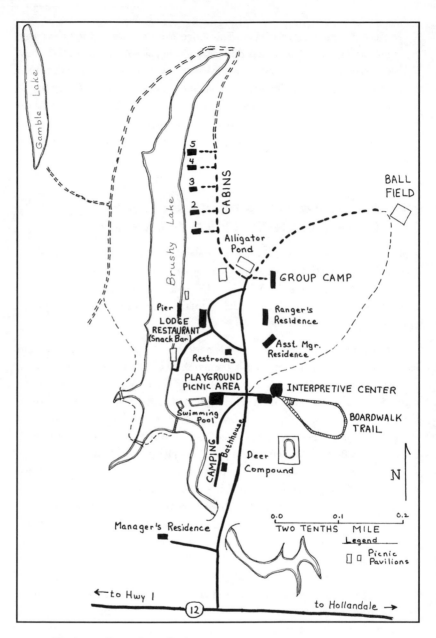

Gamble Lake

Brushy Lake

CABINS

5
4
3
2
1

BALL FIELD

Alligator Pond

GROUP CAMP

Pier

Ranger's Residence

LODGE RESTAURANT (Snack Bar)

Asst. Mgr. Residence

Restrooms

PLAYGROUND PICNIC AREA

INTERPRETIVE CENTER

Swimming Pool

BOARDWALK TRAIL

CAMPING

Bathhouse

Deer Compound

N

0.0   0.1   0.2
TWO TENTHS MILE

Legend

Picnic Pavilions

Manager's Residence

← to Hwy 1

12

to Hollandale →

MAP 59. Leroy Percy State Park

(actually a dirt road) that goes west to the Gamble Lake. Without the side trail, it's about 2.2 miles around Brushy Lake.

The second trail begins near the front of the interpretive center across from the campground and leads through hardwood bottoms to the ball playing field. Including a return on the gravel road leading to the field, it's about a 0.8-mile walk.

The third trail is an oval elevated boardwalk that begins and ends behind the wildlife interpretive center built by the Youth Conservation Corps in 1977. The center was temporarily closed for repairs in 1991.

Five thousand people were present for the dedication of the park on July 25, 1935. It was named after an able Delta planter and lawyer who was a U.S. senator from Mississippi in 1909–13. Park facilities were built by the Civilian Conservation Corps Companies 2422 and 5467 between 1934 and 1936. Only two of the seven original log cabins are left. The solid log architecture is typical of the buildings that the CCC built in parks across the nation during the Depression.

Black Bayou was once enticing to canoeists. Unfortunately it has now been channelized, confined by grass-covered levees and severed from its original meanders. These modifications are part of the ongoing Yazoo Basin project of the U.S. Army Corps of Engineers.

Best Time to Visit: The park is open all year. Parts may be flooded during the late winter and early spring, so you may want to contact the park office before planning a trip then.

Map: The Swan Lake NW topo map is recommended if you leave the immediate vicinity of Brushy Lake.

NANIH WAIYA STATE PARK,   G 10

Rt. 3, Box 251-A, Louisville, MS 39339 (601-773-7988). The park is SE of Noxapater in Winston and Neshoba counties (ca. 72 acres in two separate units)

A Choctaw legend says that the Choctaw and Chickasaw Indians were once one people who lived on the west side of the Mississippi River. They decided to move, relying on a sacred pole to guide them. Every night they set the pole upright in the ground, and every morning the pole leaned east, so they continued east. They crossed the Mississippi and eventually arrived in what is now Winston County. It was raining heavily when they stopped for the night, and the band that became the Chickasaws crossed a creek and set up camp away

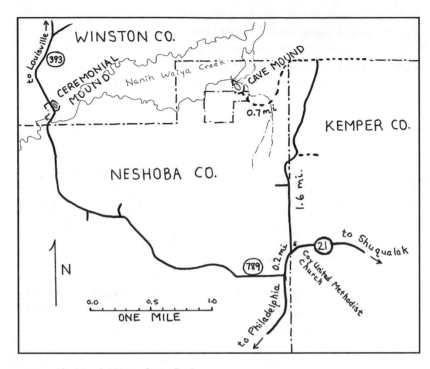

M A P 60. Nanih Waiya State Park

from the rest of the group. In the morning, this band continued traveling without checking on the position of the pole. The rest of the group, who became
the Choctaws, found the sacred pole standing upright, indicating that their
journey was over. They built Nanih Waiya at the site (in Choctaw, the name
means "bending mound.") Several other myths concerned with migrations and
the creation of the Choctaws center on Nanih Waiya. In 1918, when the federal government established the present Choctaw Reservation to give a home
to the scattered peoples who had refused to be removed to Oklahoma, most
of them had gravitated to the vicinity of their sacred mound, their "Great
Mother."

The ceremonial mound known as Nanih Waiya is in the western part of the
state park. It's about 40' high and covers about an acre of ground. It stood at
the southeastern edge of a prehistoric village that was protected by a broad
deep trough and a circular wall or rampart about a half mile in diameter. The
site was first described in 1775 and later in 1843, 1854, and 1898. The rampart
was originally at least 8' or 10' high and 20' wide. Gaps divided it into 18 seg-

ments. At least two well-worn, ancient roads led out from the site. Within the rampart stood at least one other relatively large mound, judged to be a burial mound because of numerous human bone and stone relic fragments found in it, and several remnants of smaller mounds. By 1900 most of the rampart had been eliminated by plowing, and the largest mound had been disrupted by a tunnel dug by "treasure seekers" (see Halbert's article "Nanih Waiya," in the bibliography). No traces of the rampart could be located in 1971.

Archeologists believe the mound was constructed around the time of Christ. The Choctaws probably originated much later from a confederation of survivors of several Mississippi/Alabama tribes who came together in the 16th and 17th centuries after a great die-off that began before DeSoto's expedition in 1540–41. Of Mississippi's inhabitants, 80% to 90% perished, perhaps from diseases introduced by Europeans. Many other southeastern tribes have migration myths similar to those of the Choctaws, and so the story probably goes back thousands of years.

The eastern part of the park is on the other side of Nanih Waiya Creek. It includes Nanih Waiya Cave Mound, a natural hill that is a remnant of higher ground to the south. Underneath the hill is a cave that may once have had at least four entrances, three at the base and one on top of the hill. Only one side entrance was open when I visited the site in early 1993.

In October 1973 two experienced Mississippi cavers, John Sevenair and Steven Carey, surveyed the cave with tape and compass. They were able to go 127' down a long, narrow passage that was no more than 5' wide and 10' high. They first encountered water about 35' from the entrance. The cave gradually sloped downhill, and the water grew deeper. When the water reached the ceiling, they turned back (see Knight et al., *Caves of Mississippi*, in the bibliography). This exploration was during the driest time of the year, when the underground water level in the floodplain of Nanih Waiya Creek would be lowest. Normally, even more of the cave is flooded.

Sevenair and Carey said that sections of the passageway seemed to be artificial and other portions resembled a natural cave. No one knows who dug it, if anyone did. The Choctaws, however, have known about it for generations. One Choctaw story says that a group of hunters caught in a storm dug a hole in the hillside to get out of the rain. Enlarging the hole became a pastime for the men; every time they were in the vicinity hunting or fishing, they dug some more until a cave had eventually been created.

A Choctaw creation myth tells how their ancestors emerged from a cave under a mound and dried themselves in the sun. Many living Choctaws believe Cave Mound was the site. Gideon Lincecum, who visited the Nanih Waiya ceremonial mound in 1843, said that the Choctaw migration myth regarding the journey with the pole ended at a hill with a hole in it beside a stream. Was this the place? Maybe not, because at one time there was also a water-filled chamber under the ceremonial mound. Another Choctaw tale tells of 50 children who were led into the cave by a vengeful medicine man, who stopped up the entrance and left them to be asphyxiated by "damp gas."

A picturesque swinging bridge leads across Nanih Waiya Creek from Cave Mound; it had deteriorated and was unsafe to use in 1993. This was the end of a hiking trail that once connected the ceremonial and cave mounds. It led through the swampy floodplain of Nanih Waiya Creek and had numerous bridges that frequently washed out and had to be replaced. The park people have no plans to reinstate the trail, which was said to be very interesting but "tough going."

Whether or not Choctaws originated at Nanih Waiya, it is definitely near the origin of the Pearl River, one of Mississippi's major rivers. Many meandering streams—Nanih Waiya Creek, Owl Creek, Bogue Chitto, Old Creek, Tallahaga Creek, and Big Slough—come together in a wide swamp several square miles in size and up to two miles wide. Out of the swamp the Pearl flows southwest. Most or all of this wetland is likely to be flooded in the spring.

If your visit to Nanih Waiya whets your curiosity about the Choctaw people past and present, you may want to visit the Dancing Rabbit Treaty Marker. Here, in 1830, the Choctaws were forced to cede the last of their lands and to agree to move to Oklahoma. The marker is in a Choctaw cemetery in southwestern Noxubee County along a gravel road that turns south off State Hwy 14 at the tiny community of Mashulaville.

Facilities: The western part, along State Hwy 393, has restrooms, picnic tables, three picnic pavilions that can accommodate 25 people each, a ranger station, and a visitor center for gatherings by groups of up to 75 people. The center can be reserved in advance for a fee. The eastern part has picnic tables and one pavilion. Camping is not permitted.

The park property is fenced and gated. It is open to the public six days a week except Thanksgiving, Christmas, and New Year's Day.

J 4 NATCHEZ STATE PARK,

Superintendent, 230B Wickliff Rd., Natchez, MS 39120 (601-442-2658). The park is E of Washington, Adams County (3,441 acres)

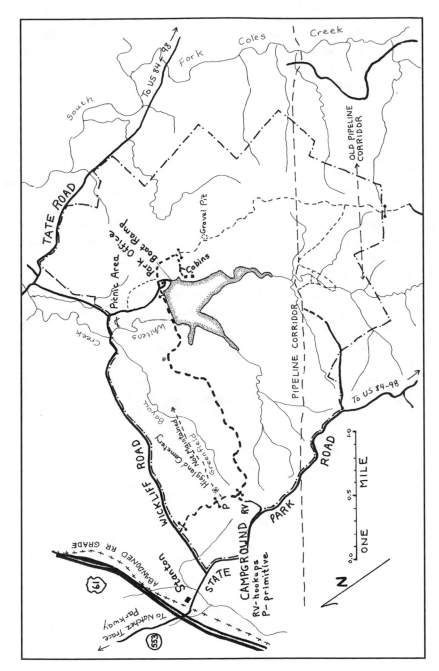

MAP 61. Natchez State Park

This is Mississippi's newest and largest state park, established in 1982 and first opened to the public in 1984. Because of the state's financial problems, it remains largely undeveloped. Horseback riders have discovered it, but it is unknown to most naturalists and hikers.

The park is within the historic Natchez District, once the territory of the Natchez Indians. They had one of the most advanced civilizations in the southeastern United States and perhaps had cleared parts of the land even before the French arrived in the early 1700s. Abandoned sunken roads and isolated cisterns that once stood alongside substantial farmhouses and plantation houses indicate that the park must have looked quite different 150 or 200 years ago.

Abandoned old Hamburg Road runs through the RV campground. A sign in the middle of it reads: "During the early and middle 1800s, this road is believed to have been one of the major thoroughfares for plantation owners, federal troops and robbers. Running from the Stanton Hall-Natchez Trace intersection to Hamburg and Union Church [to the west], this country lane winds through the site of Clover Hill Plantation, Sweet Home Place, Verona Plantation, and the Rucker Home Plantation. Some of this land, owned by Gerard Brandon, the second governor of Mississippi, was acquired by Spanish land grants."

Horseback riders have explored the park and make use of gravel and dirt roads and cleared pipeline corridors for weekend rides. State park personnel, with the assistance of Youth Conservation Corps workers, did clear a hiking trail down part of an abandoned sunken road, but brush has since reclaimed it.

The park offers a number of opportunities for hiking and horseback riding.

1. A 9.5-mile gravel road-pipeline corridor circuit begins and ends in the parking lot above the boat launch ramp and office on the east side of the dam. Follow the road around the east side of the lake, and turn left on the gated dirt road just before the lakeside cabins. Follow this road past a gravel quarry to a grassy pipeline corridor approximately 200' wide. Turn right (northwest) on the corridor and follow it all the way to paved State Park Rd. (The lake extends farther up Whitens Creek than the topo map indicates, and generally riders must turn southwest and ride upstream to find a place to cross.) Turn right on the paved road and follow it to the entrance to the campground. Ride through the campground and turn right (south) on the gravel road. Follow this road to the dam. Ride across the dam, and you will be back at the starting point. Most hikers will not care to walk the entire length of the pipeline corridor. (The gravel road from the campground to the boat launch is slated to be paved and converted to the main access route into the park.)

2. The old road continues on to the southwest beyond the junction of the pipeline corridor. It's a scenic route in deep shade. Note the abandoned cistern and sunken road on a knoll just south of the corridor. The road is gated at the park boundary, and the rest of the road is posted against trespassing. Another interesting old road branches off and goes northwest, ending in at the pipeline corridor just above the arm of the lake.

3. A hiking trail marked with yellow paint begins across the gravel road from the primitive camping area. It goes past tiny Higgland Cemetery and continues east, joining an abandoned sunken road. It is not marked with signs and will not be usable beyond the cemetery until it is cleared of brush and fallen trees.

The east side of the park remains to be explored. Generally you will not be able to enter park property unless it's right alongside a public road, because most of the surrounding land is leased to hunting clubs and posted.

Maps and Literature: None available from the state parks at this writing. The park boundary and principal roads are shown on the Cranfield topo map. It is recommended for serious exploration.

PAUL B. JOHNSON STATE PARK,   L 9

319 Geiger Lake Rd., Hattiesburg, MS 39401 (601-582-7721). The park is SE of Hattiesburg in Forrest County (580 acres, 1.5 miles of interpretive trail)

This park in the piney woods surrounds 225-acre Geiger Lake, which was constructed by soldiers at nearby Camp Shelby during World War II. To reach the nature trails, turn right at the gatehouse when you enter. The head of the Trail of the Southern Pines is framed by a gabled entrance with benches to shelter you from the sun or the rain. After you've walked about 0.2 mile, you have the choice of a short loop or a long loop. On both loops, lengthy and art-fully designed boardwalks will take you over boggy parts of the trail, and you will pass by two observation towers overlooking the lake. These structures were built in 1978–79 by young people in the Youth Conservation Corps.

Boy and Girl Scouts have earned merit badges by marking and defining trails and installing numbered posts identifying trees and shrubs along the way. They are as follows: (1) loblolly pine, (2) southern red oak, (3) white oak, (4) slash pine, (5) sourwood, (6) post oak, (7) black cherry, (8) yellow poplar, (9) water oak, (10) red maple, (11) sweetbay, (12) swamp tupelo, (13) huckleberry, (14) yaupon, (15) black tupelo, (16) American holly, (17) flowering dogwood, (18) longleaf pine, (19) swamp cyrilla, and (20) southern magnolia.

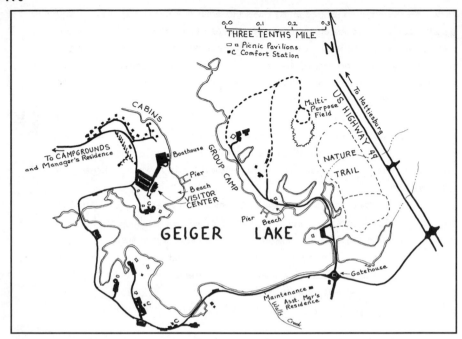

MAP 62. Paul B. Johnson State Park, southern portion

KL 6 PERCY QUIN STATE PARK,

1156 Camp Beaver Dr., McComb, MS 39648 (601-684-3938). The park is SW
of McComb, Pike County (1,731 acres, 3-mile nature trail)

Among Mississippi's 28 state parks, Percy Quin ranks high with naturalists.
The nature trail, which starts as a long boardwalk across a swamp at the
northern end of 700-acre Lake Tangipahoa, makes it a favorite with birders.
Also, the whole recreation complex blends well into the natural landscape.

The nature trail is about three miles long. Its northern end is at the end of
the road that leads north from the lodge past the picnic pavilions and playground and ends at a parking area near a restroom. The boardwalk goes on
past bald cypress and swampy thickets. Platforms with benches are at both
ends. The end of the boardwalk loops back on itself. At the edge of the loop,
the nature trail continues on west over a series of narrower boardwalks and
bridges that cross the Tangipahoa River and tributary sloughs. During the winter you are likely to flush mallards and wood ducks here. The trail gradually
curves south and continues on through loblolly pine/oak forest. Most of it is
out of sight of the lake.

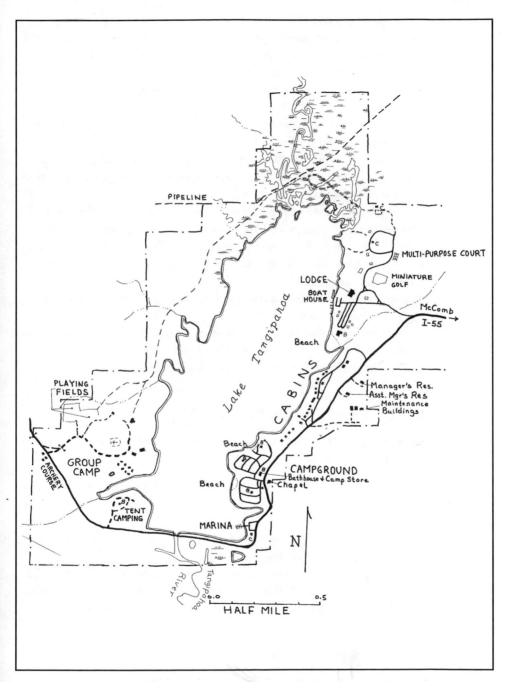

MAP 63. Percy Quin State Park

The southern end of the trail is between the two playing fields at Camp Beaver, a group camp beyond the tent camping area. Normally the road to the playing fields is gated, and a sign tells people who are not part of the group to keep out. The message is not intended for hikers who want access to the nature trail, however. It's about a five-mile walk if you follow the road back to your starting point.

For those who camp in tents, the secluded, heavily wooded tent camping area is another delight. Most tent sites face an arm of the lake.

The park is named for Percy Edwards Quin, a former congressman from Mississippi. He was descended from original settlers and longtime residents of Pike and Amite counties.

The lake, lodge, 18 of the 22 cabins, and a large brick pavilion near the lodge were constructed in the 1930s by the Civilian Conservation Corps. The lodge was constructed from timber removed from the lake site. Corps members brought the earth for the dam in wheelbarrows and made their own bricks for the lodge.

Best Time to Visit: Winter is the best time to avoid the crowds that come to this popular park.

Facilities: There is a minirailroad museum in the caboose from the Liberty White Railroad, which once ran through the park, and also a five-star archery course approved by the National Archery Association.

H 8   R O O S E V E L T   S T A T E   P A R K ,

Morton, MS 39117 (601-732-6316). The park is W of Morton, in Scott County (549 acres, 4.4 miles of trails)

This park is more than 50 years old, so the trees around the margin of 125-acre Shadow Lake have had time to grow large. You can enjoy them as you walk the four plus miles of trail on the east side of the lake. The trails are marked with blazes of spray paint. When you are distant from the lake, be sure to keep watch for these blazes so you don't lose your way.

Roosevelt is one of the original nine state parks constructed by the CCC in the 1930s. It opened in 1940 and is named after President Franklin D. Roosevelt. The site was selected because of its abundant natural springs.

N 10   S H E P A R D   S T A T E   P A R K ,

1034 Graveline Rd., Gautier, MS 39553 (601-497-2244). The park is in Gautier, Jackson County (400 acres, 2.5 miles of trail).

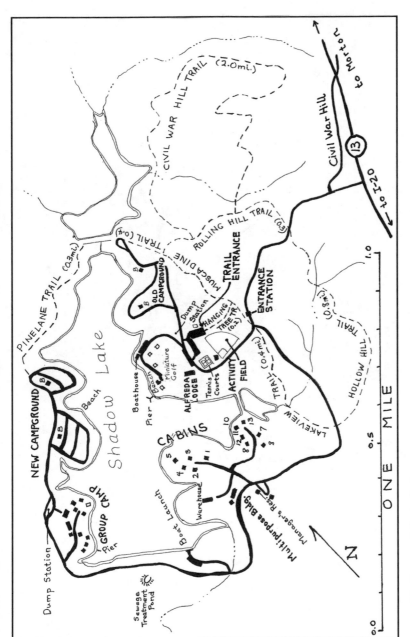

M A P 64. Roosevelt State Park

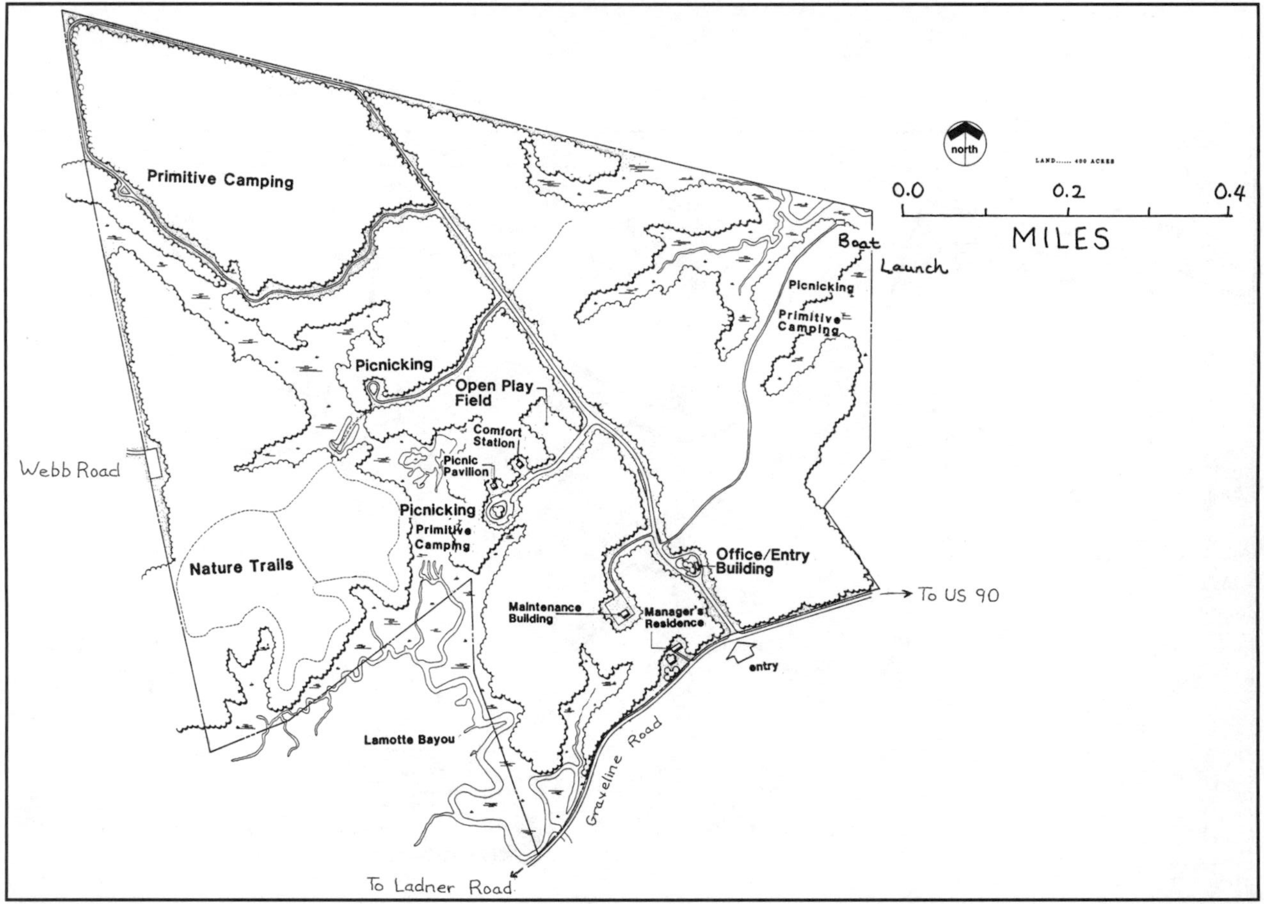

MILES

north

LAND......450 ACRES

0.0   0.2   0.4

Boat Launch

Picnicking

Primitive Camping

Office/Entry Building

Manager's Residence

Maintenance Building

entry

To US 90

Graveline Road

To Ladner Road

Lamotte Bayou

Open Play Field

Comfort Station

Picnic Pavilion

Picnicking

Picnicking

Primitive Camping

Nature Trails

Primitive Camping

Webb Road

MAP 65. Shepard State Park

This park is a well-kept secret. That's a bonus for the naturalist/hiker who likes to get away from the crowds and for campers who do not need RV hookups.

It's on the west side of the mouth of the Pascagoula River but does not front directly on the Gulf of Mexico. An arm of coastal marsh, however, extends into the park along Lamotte Bayou. A nature trail leads from the picnic area at the end of Mohawk Road across the upper end of this arm over a low dam that backs up a small freshwater pond. The trail then proceeds on through a rather mature forest of longleaf and slash pines with heavy understory of yaupon and small pines. The trail skirts the end of the marsh farther down the bayou, and here an observation platform (easy to overlook) has been built. The total length of the trail, including a cutoff, is 1.0 mile, with a maximum loop of about 0.8 mile. Horseback riding is permitted.

A looped park road, closed to the public, continues north from the intersection of Mohawk Road and the main park access road. It leads through a grassy, pine-studded savanna, and past sprawling live oaks at the edge of Lamotte Bayou. It is excellent for jogging as well as hiking and horseback riding. Total distance of the loop is 1.5 miles.

Another road leads to a second picnic area at a boat launching ramp on a bayou that parallels the L & N Railroad track, which is the northern boundary of the park. The bayou leads about 0.5 mile to the West Pascagoula River.

Primitive campsites with tables but no hookups share a common site with giant leaning live oaks, a single picnic pavilion, and playground equipment. Two campsites are right alongside the marsh, so you can watch egrets and listen to rails squawk while you eat.

Indians camped frequently at the site, although archeologists have not found any village sites. The property at one time belonged to John McCrae, a former governor of Mississippi. Later the property was acquired by the Shepard family. Horace Shepard, a naturalist and environmentalist, donated the land to the state in the late 1970s because he wanted it to remain a natural area. Conditions of the deed require the state to maintain the park in a predominantly natural condition.

Unfortunately, the lack of developed facilities and the resulting shortage of visitors means that Shepard Park is taking in little revenue—a situation that could prompt the state to abandon the park. "Friends of Shepard State Park" are trying to put the park in stable financial condition. For more information, ask the park supervisor.

Facilities: If the state legislature appropriates the funds, a separate campground with RV hookups and a bathhouse with hot showers will be constructed.

B II ## TISHOMINGO STATE PARK,

P.O. Box 880, Tishomingo, MS 38873 (601-438-6914). The park is E of Tishomingo in Tishomingo County (1,337 acres, ca. eight miles of hiking trails)

Tishomingo is a longtime favorite destination for hikers and naturalists. It's noticeably different from most other places in the state, although readers who are familiar with the southern Appalachian Mountains will feel at home.

The park takes in a portion of the watershed of Bear Creek, a wide, clear stream that originates in the Freedom Hills across the state line in Alabama, flows north through Mississippi, and then swings back into Alabama and empties into Pickwick Lake, an impounded segment of the Tennessee River. Bear Creek is a favorite with canoeists; no particular skills are needed to float it. You can rent a canoe from the park. You will be taken eight miles upstream and let off to float and paddle down to the swinging bridge in the park. (For more information on canoeing Bear Creek, see *Canoe Trails of the Deep South*, by Estes et al., in the bibliography.)

The cliffs and rock shelters are the biggest scenic attraction. Bear Creek has cut down through the Hartselle Formation, which is a thick, well-consolidated layer of sandstone, and partially through the thin layers of limestone and shales of the Pride Mountain Formation that lie beneath. These limestones and shales are softer and less resistant to erosion and weathering than the thick sandstone. Over thousands of years the Hartselle sandstone has been undercut. Occasionally huge sandstone blocks break off the overhanging cliffs and tumble down toward the creek. These rocks, which date from the Mississippian period (they are more than 320 million years old) are among the most ancient in Mississippi.

The quickest way to get to the cliffs is to park near the swinging bridge and walk across. Two formal trails are on the other side. The lower trail stays relatively close to the banks of Bear Creek, while the upper follows the lower edge of the cliffs. At least two short trails link the upper and lower routes. A particularly enchanting spot on the upper trail is a tiny box canyon with its own little waterfall.

The Saddleback Ridge Trail takes you along the top of a line of sandstone bluffs. Less than a half mile long, it begins under an elaborate arch on the south side of Haynes Lake across the road from the ranger's residence.

You will also see cliffs and rock shelters along the trails that begin at Civilian Conservation Corps Lake, a pond above a pioneer cabin. This cabin of split logs, set in the deep woods among mossy rocks, is the focus of one of Tishomingo's beauty spots. It looks as if it had been built there, but actually it

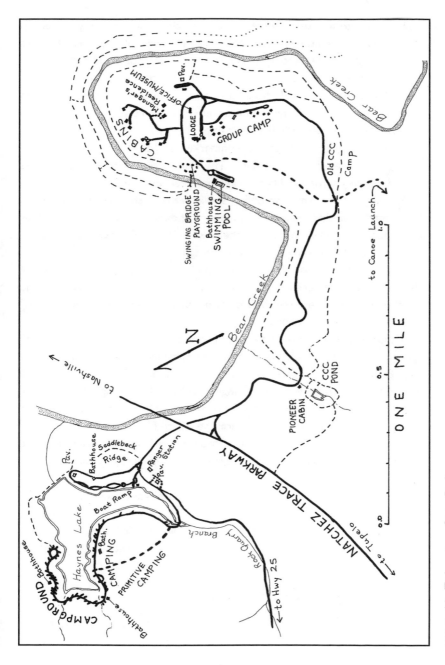

MAP 66. Tishomingo State Park

was moved into the park in 1974. Joseph Francis Barnett, an early pioneer in the area, built it on his homestead about 12 miles west of Booneville, Prentiss County, in about 1840. Later, the family added side rooms and a gallery that were eliminated when the cabin was brought to the park. Barnett died in 1855. He and his family, along with three slaves and a Confederate soldier who died in the cabin on his way home from the war, are buried on the homestead (see Howell's *Mississippi Scenes* in the bibliography).

Many of the trails in the park are unmarked, and as of 1992, only the most popular ones were being maintained. The trail section north of the Natchez Trace Parkway and west of Haynes Lake has been abandoned.

You may wish to climb into one of the larger rock shelters. Archaeologists have determined that Paleo Indians, hunters of extinct large mammals such as mastodons, camped in similar rock shelters in Colbert County just across the Alabama state line as early as 10,000 years ago.

"Tishomingo" means "warrier chief" in Chickasaw. Tishomingo was one of the last full-blooded chiefs in Mississippi. He and the other members of the Chickasaw Nation were removed from northern Mississippi to Indian Territory in what is now Oklahoma in 1832.

Tishomingo is one of the original ten state parks. The beauty of its forests is due at least in part to the 60 years they have had to recover from earlier logging. Early work in the park was done by the Civilian Conservation Corps. They started erecting the famous swinging bridge in 1933 using cables left over from the Pickwick Dam. They built the lodge, six of the cabins, the stone dam across CCC Lake, and the supports for the bridge from sandstone they quarried in the park. Many additions and improvements have been made since the park formally opened in May 1939. Haynes Lake, a 45-acre impoundment, was constructed in 1963.

Maps and Literature: You can get a map of the trails and other features from the park office, which also has a *Trails and History* and general information brochures, and information on renting canoes for float trips on Bear Creek. Brown's *Tishomingo State Park* (see the bibliography) provides a list of plants.

C 10   TOMBIGBEE STATE PARK,

Rt. 2, Box 336E, Tupelo, MS 38801 (601-842-7669). The park is SE of Tupelo, Lee County (522 acres, 1.2-mile interpretive trail)

This state park is in the Tombigbee Hills, a rugged patch of little hills up to 430′ high on the western edge of the Tennessee Hills geographic region. Lake

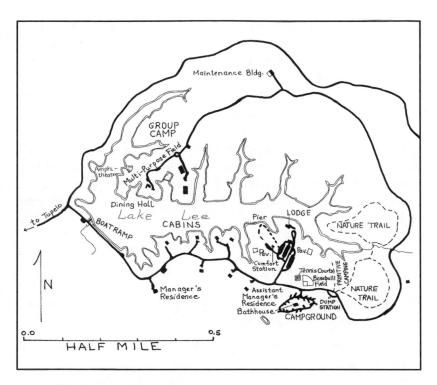

MAP 67. Tombigbee State Park

Lee, a 120-acre impoundment on the head of Garrett Creek, is the focal point of the park. It is noted for its excellent fishing. Near the park headquarters, Tombigbee State Park has large playing fields and a picnic area. The rest is predominantly hardwood forest with some shortleaf pine.

It is one of the original state parks, constructed by the Civilian Conservation Corps during the Great Depression and opened in 1938. The original lodge burned down, and the present park office was rebuilt on its foundations. Six of the seven original cabins remain. They have been fully modernized.

The Tree Trunk Trail, an interpretive nature trail laid out in a figure **8**, begins at the parking area at the gated road leading to the group camp. The trail goes up over the tops of two ridges, along hillsides, and on the shore of Lake Lee.

Twenty-four numbered posts along the way are keyed to a brochure available at the park office. The points of interest are: (1) white oak, (2) beaver sign, (3) fallen tree, (4) huckleberry bush, (5) beaver dam, (6) flowering dogwood, (7) sassafras tree, (8) coast pignut hickory, (9) love vine, (10) swamp cane, (11) yellow poplar (tulip tree), (12) overlook with cattails, (13) blackjack oak, (14) shortleaf pine, (15) sweetgum tree, (16) poison ivy, (17) red cedar, (18) bracket fungi, (19) ferns, (20) grapevine, (21) muscadine vine, (22) mosses, (23) mockernut hickory, (24) lichens.

Some of the shrubs and vines highlighted at the stops are no longer there, the beaver dam was gone in late 1992, and the observation platform at stop (12) disintegrated and was taken down. The trail was constructed by the Youth Conservation Corps in the late 1970s. Unfortunately the park people lack funding to maintain it and update the stops. Two shorter nature trails have been abandoned. The park badly needs volunteer help for trail maintenance.

Maps and Literature: Ask for guide brochure to the Tree Trunk Trail at the park office.

C 10 TRACE STATE PARK,

Rt. 1, Box 254, Belden, MS 38826 (601-489-2958). The park is E of Pontotoc, Pontotoc County (ca. 2,500 acres, ca. 25 miles of trails)

This is Mississippi's second largest state park and one of the later additions to the state park system. It has a full complement of facilties but is not as well known as the older state parks. The focus of the park is 600-acre Trace Lake, said to be the best lake in the state for bass fishing.

Located due east of Pontotoc, the area is rich in history. The park was origi-nally a county park named Old Trace Park, so called because the original Old Natchez Trace ran just to the south along what is now State Hwy 6 and then turned south at Old Pontotoc. The Natchez Trace Parkway is farther east near Tupelo, bypassing this jog in the original trail.

Tradition says that Hernando DeSoto, the first white man to set foot in Mississippi, passed the winter of 1540–41 in a Chickasaw Indian village near Redland in the southern part of Pontotoc County. At this time the area supported a large native American population. There were several villages, each with extensive fields, in the vicinity. The Chickasaws were forced to cede the last of their lands to the United States in 1832 and were moved to Oklahoma.

The park is in the Pontotoc Hills, a band of rugged terrain extending south from the Tennessee state line and ending near Houston. The land was once fertile but is also prone to erosion, exacerbated by one crop (cotton) farming. Great gullies appeared, and the impovished farmers gradually moved else-where. Today forest has reclaimed the uplands of the park.

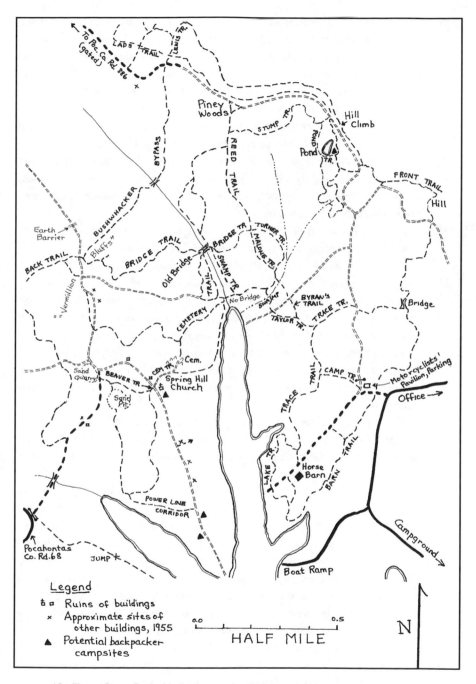

MAP 68. Trace State Park, backcountry trails in northern portion

Jason M. Stewart Nature Trail: This unlooped interpretive trail begins at the RV Campground and offers 0.5- and 0.9-mile options. Points of interest are marked and include an old homesite, a beaver lodge, demonstration of soil conservation techniques, and an opportunity to see a variety of wild plants and animals. Benches invite you to rest and observe along the way. The trail is named after a 13-year-old-boy who led in the planning of the trail; he died in a horseback riding accident before the trail was finished. Members of the local 4-H club and other civic groups completed the trail in 1992–93.

Backcountry Trails: The network of trails in the undeveloped northern and western portion of the park is what makes Trace State Park unique, however. Among the state parks, opportunities for a primitive backcountry experience are rivaled only by Natchez State Park.

The backcountry trails and a pavilion were built and marked by motorcycle clubs. They hold races in early December and at other times of the year.

The trail network is especially dense in the northwest section, and here trail signs are few. If you leave the main dirt access roads in this section, bring your compass and be sure to allow extra time for being temporarily lost. Some of the trails have steep slopes. Footing is good in dry weather, but when the soil is wet some sections are slippery. Bring your lug-soled boots.

A 1955 map shows several homes and barns in the section, and you see the collapsing ruins of at least two houses, a small barn, and a small church in here. About a tenth of a mile east of the church is tiny Spring Hill cemetery, now deep in the woods.

Backpacking is allowed as long as you inform the park office of your plans. The peninsula of land south of the old church is a popular place for backpackers to camp. A small secluded pond on the northeast side could be a nice campsite for a small party.

Legend has it that Davy Crockett—well-known hunter, Indian fighter, politician, and teller of tall tales—came to what is now the park in the 1830s. He had lost his seat as a congressman from Tennessee in 1835 and, with it, his dreams of running for the U.S. presidency. He drove a herd of horses down the Trace and built a corral in the vicinity of the old cemetery. He had a thriving business as a horse trader until he heard about the Mexican War and Sam Houston's need for help. He sold all his horses but the best saddle horse, strapped on his famous rifle "Betsey," and rode off to Texas. He died at the Alamo on March 6, 1836. The legend may not be true.

The Pontotoc Hills are an outcrop of the Ripley Formation, dating back to the Upper Cretaceous Period (65 million to 73 million years ago), when this part of Mississippi was covered with a shallow tropical sea inhabited by a diverse array of marine animals, including the giant seagoing lizards known as mosasaurs. You may find fossil shark teeth and fish vertebrae in sandstone out-croppings in the park. That rock about three inches across that you've kicked aside may well be a specimen of the large fossil clamlike mollusc *Exogyra*.

The forests are mainly oak and hickory, with some stands of pines. Deer and coyotes are abundant. From late summer through the winter, you may be treated to a coyote songfest in the dark of the night.

Near the northwest side of the park you'll find some impressive brilliant red bluffs. These and others in the county have been called the "vermillion cliffs of Pontotoc." They are something of an embarrassment to county natives because they are reminders of past agricultural abuses of the land. But the ones in the park are now deep in the woods and quite scenic.

The park was originally constructed by Pontotoc County to attract tourists to the area by providing a lake. Work began about 1969, and improvements are still being made.

Best Time to Visit: The park is open all year. If the idea of sharing the park trails with large numbers of motorcyclists bothers you, contact the park office in advance to learn which weekends the races will be held.

Facilities: In addition to the facilities listed in table 2, the Pontotoc Country Club's 18-hole golf course adjacent to the park is open to park visitors for a green fee. The park also has a unique Horse Barn with eight box stalls. For a nominal fee you can put your horse in a stall while you stay in the campground.

Access: The park entrance and office are north of State Hwy 6 between Tu-pelo and Pontotoc. The best starting points for trail exploration are the Horse Barn, which has a large parking area, and the motorcyclists' "Bushwhacker Pavilion," which is on the way to the Horse Barn. You can also access the trail network on the west side of the park via Pontotoc County Rd. 60.

Maps and Literature: Ask for an overall map of the park and a brochure on the nature trail at the office. They don't show the backcountry trails. The topo maps (Northeast Pontotoc and Southeast Pontotoc) are recommended be-cause they show the location of clearings adjacent to the park—just in case you get lost.

WALL DOXEY STATE PARK, B 8

Rt. 5, Box 245, Holly Springs, MS 38635 (601-252-4231). The park is S of Holly Springs, Marshall County (810 acres, 2.5-mile loop hiking trail)

This is another of Mississippi's original state parks, built by the Civilian Conservation Corps in the 1930s. The 60-year-old trees, stone picnic pavil-ions and lodge, and extensive natural wetlands make this park one of the

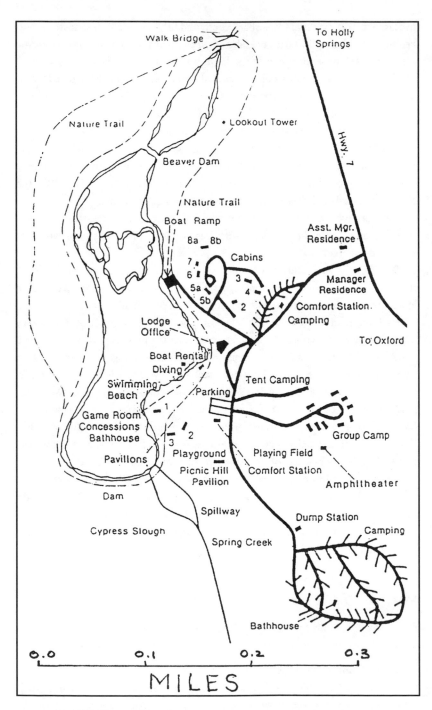

MAP 69. Wall Doxey State Park

most attractive to naturalists. The lake invites exploration by canoes, which can be rented at the park.

The trail that circles the lake begins as a dirt road in the playground area. You can also access it from a short footpath that begins at the paved road near "Picnic Hill Pavilion," an example of the CCC's fine stone architecture. The trail follows the dirt road over the dam. As you walk across the dam, you will see extensive alder thickets below you and, just beyond the dam, a small grove of cypress growing in the lake. Beyond that is a walk-in camping area for Boy Scouts and anyone else who cares to use it. It has tap water, a picnic table, and a campfire ring.

Just north of the campsite, the dirt road diverges on the left and climbs to the top of a ridge overlooking the lake. The foot trail follows the edge of the lake, taking you past some large trees, many of them tulip poplar. A narrow, rustic footbridge crosses the wetlands above the upper end of the lake. Keep an eye out for beaver dams, lodges, and small trees "harvested" by beavers. As the trail starts back toward the developed part of the park, you pass through alder thickets. An observation platform gives you an overview, with excellent birding potential.

Spring Lake is near the headwaters of Little Spring Creek, which is fed by numerous natural springs from the surrounding steep hills. The lake (or a smaller predecessor) dates back more than 150 years. Slaves owned by William Blanton Lumpkin built the first dam. Lumpkin had moved to Mississippi from Georgia in 1836, only four years after the Chickasaws ceded the land to the whites. He purchased 160 acres on what is now the upper end of the present lake (northeast quarter of Sec. 12) as well as an additional 1,000 acres to the northeast.

Here he put his slaves to work building two dams and, between the two impoundments, a four-story mill built of "native rock from Caledonia Mountains." An elevated raceway from the upper lake led to a big water wheel. The mill ground wheat and corn into flour and meal. The big stone building has had a water-powered sawmill and a cotton gin. An oil painting of the old mill hangs in the foyer of the park lodge today.

Dora Brooks McGowan reminisced about idyllic pre–Civil War times at her grandfather's mill in a letter written in 1928. The two ponds were "beauty places known and loved by all. Nature's garden, a natural grove of lofty and beautiful forest trees—birch, willow, oak, and many others, at whose base grew moss and wild flowers of every description—surrounded the ponds. It was here we enjoyed life to the fullest extent. The cold, crystal clear waters were stocked with fish of all kinds—white perch, goggle-eyed perch, bream, and trout. Nowhere could fish be caught that were so good as at the mill."

Mr. Lumpkin began to build a brick mansion on a hill about a mile away. It was so enormous that it was named Morro Castle. Elaborate flower gardens and a summerhouse made of living cedars were planted around it.

The Civil War halted construction, and the mansion was never completed. In the winter of 1862 General Grant's troops marched through, following the route of the Mississippi Central Railroad toward Vicksburg. Major General J. B. McPherson's entire force of 10,000 men camped around the lakes on November 29, 1862. The Union forces took everything they could find near the mill—livestock, meal, flour, and cotton. The mill was filled with recently ginned cotton. Grant took 65 bales and issued receipts for their market value. Then the troops set the mill on fire. The cotton-filled mill burned and smoldered for months.

The CCC began converting the site into a state park on June 25, 1935. It was opened to the public in 1938. Originally it was named Spring Lake State Park. Later it was renamed after U.S. senator Wall Doxey, an influential legislator whose home base was Holly Springs.

Literature: You may request a copy of a two-page excerpt on Lumpkin's Mill from Ben Gray Lumpkin and Martha Neville Lumpkin's book (see the bibliography).

6. State Wildlife Management Areas, Water Parks, and Natural Areas

State parks aren't the only state-owned lands with trails. Wildlife management areas owned by the Department of Wildlife, Fisheries and Parks have some trails, and more significantly, include outstanding swamps threaded with natural rivers and bayous awaiting exploration by canoe. The larger water parks are similar to state parks in the array of recreational facilities they offer, including nature trails. Mississippi's only designated state natural area, Clark Creek, is a favorite beauty spot with six natural waterfalls.

STATE WILDLIFE MANAGEMENT AREAS,

Mississippi Department of Wildlife, Fisheries, and Parks, P.O. Box 451, Jackson, MS 39205-0451 (601-364-2180)

The Mississippi Department of Wildlife, Fisheries, and Parks (MDWFP) administers at least 33 state wildlife management areas (WMAs) and waterfowl areas. The state highway map shows all but the most recently acquired WMAs in gold and the waterfowl areas in green.

The first state wildlife areas were set up as wildlife refuges in the 1930s. Their purpose was to restore wildlife populations that had been reduced to near zero by unrestricted hunting. In 1929, for example, no more than 200 deer and 1,500 turkeys survived in the entire state. Wildlife refuges were established in the new national forests, in state parks, and on private lands. Deer were imported from out of state and released in the refuges. Strictly protected from hunters, they multiplied in the regenerating cutover forests. As their numbers grew, they were trapped and reintroduced elsewhere.

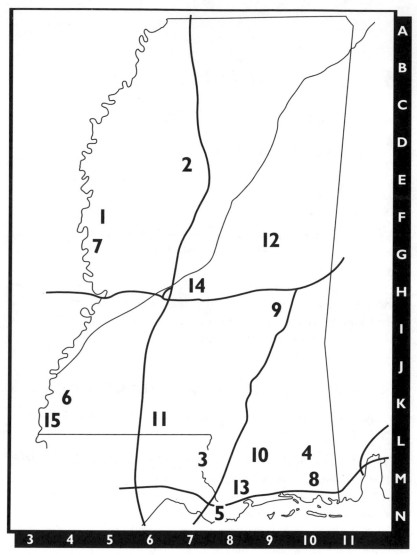

MAP 70. Wildlife management areas, water development district parks, and natural areas in Mississippi

LEGEND

1 = Leroy Percy WMA	8 = Ward Bayou WMA
2 = Malmaison WMA and Greentree Waterfowl Area	9 = Dunn's Falls WP
	10 = Flint Creek WP
3 = Old River WMA	11 = Bogue Chitto WP
4 = Pascagoula River WMA	12 = Burnside Lake WP
5 = Pearl River WMA	13 = McLeod Water Park
6 = Sandy Creek WMA	14 = Reservoir Botanical Garden
7 = Shipland WMA	15 = Clark Creek Natural Area

A similar trap-and-release program was instituted for turkeys in the mid-1950s, when newly invented cannon-propelled nets made it possible to capture and transfer entire flocks to new areas. By the mid-1980s, hunters were taking 200,000 to 250,000 deer annually, and more than 50,000 turkeys. Gradually the refuges were declassified; the last was discontinued in 1991.

Most of the present state wildlife and waterfowl areas are not owned by the state. Eleven are within national forests. (WMAs within the national forests are described as parts of those forests in this guide.) Many other WMAs are on timber lands owned and managed by timber corporations and two state universities. Within these areas, state wildlife managers are responsible for supervising hunters and maintaining small openings planted with wildlife foods. The Forest Service and private owners are responsible for logging, roads, and other development. Areas owned by timber corporations are likely to be managed for pine timber and pulpwood on short rotation periods. Filled with wide, dusty logging access roads, they are not especially attractive for off-road exploration.

Since the 1970s, the MDWFP has begun to acquire areas of its own in critical wetlands. All the areas described below are of this kind. Only one state-owned WMA has a trail designed specifically for hiking and nature study; many are largely swamps, accessible mainly by water. Other WMAs may also be interesting places for hikers and could be promising sites for future trails.

Bulletin boards with posted regulations are placed beside the main access roads into each WMA. During the hunting seasons they will be supplied with forms for hunters to fill out. Even if you aren't hunting, you should fill out a form. The state wildlife managers are interested in documenting use of the WMAs by nonhunters as well as hunters.

Facilities: During the hunting seasons camping is likely to be restricted to "designated sites" in WMAs, including those in the national forests. The designated sites may be Forest Service campgrounds, but most WMAs also have primitive camping areas. They consist of a place to park off the road and pitch a tent and sometimes a trash can. You may be required to get written permission from the area manager before occupying a campsite during the fall-winter hunting seasons. You can use the campsites without permission at other times of the year except in the Delta National Forest.

Maps and Other Literature: The MDWFP distributes a brochure listing all the WMAs and waterfowl areas with addresses and phone numbers of area managers. It also issues small maps of each WMA with hunting seasons and rules printed on the back. Some of the maps are excellent, while others are hardly worth having. During the hunting seasons the bulletin boards will usually have a supply of the map for the relevant WMA.

F5 **LEROY PERCY WILDLIFE MANAGEMENT AREA.**
See Leroy Percy State Park.

E7 **MALMAISON WILDLIFE MANAGEMENT AREA
AND GREENTREE WATERFOWL AREA,**
Manager, 628 Malmaison Headquarters Rd., Holcomb, MS 38490 (601-453-5409). The area is between Grenada and Greenwood in Grenada and Leflore counties (9,483 acres, three-mile trail network)

Malmaison is one of the most varied of the state wildlife management areas (WMAs) because it encompasses both loess bluffs and hardwood bottoms and oxbow lakes along a six-mile stretch of the Yalobusha River. It is the only WMA with a designated trail specifically for naturalists, hikers, and history buffs.

LeFlore Trail Network: A map stand at the beginning of the trail presents an overview of the trail network. Underneath the map you should find copies of four different leaflets: yellow (a detailed guide to the trails); green (a list of plants along the trails, including some native species that have been planted); blue (a history of the area focusing on Greenwood LeFlore and his relatives and descendants); and white (a guide to the small cemetery along the Historic Trail).

The area in which the trails have been built originally belonged to the famous mixed-blood Choctaw Indian chief Greenwood LeFlore (1800–65). He was a son of Louis LeFleur, a French-Canadian trader who set up at least one trading post along the Old Natchez Trace. Educated in Nashville, Greenwood was elected a chief of the Choctaw Nation in 1824.

While Greenwood was growing up, more and more land-hungry white settlers were pouring into Mississippi. The resident Indians were forced to sign away their land piece by piece. On September 18, 1830, the Choctaws reluctantly agreed to give up all their remaining territory and move to Indian Territory in Oklahoma. Greenwood persuaded other Choctaw chiefs to sign the agreement, known as the Treaty of Dancing Rabbit Creek. He was also responsible for an article in the treaty that allowed individual Choctaw families to remain in the state and apply for parcels of land. Greenwood himself received for his efforts a gift of 2,500 acres from the U.S. commissioners who negotiated the treaty. The trails are on part of that allotment.

Greenwood LeFlore went on to become a wealthy planter, owning 15,000 acres in Mississippi, 60,000 acres in Texas, more than 400 slaves, and a mansion east of Greenwood. Few other Choctaws succeeded in acquiring parcels of land.

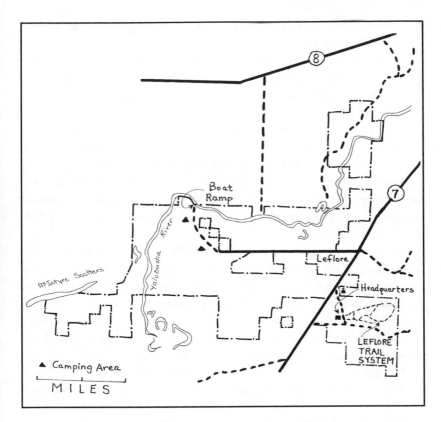

MAP 71. Malmaison Wildlife Management Area. Filled triangles indicate camping areas.

The Historic Trail leads to an abandoned cemetery. Legible headstones date from 1891 to 1959. Among them are three monuments to LeFlores. One is for Cuffie LeFlore, who died in 1935 at age 80. Cuffie's name appears in a list of 91 slaves who were deeded, along with this land, to Greenwood's son, John Donley LeFlore, in 1858. Cuffie was only four years old at the time.

If you turn left and go uphill just before crossing a bridge over an intermittent creek that runs in front of the cemetery, you will reach the site of Jackson LeFlore's house in about a mile. Jackson (1815–54) was Greenwood's youngest brother. The house stood as late as 1937 and is said to have resembled the reconstructed plantation house at Florewood Plantation State Park. What you will find today are scattered bricks beside huge red cedars growing from a carpet of low-growing *Vinca minor* on a hilltop. Beyond the house site the trail may be posted against trespassing. If so, you can follow a woods road on your left back down to the cemetery.

The Footbridge Trail is a shorter loop that takes you up and down steep stairways in the loess bluffs, past huge beech trees clinging to eroding bluffs on a tributary of Potacocowa Creek. The short Pecan Trail leads past the edge of a pecan grove and a cabin.

The trail network is a cooperative venture between the Mississippi Department of Wildlife, Fisheries, and Parks and the Greenwood Garden Club, headed by Mrs. Mary Deaton. It was dedicated in April 1983 by Governor William Winter, who cut the ceremonial ribbon with a sword that General Andrew Jackson had given to his friend Greenwood LeFlore. A considerable amount of federal funding was needed to construct the trail—funds that are not available today.

The largest portion of the WMA, however, is in the swampy forested bottomlands along the Yalobusha River. It is an important wintering ground for ducks and other waterfowl. There are several oxbow lakes along both sides of the river. A levee has outlets that can be closed during the late fall and early winter. Shallow water collects in this greentree reservoir, creating additional habitat for ducks and migratory waterfowl. In late February the water is released. If the reservoir were permanently flooded, the trees would be killed.

The state purchased most of the wildlife management area from E. F. Glaser in 1970. The 808 acres in the McIntyre Scatters were purchased by the Nature Conservancy in 1977 and later transferred to the state as an addition to the WMA. It is mainly forested bottomlands that are usually flooded late in the winter and in the spring. The name refers to scattered flooded patches that expand, contract, and disappear with the changing level of the Yazoo River.

Best Times to Visit: Wildflowers along the nature trails are at their best in the spring, from mid-February to late April. A succession of flowers continue to bloom into late fall, however. The best time for waterfowl viewing is November through January. Nonhunters are urged to stay away during the two-week conventional weapon deer season, which always begins the Saturday before Thanksgiving.

Facilities: Primitive campsites are located near the levee that bounds the large greentree reservoir west of Highway 7. You must get a free permit from the area headquarters to stay there.

Access: Malmaison headquarters and the nature trails are east of Highway 7 about 0.1 mile south of the nearly extinct town of LeFlore. The gravel road turns off the highway just south of the LeFlore Baptist Church.

Maps and Literature: You don't need a map to explore the LeFlore Trail

System. Copies of the brochures may be available at the trailhead. These brochures contain such a wealth of information that you may want to peruse them before starting on your hike.

The relevant topo maps, Avalon, for the eastern two-thirds of the areas, and Money, for the western portion, are recommended for exploring all but the LeFlore Trail and roads. For copies of the trail brochures, send a stamped, self-addressed, legal-sized envelope to Mrs. Mary Deaton, 807 Robert E. Lee Dr., Greenwood, MS 38930 (601-453-6537).

OLD RIVER WILDLIFE MANAGEMENT AREA, M 8
James P. Carver, Manager, Rt. 1, Box 251-E, Poplarville, MS 39470 (601-772-9024). The area is S of Bogalusa, LA, in Pearl River County, MS (14,764 acres)

The Old River is an accessory channel of the Pearl that diverges from the main river in the northern part of the WMA and rejoins it in the southern end. In between is a complex drainage with 10 named oxbow lakes. The area was purchased by the Nature Conservancy in the early 1980s and was transferred to the Department of Wildlife, Fisheries, and Parks in 1985. It is the northernmost of three public wildlife areas on the lower Pearl River floodway, often called Honey Island Swamp.

At least two-thirds of the area lies between the Old River and the main Pearl River. It is closed to motor vehicles and is accessible only by boat. A suggested float trip begins on the west side of the Pearl River at Richardson Landing, which is at the end of Riverside Drive just east of Bogalusa. Float down the Pearl 2.5 miles to a cutoff bend. From the easternmost point of the bend, take an unnamed stream to Pine Island Lake (erroneously designated Horseshoe Lake on the Henleyfield topo map). From here proceed south on the Old River to the takeout point on Ten Landing Lake. The total length of the float trip is approximately 8.5 miles.

Another canoe trip is a visit to Socias Lake. You put into the Pearl on the Louisiana side, paddle down the Pearl River, and turn up Gum Bayou, said to be a classic stream overhung with hardwoods. When the Pearl is low, you can easily paddle back upstream to your starting point. You will want to have a copy of the Henleyfield topo map with you.

For additional general information on Honey Island Swamp, more detailed descriptions of suggested canoe trips, how to learn the level of the Pearl River at Bogalusa, and the names of canoe outfitters, see the section on Bogue Chitto National Wildlife Refuge.

Best Time to Visit: The area is open all year. Normally much of the area will be flooded in the late winter and spring.

Access: The Department maintains three gravel access roads. Each has a signboard with hunting information and leaflets at its entrance. The first road turns south off State Hwy 26 on the east side of the Pearl River, just after crossing an oxbow lake, at a sign announcing the boundary of Washington Parish, Louisiana. It leads past a boat ramp at Crossroads Landing on the Pearl and ends at Horseshoe Lake. Trails following the outer ledge of the lake lead in both directions from an informal campsite.

The second is via Dillard Rd., which crosses Hwy 43 1.0 mile south of Hwy 26. Short trails lead in either direction along a slough from the end of this road. The third turns west off Hwy 43 at Henleyfield beside a brick church with a large cemetery behind it. In about a half mile take the right fork (Albert Prince Rd.) and proceed down a hill to Ten Landing Lake.

Facilities: Each access road has one or more boat launching ramps and ends in a camping area. Ten Landing Lake has two camping areas; the northern one is in large pines. No facilities except a cleared grassy area are provided. Camping is limited to these four designated sites and on sandbars and banks of the Pearl River and other streams.

You must get a camping permit from the area manager first. His headquarters is prominently marked on the west side of Hwy 43 about halfway between Henleyfield and the intersection of Hwys 26 and 43. If he isn't in, you can fill out a permit form at headquarters and put the manager's portion in a box.

Maps and Literature: The Department has an excellent map of the area. The Bogalusa East and Heneyfield topo maps are recommended for canoe exploration.

LM 10 PASCAGOULA RIVER WILDLIFE MANAGEMENT AREA,

Managers: for Jackson Co. portion, Michael E. Everett, 816 Wade-Vancleave Rd., Pascagoula, MS 39567 (601-588-3878); and for George Co. portion, Herman W. Murrah, Rt. 6, Box 350, Lucedale, MS 39452 (601-947-6376). The area is W of Lucedale and Wade in George and Jackson counties (37,994 acres)

The WMA encompasses a large portion of the floodplain of the Pascagoula River—a complex of hardwood bottoms, streams, and abandoned river channels, and more than 36 cypress-lined oxbow lakes. The ever-shifting channel of the river is lined with white sand.

The Pascagoula is one of Mississippi's larger rivers. It originates at the junction of the Leaf and Chickasawhay rivers and flows south through George and

Jackson counties to empty into the Gulf between the cities of Pascagoula and Moss Point. On its way it meanders through a wide floodway of bottomland hardwoods and swamps that merge with tidal marshlands near the Gulf. Much of the nontidal part of the floodway is protected in the WMA. The most remote part of the area is on the west side of the river where Black Creek and Red Creek come together and flow into the river.

The area protects the habitat of species such as the swallow-tailed kite and the alligator. The yellow-blotched map turtle, a federally listed threatened species, is found only in the Pascagoula and its major tributaries. Louisiana black bears, also listed as threatened, are occasionally sighted in the area. Here and there are some giant cypress left over from the original virgin forests because they were hollow or otherwise defective as lumber.

The Pascagoula WMA is the largest tract ever acquired by the state. Approximately 32,000 acres were purchased for $13.5 million in 1976 from the Pascagoula Hardwoods Company. The company was a group of shareholders descended from families who had moved to Laurel at the turn of the century and made their fortunes logging the virgin pine forests. Fearing that the relatively undisturbed swamp forests would be acquired by a major lumber corporation and clearcut, Avery Wood, then director of the Fish and Game Commission, members of his staff, and Dave Morine of the Nature Conservancy instigated an intensive lobbying and public education campaign and successfully persuaded the shareholders to sell and the state legislature to appropriate the funds (see Schueler's book *Preserving the Pascagoula* in the bibliography). The protected area along the river was recently expanded on the south by the new Ward Bayou WMA.

Camping is allowed along the river and large streams as long as the site is visible by boat. You can also camp anywhere along roads open to the public. Most of these roads have grassy berms wide enough for parking and pitching a tent. At one time camping was also allowed anywhere in the swamp, but Wildlife people got tired of searching for hunting and fishing parties whose families had emergencies. During the hunting seasons, you must have a written permit from the relevant area manager. Sunday hunting is not permitted in the area.

Best Time to Visit: The WMA is open all year. Much or almost all of the area may be flooded from late winter through spring. During that time a boat or canoe is essential. Summers are hot and humid.

Access: Roads shown on the maps issued by the Mississippi Department of Wildlife, Fisheries, and Parks are all-weather roads negotiable by all vehicles (if they aren't flooded). There are no designated hiking trails, but numerous lanes that are gated to exclude public vehicles branch off from the public roads. They are not shown on any map. Most of them are less than a mile long. The entire boundary of the WMA is marked by a cleared lane that is supposed to be 30' wide but is actually much narrower. It could also be used as a hiking trail.

The remote west side, sometimes called the "Big Swamp," is accessible by dirt roads leading east from State Hwy 57, but they cross private lands and are not open to the public. So you get there by crossing the Pascagoula by boat or taking a canoe or johnboat down Black Creek or Red Creek. Mills Ditch, which joins Black Creek about a mile upstream from the junction of Red Creek, is not passable to boats when the water level is low.

If you choose to float down to the Big Swamp, you can put in either Black Creek or Red Creek from State Hwy 57. Either way, it's about a 23-mile float down to the Hwy 26 bridge over the Pascagoula River including a 3-mile paddle on the river. Without allowing any time for exploring the swamp itself, it's an excellent overnight trip, with fine fishing for bass, bluegill, crappie, and catfish. The Pascagoula is too wide for scenic canoeing. Black Creek and Red Creek average about one mile per hour, and it's usually not difficult to paddle back upstream and make a round trip of it with a short car shuttle between the Black Creek and Red Creek bridges.

Facilities: The only developed facilities are the gravel roads and boat ramps.

Maps: The Mississippi Department of Wildlife, Fisheries, and Parks has issued two maps of the area—one for George County and one for Jackson County. Request them from the area managers. For serious off-road exploration by canoe, topo maps are recommended (see map 72 for area covered by topo maps).

N 8 PEARL RIVER WILDLIFE MANAGEMENT AREA,

Louisiana Department of Wildlife and Fisheries, District VII, P.O. Box 98000, Baton Rouge, LA 70898-9000; (504-765-2360). The superintendent, Mark Bible, lives at Crawford Landing (504-643-3958). The area is W of Slidell, St. Tammany Parish, Louisiana (34,818 acres, one-mile nature trail)

This is the southernmost of the three public wildlife management areas in the lower floodway of the Pearl River, the so-called Honey Island Swamp. It is entirely in Louisiana, but I include it here because it has facilities and services not available in the Old River Wildlife Management Area and the Bogue Chitto National Wildlife Refuge.

The Honey Island Swamp Nature Trail, a one-mile loop, is in the northern part of the WMA just south of old U.S. Hwy 11. Brochures that should be available in a box about 20 yards down the trail from the parking area are keyed to numbered posts identifying swamp plants. To be sure of having one,

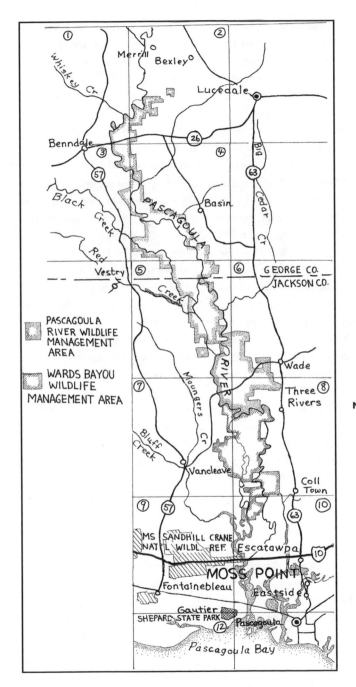

MAP 72. Public lands on the Pascagoula River showing relevant topographic maps:
1) Avent
2) Merrill
3) Benndale
4) Basin
5) Easen Hill
6) Harleston
7) Vancleave
8) Three Rivers
9) Gautier North
10) Pascagoula North
12) Pascagoula South

call the area superintendent and order in advance. The route leads past a small oxbow lake. Chances of encountering wood ducks and turkeys are excellent.

For additional general information on Honey Island Swamp, more detailed descriptions of suggested canoe trips, how to learn the level of the Pearl River at Bogalusa, and the names of canoe outfitters, see the section on Bogue Chitto National Wildlife Refuge.

Fee: The Louisiana legislature recently passed a law requiring people between the ages of 16 and 59 who enter state WMAs at any time of the year to have a Wild Louisiana stamp, a hunting license, or a fishing license. This group includes hikers on the nature trail. The stamp and licenses may be purchased from any store in Louisiana that sells hunting and fishing equipment, including hardware stores and WalMart. The closest store to the Honey Island Swamp Nature Trail is probably the WalMart in Slidell. In 1993, the fees were $2.50 for a cane fishing license, $5.00 for a stamp, and $5.50 for a regular hunting or fishing license.

Fees for nonconsumptive users of state WMAs (people who neither hunt nor fish) are becoming more popular nationwide, and Mississippi might adopt them in the future. WMAs have traditionally been funded by a combination of general tax revenues, taxes on firearms and ammunition, and hunting and fishing licenses. It's not surprising that most management funds go into programs to increase the numbers of game animals and fish. If nonconsumptive users contribute revenue directly, programs to benefit nongame species and natural ecosystems may receive more attention.

Best Time to Visit: The area is accessible all year. From late winter through spring, however, much of it will be flooded, and you will need a boat. During the fall you can walk long distances on dry land. Louisiana's three-day deer season begins the day after Thanksgiving. Another busy time in the woods is the opening of squirrel season in the first week of October.

Facilities: Camping area at Crawford Landing on the West Pearl River just north of Interstate 10 with a concrete boat launch pad, water, toilets, and grassy area. There is at least one privately owned campground in Slidell with RV hookups.

The St. Tammany Parish Tourist and Convention Commission (1-800-634-9443) has brochures from outfits that conduct daily motorboat tours of Honey Island Swamp.

Access: To reach the nature trail, take the Honey Island Swamp exit off Interstate 59 between Slidell and the bridges over the Pearl River floodway. Follow old U.S. Hwy 11 east to the intersection of Oil Well Rd., a gravel road. Turn right. The trailhead is a short distance down the road on your left.

The Crawford Landing boat launch/camping area is close to I-10, but you have to drive a long way around to reach it. From I-10, turn north on I-59 and proceed to the next exit (Hwy 11 west). Follow Rt. 1090 south on the east side I-59 almost to I-10. Here Rt. 1090 swings east alongside I-10, then angles away from the interstate and ends at the landing.

Maps and Literature: The Louisiana Department of Wildlife and Fisheries distributes a free map of the area. Topo maps are recommended for canoe exploration (see map 29).

SANDY CREEK WILDLIFE MANAGEMENT AREA.   K 4
See Homochitto National Forest.

SHIPLAND WILDLIFE MANAGEMENT AREA,   G 5
Manager, Randy Bishop, P.O. Box 274, Rolling Fork, MS 39159 (601-873-6968). NW of Fitler, Issaquena County (3,642 acres, informal 2.0-mile hiking trail)

This wildlife management area includes 2.5 miles of frontage on the Mississippi River, tracts of bottomland hardwood and riparian forests, and a large sandy meadow—habitat for an array of game and nongame species. Scissor-tailed flycatchers, rare in Mississippi, are sometimes seen here. From late fall through early spring, you are likely to see ducks in a leveed-off strait of the river. It was set up in 1984 with the cooperation of the Nature Conservancy.

Between the main levee and the river are remnants of earlier attempts to contain the floodwaters of the Mississippi. Some of these old levees are said to have been built by slaves before the Civil War.

Almost exactly a mile from the point where the access road turns off the mainline levee, you will drive past a gated woods road on your left. (This makes an excellent hiking trail, and you are likely to see birds and other wildlife.) You pass an informal campsite in another 0.3 mile and enter the meadow. The improved road swings left and continues on, reentering the woods and paralleling the river. If you park near the edge of the river and walk down the bank, you may see ducks.

Best Time to Visit: The area is open all year. Early winter through spring is the best time to see waterfowl. Many migratory songbirds can be seen in the spring, beginning in mid-March. You should avoid the area during the regular deer season, which begins the Saturday before Thanksgiving and lasts one or two weeks. When the Mississippi River is high, much of the area will be flooded.

Facilities: There is an informal shaded campsite with a trash can, 1.3 miles from the road on the mainline levee. No water, tables, or toilets are provided. You must have written permission from the area manager to camp there.

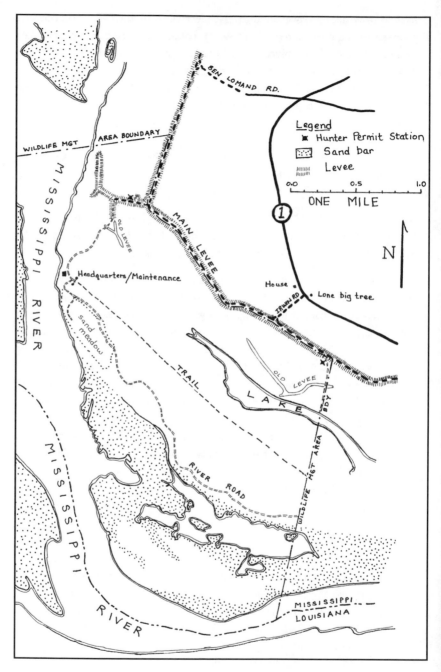

MAP 73. Shipland Wildlife Management Area

WARD BAYOU WILDLIFE MANAGEMENT AREA,

Manager: Frank Evans, 19001 Larue Rd., Ocean Springs, MS 39564 (601-392-5138). The area is NE of Vancleave, Jackson County (at least 12,000 acres)

One of the newest state wildlife management areas, Ward Bayou WMA is just south of the Pascagoula WMA. The Pascagoula River makes a wide swing east and then south, bounding the basin on the north and east. Ward Bayou is a major tributary of the Pascagoula.

Palmettos are lush within the area. Wildflowers bloom along the bayous. There are many species of birds, turtles, and snakes. Chances of encountering an alligator are good.

The entire area is likely to be flooded between late January and late March. Area Manager Frank Evans does not recommend taking a canoe into the flooded area, because currents in the basin can be very strong. When the area floods, the water rises very quickly. The best way to see the area is to take a motor boat in, stop, and walk.

Camping is permitted only on sandbars along the Pascagoula and principal streams. This policy allows managers to keep track of visitors and limits damage to the area.

In 1993 the only access road was Ward Bayou Road, a dirt road that is frequently flooded. Only minimal development is planned. An all-weather road will eventually be built around the area. Trails for hikers and four-wheelers are planned. The four-wheeler trails will be open to handicapped hunters during the deer seasons. Overall, the goal will be to keep the area natural.

The area was purchased by the U.S. Army Corps of Engineers and turned over to the state to compensate for the loss of fish and wildlife habitat caused by construction of the Tennessee-Tombigbee Waterway. Land is still being purchased from willing sellers for addition to the WMA.

Best Time to Visit: October is probably the best month for exploring the area on foot, late winter and spring by boat.

Facilities: None in 1993.

Access: The only public access overland is from the west side of the area via Ward Bayou, which is reached by Ward Bayou Rd. north of Vancleave.

Maps: Three Rivers and Vancleave topo maps are recommended. The U.S. Army Corps of Engineers is preparing a map that should be available from the area manager by spring 1994.

WATER DEVELOPMENT DISTRICTS

Mississippi's water development districts were established to provide, promote, and improve navigation, flood control, beneficial water distribution, and recreation. All three contain public recreation areas that are usually known as water parks because they are along lakes and streams. On the official state highway map they are indicated by red teepee symbols. (Within the national forests, the teepees are national forest recreation areas.)

Some water parks are large enough to rival the state parks. They may have water slides, campgrounds, cabins, playing fields (some lighted for night use), picnic pavilions, water skiing, and even tennis courts. A few are merely put in/take out spots for canoeists. Other water parks are for day use only. Most are too small to have half-mile-long trails and are thus not included in this guide.

PAT HARRISON WATERWAY DISTRICT

The Pat Harrison Waterway District is responsible for the watershed of the Pascagoula River, mainly in southeastern Mississippi. It has 10 water parks. Of these, 8 have overnight camping facilities, and 6 also have rental cabins.

For Further Information: The district has a large booklet and a brochure describing all 10 water parks. Call 1-800-748-9403 for literature and to reserve campsites and cabins.

- **Dunn's Falls Water Park,** Rt. 1, Box 115, Enterprise, MS 39330 (601-655-9511). The water park is NW of Enterprise, Lauderdale County (69 acres, ca. 1.5-mile trail network). The main attractions at this atypical water park are the lovely waterfall cascading down a steep rocky slope into the Chunky River and the old mill with its waterwheel at the top. The mill was built in Cave Springs, Georgia, in 1857 and operated there until the 1950s.

The original mill at the site was also built in the 1850s by John Dunn, a young Irish immigrant. He noted that a stream ran parallel to the river only 70 yards away. He built a dam to divert the stream down the bank and put the water power to use in his mill. Local farmers brought their corn here for grinding. During the Civil War, Dunn manufactured blankets, hats, knives and clothing for Confederate troops. General Sherman's troops burned the mill down in 1864.

The Georgia mill was carefully disassembled during the 1980s and put back together at Dunn's Falls, complete with its inner workings. It was formally reopened in 1988. There is also a homesteader cabin and the millpond at the site.

A staircase runs down to the river beside the falls. An old road, perhaps from antebellum times, angles down to the river from the mill. It is now an interesting trail. A narrow foot trail runs back up to the picnic area from this road. A clearing along the old road is used as a backcountry campsite by Scouts and other youth groups. A variety of wild animals, including turkeys, deer, squirrels, rabbits, quail, hawks, owls, doves, coyotes, and bobcats, inhabit these wooded slopes.

Facilities: Picnic ground, primitive walk-in camping for youth groups, swimming in the river, and fishing in the millpond.

- **Flint Creek Water Park,** 1216 Parkway Dr., Wiggins, MS 39577 (601-928-3051). For information on cabins and to make reservations, contact Flint Creek Water Park, P.O. Drawer 1509, Hattiesburg, MS 39401 (1-800-748-9403). The water park is adjacent to Wiggins in Stone County (1,900 acres, 3.5-mile trail).

The Nature Trail takes you through rolling hills on the remote north side of the 600 acre reservoir, staying out of sight of the lake. You will find huckleberries in May and a variety of wildflowers changing with the seasons. A campsite for Boy Scouts and other groups has been established about 1.5 or 2 miles from the start of the trail (see below).

The trail used to be 7.5 miles long and connected with the northwest side of the lake with Fisherman's Ramp on the northeast side. Logging has converted four miles of the trail into a fire lane, and the Nature Trail dead-ends at the start of the lane.

Facilities: The Boy Scout Area is a walk-in primitive campsite. It's a three- or four-acre clearing near the lake shore and has a hand pump for water and an outhouse. Usually the kids and their leaders backpack in, but some Scout leaders get a key to the locked gate at the trailhead from the park office and use a four-wheel-drive vehicle to take supplies into the site via a separate dirt road. It's okay to camp elsewhere along the lake off the Nature Trail, and the campsite is not restricted to youth groups.

Developed facilities include cabins, campgrounds with RV hookups, primitive campgrounds, boat ramps, water skiing, fishing, a picnic area, baseball field, swimming, and Watertown USA, with four waterslides for children and adults. (Swimming is allowed only in developed swimming areas. Fees are charged for day use and for overnight camping.)

Maps: Get a map at the park office at the entrance.

PEARL RIVER BASIN DEVELOPMENT DISTRICT,

P.O. Box 5332, Jackson, MS 39296 (601-354-6301). The development district includes the watersheds of the Pearl River and two adjacent rivers, the Bogue Chitto and the Jourdan in south central Mississippi

Eighteen separate water parks (WPs) were listed in the out-of-date brochure *Pearl River Boatway Parks* distributed to the public in 1992. Some of these parks have been abandoned, transferred to another agency or private concern, or upgraded. Note the following changes if you have a brochure listing 18 water parks: (3) Schockaloe Horse Trail is in the Bienville National Forest; (4) Riverside Park is now LeFleur's Bluff State Park; (7) Georgetown WP has been abandoned; (8) Wanilla WP is now only a boat ramp; (10) more campsites have been added to Atwood WP; (11) Columbia WP now has campsites with RV hookups; (12) Summit WP has been sold to a private concern; (14) Walker's Bridge WP is primarily for day use, as is (15) Holmes WP; (16) Crossroads WP is now only a picnic area; (17) Walkiah Bluff WP may be closed or abandoned.

L 6

• **Bogue Chitto Water Park,** 1068 Dogwood Trail, McComb, MS 39648 (601-684-9568). The water park is W of Tylertown, Pike County (270 acres; ca. one mile of hiking trail). Besides a boat launch, campgrounds, and other facilities, the park has at least a mile of hiking trails along abandoned roads. Much of the natural hardwood forest has been preserved, but there are also two large playing fields.

The park is on a bend of the Bogue Chitto River. This lovely river begins near Brookhaven and meanders south into Louisiana. Curving east, it eventually joins the Pearl River in the Bogue Chitto National Wildlife Refuge. More than 100 miles are canoeable.

Facilities: Playing fields, large pavilion, two playgrounds for children, 80 campsites with hookups, a primitive camping area, and a hard-surface multiuse court for basketball, volleyball, and badminton.

A single "cabin" overlooking the river in a remote part of the park is available for rent. It's a converted railroad boxcar with a heater, bathroom, kitchen, screened porch, and four beds.

Three different outfitters rent canoes and inner tubes for float trips down the Bogue Chitto as well as providing shuttle service. The park office can give you numbers of canoe and tube outfitters. For detailed information on canoeing the entire Bogue Chitto, see Sevenair's *Trail Guide to the Delta Country* or *Canoe Trails of the Deep South,* edited by Estes et al., in the bibliography.

G 9

• **Burnside Lake Water Park,** Rt. 6, Box 54, Philadelphia, MS 39350 (601-656-7621). The water park is N of Philadelphia, Neshoba County (115.3 acres, ca. 0.5-mile trail network). This park includes a beautiful oxbow lake set

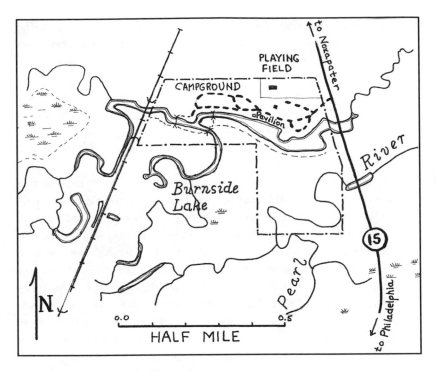

MAP 74. Burnside Lake Water Park

with stately cypress and tupelos. A trail with several boardwalks and bridges leads from the campground across the upper end of the lake and along the far side.

The park is on the north side of the Pearl River just off State Hwy 15. It is an excellent base camp for exploring other interesting sites nearby, such as Nanih Waiya State Park and the Noxubee National Wildlife Refuge.

Facilities: Campground with RV hookups, primitive campsites, lighted ball-fields, picnic pavilions, boat launching ramp, playground, bathhouse.

● **McLeod Water Park,** 8100 Texas Flat Rd., Kiln, MS 39556; (601-467-1894). The water park is SW of Kiln, Hancock County (428 acres; one-mile loop nature trail and old roads usable as trails). McLeod Park is well known locally, but most tourists have not heard of it. That's their loss, because this backwater park is full of interesting and beautiful spots.

McLeod Park is located on the south side of the Jourdan River, one of Mississippi's shortest rivers. Just a few miles upstream, it grows so shallow that it becomes Catahoula Creek. Downstream, it leaves the woods and winds through coastal marshland on its way to the Gulf through Bay St. Louis. The park contains two oxbow lakes. A concrete boat ramp and two fishing piers have been built into the larger of the two lakes, and a channel connects it with the Jourdan.

You can rent a canoe in the park or bring your own boat for a leisurely exploration of the river up- and downstream from the park. If you wish, you can drop a hook and catch channel catfish, bass, crappie, and spotted trout. Swimming is not encouraged in the Jourdan because of dangerous currents and steep dropoffs.

A nature trail about a mile long begins at the edge of the RV camping area just beyond the playing field. Leading over boardwalks and along the sandy banks of the Jourdan, the trail takes you through a forest of pine and magnolia with understories of palmetto and wax myrtle. In early spring wild azaleas, redbuds, and dogwoods will be in bloom. The route loops around a cemetery.

The park is named after the McLeod family, who settled at Kiln and set up a sawmill in the late 1800s. (Kiln takes its name from the charcoal kiln that operated there in the early 1900s.) The park had several houses on it until the mid-1960s. When the Stennis Space Center was established in the early 1960s, all dwellings within approximately 10 miles of its center were removed because the government did not want to be liable for any adverse effects of excessive noise from the rocket engines it was testing. Not only were scattered homes removed but also three whole villages. The area that is now McLeod Park is at the extreme southeast border of this easement area. After the government purchased the land and the houses were removed, 428 acres were turned over to the Hancock County Park Commission for a park.

Best Time to Visit: The park is open all year. Spring is the best for wildflowers. June, July, and August days are generally hot and humid. Temperatures sometimes drop below freezing in January and February. The campground may be full during spring weekends, especially Memorial Day weekend. Most visitors come to fish, so the park will be most crowded in the fishing season.

Facilities: Picnic ground with large playground for children, 36 campsites with RV hookups, and a primitive camping area (my favorite in Mississippi) with isolated riverside sites and chemical toilets but no tables or fireplaces. (The gate to the park is locked after dark for security, so you may not be able to get into the park if you arrive late at night.) There are also bathhouses with hot showers; two open air pavilions that are rented to groups; a concrete boat launching ramp; fishing piers; a playing field with bleachers and night lights; a volleyball, soccer, and horseshoe playing area; an indoor assembly room; and canoes for rent.

Maps and Literature: A brochure and detailed map of the park are available from the park office. The Kiln topo map is useful. The park is not shown on the 1976 version, but it is in Secs. 35, 36, 1, and 2 at the bottom left of the map.

• **Reservoir Botanical Gardens,** N of Jackson, Rankin County (42   H 7 acres, 0.5-mile loop trail). A wide, paved trail winds through a natural hard- wood forest planted with azaleas abloom in multiple shades of pink and red in midspring. The azaleas were planted in the early 1970s and look as if they had always grown in the woods. The trail is suitable for the handicapped. Benches invite a pause along Mill Creek.

This is a new trail formally opened on June 5, 1993. It was built and is maintained in cooperation with the Garden Clubs of Mississippi.

Best Time to Visit: The azaleas bloom in March and April.

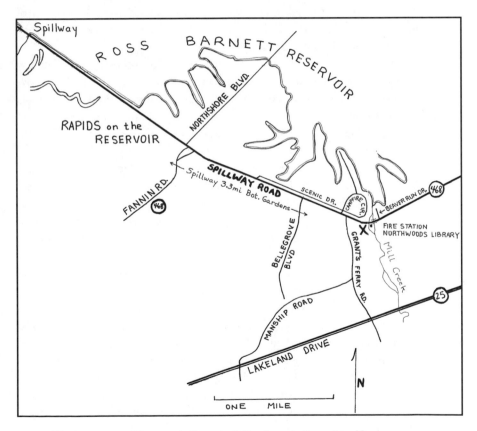

M A P 75. Location of Reservoir Botanical Gardens, indicated by X

STATE NATURAL AREA

L 4 ## CLARK CREEK NATURAL AREA,
Mississippi Department of Wildlife, Fisheries, and Parks, P.O. Box 451, Jackson, MS 39205 (601-362-9212). The natural area is W of Pond, Wilkinson County (2,000+ acres, 1.5-mile partially looped trail)

When you are in this area, you'll find it hard to believe you're in Mississippi. The Appalachians or the Ozarks, maybe, but who would expect to be standing on a huge boulder at the base of a waterfall 40' high in Mississippi?

The waterfalls, averaging about 15' high, make Clark Creek one of Mississippi's most popular destinations for hikers. In warm weather, there's the opportunity to frolic under a giant natural shower, and at any time of the year you can clamber over automobile-sized chunks of limestone that have fallen into the streambed. There are also deep hollows festooned with ferns typical of more northern latitudes. Elevations from stream bottoms to ridgetops range up to 200', unusually rugged for Mississippi.

For naturalists, Clark Creek is much more than waterfalls. The narrow ridges 300' to 400' high that separate the tributaries of Clark Creek are covered with a mixed hardwood forest, with beech and magnolia predominating, and a roseaucane understory. The cool damp hollows contain violets and maidenhair and christmas ferns. A great variety of mosses, lichens, and mushrooms grow on rocks and fallen tree trunks.

A fish endangered in the state, the southern red-bellied dace, lives in Clark Creek. A rare snail, the Carolina magnolia vine, which is on the state endangered species list, and the Louisiana black bear, a federally listed threatened species, are also found here. Especially in the spring, birders report an array of warblers, vireos, and other passerine species as well as Mississippi kites and other raptors.

Clark Creek is the crown jewel of natural areas in the state. It's the best example of natural diversity that we have, according to Bill Quisenberry, of the State Department of Wildlife, Fisheries, and Parks. Appropriately, it became the state's first formally designated natural area in 1978. Concern for potential damage from exploration and drilling for oil—polluting the stream with drilling mud, brine, and oil and disrupting and eroding the slopes with bulldozed access roads—led the state's Natural Heritage Program to work with Wilkinson County, International Paper, the Nature Conservancy, and others to purchase the area. The land is now managed by the Department of Wildlife, Fisheries, and Parks.

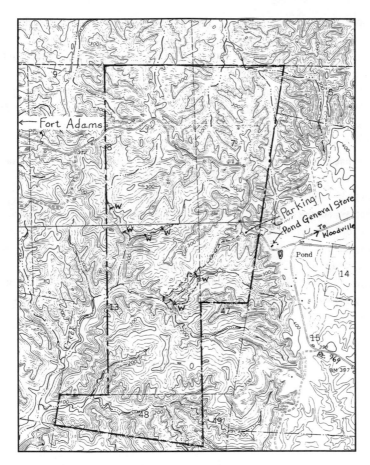

MAP 76. Clark Creek Natural Area. The contour interval is 20'. "W" indicates waterfall.

Because of the rugged terrain with very steep slopes, even on the trails, people with physical infirmities may have trouble. A single trail leads down from the parking lot near the Pond to the main fork of Clark Creek and the tops of two of the waterfalls. Three steep staircases (in poor repair in 1991) lead down to the bed of the stream below the waterfalls. Downstream from the natural area, Clark Creek runs through private land that is posted against trespassing.

Clark Creek Natural Area is probably the only area in Mississippi that is in danger of being loved too much by hikers and naturalists. Thousands of tramping feet have eliminated leaf litter and low-growing vegetation alongside the trails, exposing tree roots and initiating erosion. To minimize your impact on this very special place, stay on established trails. Camping and backpacking are not permitted.

Best Time to Visit: Spring is the best time for wildflowers and birding. The weather is nicest in the fall. In midwinter you may have the area to yourself. The waterfalls will be most impressive after periods of heavy rain.

Facilities: All you will find in the natural area is the trail and a parking lot. Note that there are no restrooms and that the Pond Store does not have a public restroom. Bring some toilet paper and a trowel with you, and bury your stool at least 200' from water.

Access: Follow the signs to Clark Creek Natural Area from Woodville 13 miles to Pond, which has only two or three buildings and hardly qualifies as a town. Keep an eye out for the Pond Store, a large white building on the west side of the road. Turn west on the road that goes past the store toward Fort Adams. The parking lot and trailhead are in the woods on the left side of the road just beyond the cleared area near the store (a genuine old-time general store built in 1881).

7. Other Public Lands

A variety of state agencies, universities, and municipalities are responsible for these areas.

GRAND GULF MILITARY MONUMENT,

Rt. 2, Box 389, Port Gibson, MS 39150 (601-437-5911). The monument is NW of Port Gibson, Claiborne County (450-acre park, ca. 0.5-mile trail)

This park exists because its site was once strategically located on the Mississippi River. There is a restored Spanish house here that was built in the 1790s. In the early 1800s the thriving port town of Grand Gulf grew up on the bank of the Mississippi. A thousand people lived there in 1833. Then the river shifted its course and began to undercut the town site itself. Soon only 158 people were left. In 1929 the U.S. Army Corps of Engineers cut off the bend of the Mississippi, leaving what remained of the town more than a half mile from the river. The site remains—romantic and overhung with moss-draped trees.

The name Grand Gulf was derived from a whirlpool at Point of Rocks where the Big Black River once emptied into the Mississippi. The overlooks from the point and steep loess bluffs above the floodplain of the Mississippi River proved crucial in the Civil War. Two major naval battles occurred here, the first between May 26 and June 8, 1862, and the second on April 29, 1863. In both cases the Confederates successfully prevented federal gunboats from proceeding up the Mississippi. After the second engagement, General Ulysses S. Grant and his troops crossed the Mississippi three miles downstream and began his famous march that ended with the fall of Vicksburg on July 4. You can still see redoubts, gun emplacements, and a Confederate cemetery.

The park has three minor trails, probably less than 0.2 mile each, and one "nature trail" about 0.5 mile long. This trail begins at the rifle pits and gun emplacements on Virgil D. Wheeless Dr. As of the fall of 1991, it was poorly marked with red and yellow paint blazes and surveyors tape and was easy to

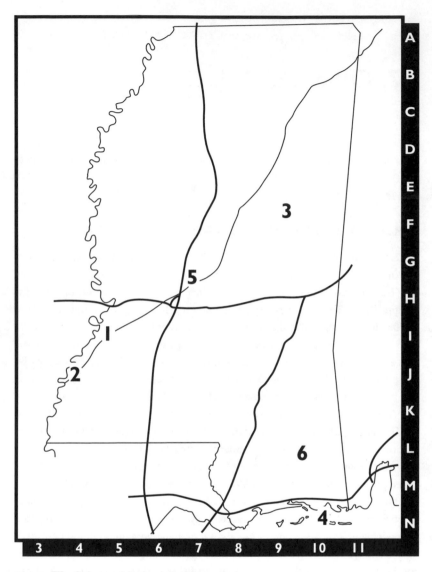

MAP 77. Other public lands in Mississippi

LEGEND

1	=	Grand Gulf Military Monument
2	=	Historic Jefferson College
3	=	Dorman Lake Nature Trail and Pine Natural Area
4	=	Round Island
5	=	Simmons Arboretum
6	=	Wyatt Hills

lose after it crossed an intermittent stream. After transversing ridges in some typically rugged loess terrain, the trail ends on Rocky Springs Road, a gravel road, at a tiny cemetery in the woods. Since this end of the trail is on private property, it is not marked. It is 0.35 mile from the junction of Rocky Springs Road with the paved access road to the park.

The half-mile trail was once part of a 14-mile loop route that was marked and used by the Boy Scouts. Unfortunately much of the route was on private land and had to be abandoned. The Scouts and park personnel are planning a new 8-mile circuit hiking route that will probably go along public roads for a good part of the way.

Unfortunately, nature at the park seems to be a distant third to developed recreation. An elevated boardwalk once led to the old channel of the Mississippi River, now a chain of lakes that are attractive to a variety of water and shore birds. It's now fallen down and unusable. The intermittent stream that the half-mile hiking trail crosses may be dammed and made into a recreational lake. Given the recently constructed extensive paved RV campground, a lot of development will have been crowded into a small park.

Facilities: Museum, blacksmith shop, picnic area with pavilions for rent, lookout tower, RV campground with hookups, primitive camping area (a long way from the restrooms!).

Maps: A color brochure and a map showing the approximate routes of the trails are available from the office. The Grand Gulf topo map is useful.

HISTORIC JEFFERSON COLLEGE,   J4

P.O. Box 700, Washington, MS 39190 (601-442-2901) (1.4 miles of interpretive trail)

Historic Jefferson College, named after President Thomas Jefferson, opened as a preparatory school with 15 students in 1811. Six years later it became a full-fledged college. It closed during the Civil War but reopened in 1866 again as a preparatory school. It was later a private military academy until it shut down for good in 1964. The Mississippi State Department of Archives and History now owns the site and is restoring the buildings.

The park has a network of interpretive trails. Some people consider them the most beautiful trails in the state. You have a choice of a 0.5-mile or 0.9-mile loop. Both trails take you past the tiny college cemetery, through mature forests of oaks and other hardwoods, and past Ellicott Springs (now emptying into an interesting concrete-walled pond set in steep loess bluffs). The springs are named after Andrew Ellicott, who camped here in 1797 before he surveyed the 31st parallel, which at the time was the dividing line between territories of the United States and Spain. Some of the terrain is rugged, and part of the trail is narrow with log treads, rustic wooden handrails, and narrow bridges. The longer loop takes you almost down to St. Catherine Creek's wide sandy bottom. Many of the trees and vines are labeled.

Best Time to Visit: The park is open seven days a week all year.

Facilities: Restrooms, picnic area adjacent to the parking area.

Access: The college is in the small town of Washington, which is on U.S. Hwy 61 seven miles east of Natchez. It is marked by signs on the north side of the highway.

Maps: A map of the grounds, including the trails, is available from the visitor center.

F 10 JOHN W. STARR MEMORIAL FOREST,

Manager, Charles E. Burkhardt, P.O. Box 9680, Mississippi State, MS 39762 (601-325-2191). The forest is between Starkville and Louisville in Oktibbeha, and Winston counties (8,244 acres, 0.7-mile interpretive trail)

Starr Memorial Forest is owned by Mississippi State University and is managed by its School of Forest of Resources as an outdoor laboratory for teaching, research, and demonstration. The terrain is gently rolling to almost flat. The "uplands" are loblolly and shortleaf pine forest, with extensive hardwood bottoms along streams, which are all tributaries of the Noxubee River. The forest is accessible via many roads, some of which are closed to vehicles and popular with horseback riders.

The Memorial Forest is divided into three separate units separated from one another by the Noxubee National Wildlife Refuge. The Mississippi Department of Wildlife, Fisheries, and Parks is responsible for wildlife management; hunters and trappers must have a special permit.

The federal government purchased the land in the 1930s and turned it over to the university in 1955. Other adjacent lands acquired at the same time are now the Noxubee National Wildlife Refuge and the Ackerman Unit of the Tombigbee National Forest.

Dorman Lake Nature Trail and Pine Natural Area: This is the only foot trail. Dorman Lake (ca. 13 acres) is fringed with beautiful mature loblolly pine. An interpretive trail begins at the picnic area and runs around the lake. Many trees and shrubs are labeled along the way, including cherrybark oak, black gum, red maple, willow oak, water oak, post oak, and common persimmon. Unfortunately only a narrow fringe of trees was left around the lake when the surrounding timber was clearcut to pay for a new building for the School of Forest Resources.

The picnic area has restrooms, water, tables, and a pavilion. It is closed to fishing, and overnight camping is not permitted. The restrooms and water may be shut down.

You can reach Dorman Lake from State Hwy 25 via Dorman Lake Rd., a gravel road that is marked by a large sign on the east side of the highway. If you are driving north on Hwy 25, the intersection of Dorman Lake Rd. is 5.0 miles from the junction of Loakfoma Rd. On the way to the lake, you will drive past the "Pine Natural Area," a small area of unmanaged pine.

Map: A map is available from the office of the forest manager.

UNIVERSITY OF MISSISSIPPI FOREST,   M 10

Manager, 2635 Wire Rd. E, Perkinston, MS 39573 (601-928-3461). The forest is between Lucedale and Saucier in George, Jackson, and Stone counties (approximately 22,000 acres)

The University of Mississippi Forest lies mostly between the Black Creek and Biloxi ranger districts of the DeSoto National Forest. Part of it is shown in orange as Red Creek Game Management Area on the state highway map. The land is managed for timber production, with the proceeds going to the university. Pines are managed on a 50-year rotation, longer than that used by private timber companies, which average 30 years, and shorter than that used by the Forest Service, which has its pine stands clearcut every 50 to 80 years.

Hunting is regulated by the state. The eastern edge of the university forest was designated as the Red Creek Game Refuge until it was declassified in 1991. It was one of the two original state wildlife refuges set aside in the 1930s or 1940s as breeding areas for deer and turkeys, which were captured for restocking elsewhere in the state. The Red Creek Refuge was the last such refuge.

The U.S. government granted the land to the university during the 1890s. The area was originally part of a naval reserve (timber set aside for turpentine and resin needed for sealing wooden ships) established by Congress in 1858. Four institutions of higher learning were given grants. The other three colleges sold their lands to timber companies at four to six dollars per acre.

Facilities: No trails, campgrounds, or picnic areas are provided, but the general public is welcome to hunt and hike on the area. Overnight camping is not allowed.

Maps: The area is shown in purple on the U.S. Forest Service's map of the DeSoto National Forest. Copies are sold at the offices of the Black Creek Ranger District and the Biloxi Ranger District as well as by the forest supervisor's office in Jackson.

● **Wyatt Hills Natural Area,** E of Perkinston, George County (60 acres)

The Wyatt Hills extend east-west for more than three miles on the south side of Black Creek. They are similar to the Red Hills to the west, which are traversed by the Black Creek Trail. As in the Red Hills, the distinctive terrain is caused by the red sands and white clays of the Citronelle Formation of the Pleistocene Age.

The University of Mississippi owns only a small part of the Wyatt Hills in T. 3S, R. 9W, Sec. 2. Its property lines are marked by orange paint blazes. International Paper Company owns the western end of the hills, and Scott Paper Company's land abuts on the east. Both these companies have clearcut their properties in the hills, and so if you are interested in scenery, you won't be inclined to set foot on these private lands. Even if you do, you shouldn't, because the land is leased to private hunting clubs.

Access: The Wyatt Hills are accessible by a dirt road that diverges from Old Hwy 26 (FS 396 on the DeSoto NF map). Drive east 1.7 miles from the junction of the New Zion Church Rd. to the Pine Bluff Missionary Baptist Church on the north side of the highway. Continue another 1.0 mile on the highway to the intersection of a dirt road on the ridgeline between Pinelog and Bridge branches. Turn north and follow the dirt road 1.7 miles to the Wyatt Hills. The road is rough and slick during wet weather. It is better for pickups and four-wheel-drive vehicles than for ordinary passenger cars. (You cannot reach university land via the gravel road that runs north past the Pine Bluff Church.)

Maps: The Benndale topo map is useful.

N 10 **R O U N D I S L A N D,**

Contact: Betty Bensey, City of Pascagoula, P.O. Drawer 908, Pascagoula, MS 39568 (601-938-6651). The island is in the Mississippi Sound S of Pascagoula, Jackson County (110 acres)

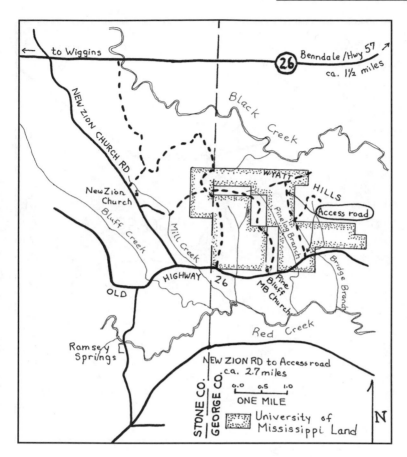

M A P 78. Wyatt Hills Natural Area in the University of Mississippi Forest. The shaded area is land owned by the university.

On the state road map, this island is a fleck in the Mississippi Sound about halfway between the mouth of the Pascagoula River and Horn Island. It's about three miles from Pascagoula.

Despite its name, the island is triangular in shape, with the narrow point of the triangle pointing northwest. The southern end, about 49 acres, belongs to the city of Pascagoula. The rest is private.

Slash pine with an understory of palmetto and salt bush predominates on the island. Its highest point is no more than seven feet above sea level, and much of the interior is marshy. Great blue herons have a rookery on the island, and six pairs of ospreys nest there. The beaches are narrow.

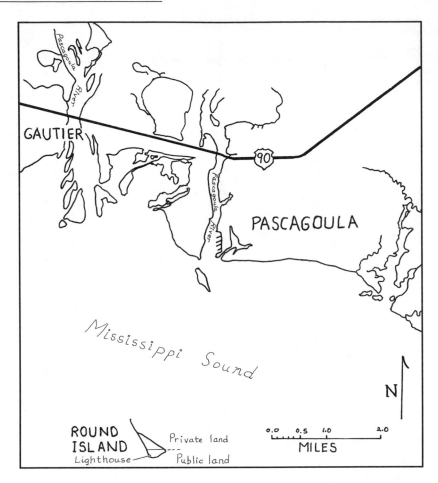

MAP 79. Round Island

D'Iberville discovered the island in 1699 and named it Isle Ronde reportedly "on account of its form." On a 1719–20 map it is shown as U-shaped. By the mid-1800s it was teardrop shaped, and now it's triangular. It has been steadily shrinking at least since 1886, when it was 232 acres.

A round brick lighthouse 60' high stands at the southwest corner of the island. It was built in 1859 because the shoreline had retreated to the edge of the original lighthouse, constructed in 1833, making it unstable. A succession of keepers manned the lighthouse until 1944. They lived in a nearby keeper's dwelling. This and associated outbuildings, henhouse, cowshed, and a garden are gone today. The federal government turned its landholding and the lighthouse over to the city of Pascagoula in 1989. It has been designated a state and national landmark.

Today the lighthouse stands at the very edge of the island, lapped by waves at high tide. It is in an excellent state of preservation, but eventually it is likely to be undermined in a severe storm. The city is soliciting donations to stabilize it and restore the keeper's house and outbuildings.

The federal government also maintained a quarantine and inspection station for yellow fever in the late 1800s after the Civil War. During prohibition it was a way station for running bootleg liquor to the coast.

Access: The island is easily accessible by private boat. The best place to anchor is off the northwestern shore. Watch out for stumps and tree roots near the shore. If you don't have a boat of your own or a friend who can take you, one of the charter boat services that take people to the barrier islands might take you. Ask the office of the Gulf Islands National Seashore in Ocean Springs for a list.

SIMMONS ARBORETUM,

H 7

Madison Parks and Recreation, P.O. Box 40, Madison, MS 39130 (601-856-8958). The arboretum is in Madison, Madison County (10 acres, one-mile trail network)

The arboretum is adjacent to the Natchez Trace Parkway and includes hills and a wetland. Dr. Walter and Ruth Simmons donated the land, and the arboretum has become a community project. Scouts, craftsmen, landscape architects, and a local homebuilder are involved. The area is being landscaped and planted with native trees, shrubs, and herbaceous plants. The park, scheduled for completion in 1997, will have a pond and may eventually have a specimen of every tree native to Mississippi.

To raise money for the project, the Simmons Arboretum Committee is sell-ing individual bricks for $30 to individuals and $50 to businesses. The bricks will be engraved with the donor's name and will be used to pave the pathways. To contribute a brick or to donate time or materials, inquire at the Madison Chamber of Commerce, City Hall (856-7060).

Access: The arboretum is at the end of St. Augustine Dr. in Madison. To reach it from I-55, take the Madison exit, which puts you on Main St. Follow Main St. to State Hwy 51. Turn right on 51 and left on St. Augustine Dr. The entrance to the arboretum is marked with a sign and adjoins a parking area.

8. Private Natural Areas and Resorts

Only a few private lands qualify for inclusion in this guide—those that are large enough to contain trails at least a half mile long and are open to the general public with or without an admission fee. The Crosby Arboretum and the Mississippi Petrified Forest are comparable to federal and state parks in the quality of their educational exhibits and in their commitment to the preservation of the state's natural heritage.

M 8 PINECOTE AND THE CROSBY ARBORETUM,

Crosby Arboretum, P.O. Box 190, Picayune, MS 39466 (601-799-2311). Pinecote and the arboretum are in Picayune, Hancock County (Pinecote has 64 acres, with interpretive trail; also several other natural areas in the Pearl River Basin)

This area is a living museum of plants native to the piney woods and coastal plain of the Pearl River Basin, with a self-guiding interpretive trail and pre-arranged tours of Pinecote, the arboretum's native plant center. Crosby Arboretum also owns several ecologically significant natural areas in southern Mississippi. It sponsors a variety of educational and scientific activities related to native plants and their interrelationships with man.

The Crosby Arboretum is unique in the state, and there are few of its kind in the Southeast. Its mission is to preserve, restore, and study native plants and landscapes in southern Mississippi and to foster public appreciation of them.

The focal point of the arboretum is its interpretive center, Pinecote. A second-growth forest of slash pine is slowly being converted to a living and natural-appearing complex of plants as they once grew on the coastal plain savanna before the landscape was drastically altered by clearcut logging in the early 1900s. A self-guiding trail winds around an irregularly shaped pond sur-

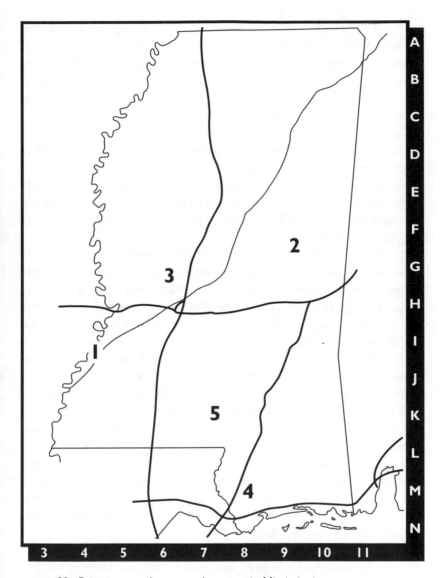

MAP 80. Private natural areas and resorts in Mississippi

LEGEND

1 = Canemount Plantation

2 = Lake Tiak-O'Khata

3 = Mississippi Petrified Forest

4 = Pinecote and the Crosby Arboretum

5 = Red Bluff

rounded by vegetation adapted to damp forests. Nearby, a grassy pine savanna is slowly and surely emerging with the help of judicious prescribed burning. Pitcher plants and other bog plants have been transplanted into the savanna. More than 400 species of native plants now grow at Pinecote. At the edge of the pond is an inspiring open air pavilion designed by the award-winning Arkansas architect Euine Fay Jones. It is used for lectures and even symphonies.

The arboretum's mission goes far beyond Pinecote. Arboretum staff and associates conduct botanical field trips in the surrounding areas, sell native plants to gardeners, sponsor educational sessions in garden design, and have sponsored symposiums and forums on the piney woods and wetlands and photographic exhibits of the local landscape, past and present. The arboretum works with scientific researchers and provides educational material on the benefits and uses of native plants.

The founders of the arboretum realized that it would be impossible to establish examples of all the types of plant communities in the Pearl River Basin at Pinecote and have also acquired 11 other natural areas scattered over Mississippi and adjacent parts of Louisiana. They include beautiful pitcher plant bogs that contain native orchids and insect-eating plants. A longleaf pine ridge, an Atlantic white cedar swamp, a beech-magnolia woods, a hardwood and mesic bluff preserve, a cypress-gum swamp, a hardwood hammock, a slash pine savanna, and a hardwood creek bottom are represented.

The Crosby Arboretum was established in 1980 as a living memorial to L. O. Crosby, Jr. (1907–78). His father, L. O. Crosby, Sr., was one of many timber magnates who made a fortune stripping the virgin longleaf and slash pine timber from the piney woods and coastal plain in the early 1900s. Unlike the others, who then left the denuded region for the Pacific Northwest, Crosby stayed and helped his idle sawmill employees through the Great Depression by growing strawberries and tung trees (valued at the time by the Chinese for their oil). The arboretum is just one of the philanthropic endeavors of his descendants in the Pearl River Basin.

Best Time to Visit: Pinecote is open six days a week year round. The best displays of wildflowers are in the spring, but there is always something to see. The interpretive material is constantly updated to fit the changing seasons.

Access: To reach Pinecote, take the exit for State Hwy 43 off Interstate 59 just south of Picayune. Turn east and take the first road to the south, following the signs to the Crosby Arboretum 1.3 miles down the road.

Facilities: Drinking water and restroom.

Maps and Literature: A map and botanical literature are available at Pinecote.

Activities: Tours for classes and groups can be arranged. The arboretum has

more than 500 members and welcomes new members. Volunteer horticultur-
ists have put in many hours at Pinecote.

MISSISSIPPI PETRIFIED FOREST, H 6

P.O. Box 37, Flora, MS 39071 (601- 879-8189). The petrified forest is adjacent
to Flora in Madison County (0.5-mile interpretive trail)

The Petrified Forest was discovered sometime before 1845 and was well
known when the R. J. Schabilion family purchased the property in 1963. For
decades, collectors had been hauling off hundreds of tons of fossil logs and
chipping samples off the pieces they couldn't carry. The Schabilions developed
the site as a "show and tell" outdoor museum, and through their efforts, it was
designated a Natural Landmark in 1966.

The logs are up to seven feet in diameter. They are embedded in colorful
reddish orange, yellowish white, and pale brown sands up to 75' thick. Erosion
is proceeding rapidly, and as the sand washes away, new logs are revealed.
Geologists have named the geologic formation in which the logs are buried
the Forest Hill Formation. It was deposited on land an estimated 36 million to
38 million years ago.

The logs were apparently buried in sand washed down by prehistoric
streams. Burial must have been rapid, because they were only slightly decayed
when fossilization began. When thin sections of the petrified wood are cut,
polished, and examined under a microscope, the cellular structure is clear, but
all of the original organic cellulose or lignin has been replaced by chalcedony
and other silicates.

Only two species of trees have been identified. An earlier study identified
them as a conifer and a broad-leaved tree of northern origin. It was difficult to
reconcile these identifications with other geologic evidence in Mississippi and
adjacent states, which suggests a subtropical climate where palms thrived at
the time the logs were buried.

In 1981, a new study (by Blackwell et al.; see the bibliography) determined
that the presumed northern species identifications were incorrect. The most
common species was reassigned to *Cupressinoxylon florense* in the family Cu-
pressaceae, which are conifers. The closest living relative to *Cupressinoxylon* occurs in South Africa. Presently these conifers live only in the Old World, but
for most of their history they were also widespread in North America.

The less numerous species was identified as *Floroxylon variabile* in the family
Euphorbiaceae. This family of broad-leaved trees is neotropical. The closest

extant species are found in the West Indies and northern South America.

Another indication that the climate in Mississippi at the time the petrified forest grew was subtropical is the fact that growth rings are missing or are poorly defined in the logs, as they would be if winters were exceedingly mild or almost nonexistent.

The trees possibly grew in a swamp near the stream or river in which they were buried. Similar types of fossil wood are known in many other sites in Mississippi, Arkansas, Louisiana, and eastern Texas.

Within the last decades, the configuration of the badlands at the Petrified Forest has changed noticeably, and the site is now sheltered by a maturing forest dominated by loblolly pines and red cedar.

Visitors are given a self-guiding brochure corresponding to numbers along the trail when they buy their admission tickets. Many of the living trees and vines are identified by signs.

Facilities: There are a museum with displays of petrified wood and fossil animals from many localities; a gift shop with fossils, minerals, and lapidary supplies for sale; a campground with showers; and a picnic area.

Maps and Literature: Maps and literature are available at the gift shop.

K7 RED BLUFF,

SE of Morgantown in Marion County (40 acres, informal trails)

This bluff on the west side of the Pearl River just might be Mississippi's largest gully. Photographs can't do it justice. You have to be there, looking over the edge. The 40 acres that include the gully are privately owned, but the public is free to visit the site.

Red Bluff is about 150' high. The Citronelle Formation (Pleistocene Age) on top contributes the red, white, and gold. Underneath is the Pascagoula/Hattiesburg Formation (Miocene Age), with its green, bluish green, and gray clays and siltstones.

The bluff has existed a long time, and the gully is still growing. State Hwy 587, which runs along the top, has had to be relocated at least once as the gully continues to cut back away from the river.

Once you've enjoyed the view from the top, it's worth an hour or two of your time to hike to the bottom and back up. Informal but well-worn trails lead down both steep sides of the gully. People who don't have knee problems and who are in good physical condition should have no trouble making the trip.

Once you are on the bottom, you can walk across the railroad track and through a bottomland hardwood forest to the Pearl River.

Facilities: All you will find at the bluff overlook is a place to park and informal hiking trails. The Columbia Water Park (601-736-2691) is a good base for exploring the area, however. It has a public boat launch, huge pavilion, picnic and camping areas (no RV hookups), and lighted ballfields. Columbia Water Park is on the Pearl River off the Hwy 35 bypass, two miles north of Columbia.

Access: Red Bluff is alongside State Hwy 587, 2.2 miles north of Morgantown. You can park on either side, but the best place to stop and gawk is at the end of a short spur road on the north side of the gully.

If you want to see the bluff from the bottom but aren't physically equal to the steep slopes, you could drive 1.0 mile south on the highway from the southern edge of the gully to a point where two roads come in on your right (Pearl River side). Park near the railroad track. From here you can walk 1.0 mile north along the track to the base of the bluff.

Map: The Morgantown topo map is useful.

CANEMOUNT PLANTATION,

I 5

W of Port Gibson in Claiborne County (three-mile hiking trail on 6,000-acre plantation)

A path through the woods and along a creek bank awaits hikers at this historic antebellum plantation. More than 50 stands for viewing deer and other wildlife have been erected on the property. The path is open to paying guests only.

The "big house" was built in 1855. A former slave cabin, pond house and the original kitchen have been restored and are rented to bed-and-breakfast guests. Bicyclists riding the Natchez Trace Parkway often stay overnight here. For further information, call 1-800-423-0684.

LAKE TIAK-O'KHATA,

F 9

P.O. Box 160, Louisville, MS 39339 (601-773-7853). The lake is SW of Louisville in Winston County (two-mile-round-trip nature trail)

When Mississippians think of Lake Tiak-O'Khata, conventions, good cuisine, and parties are likely to come to mind. But along with its two convention centers, the 100-acre lake has a 74-unit motel, an RV park with hookups, and five duplex cabins.

According to the manager, the nature trail has breathtaking views of the lake. You will find benches at three points along the way and a picnic area. "After a rollercoaster beginning," he says, "the trail becomes fairly level and is a fun walk for people of all ages." The trail is open only to paying guests.

Once you've finished your walk, there are many other things you can do, such as fishing for largemouth bass, swimming, sliding down a spiral water slide, or suntanning on a white sand beach. Also, you can play tennis, basketball, and volleyball. Excellent golf courses are nearby. The name is Choctaw for "Pine Lake."

Appendix 1   Coping with Natural Hazards

Snakes: Fear of snakes is probably the single biggest reason why more people don't explore the wild areas of Mississippi. Yet according to the Poison Control Center (University of Mississippi, 2500 N. State St., Jackson, MS 39216; 601-354-7660), no snakebite fatalities have been recorded here for more than 30 years. A macho attitude is conducive to snakebites; of the 50 to 60 people who are treated for snake bite annually, most are males. Some people have been bitten more than once because they were trying to kill the snake.

To avoid trouble with poisonous snakes, be watchful and respectful. Look before you step over large fallen trees in swampy areas or sit down on one; a cottonmouth might be coiled on the other side. If you aren't sure whether a snake is poisonous, keep away. Any snake will do its best to avoid you. Unless it's taken by surprise, a cottonmouth or rattlesnake will warn you when you come too close and will bite only as a last resort, to save its own life. Remember that the snake is a resident of the natural area and that you are only a visitor. The Poison Control Center distributes a free one-page set of up-to-date instructions, "First Aid for Snakebite," that you can add to your first aid kit.

Mosquitoes: Mosquitoes aren't as bad in Mississippi as most people think except in wooded areas on the Delta in summer and at certain times and places on the barrier islands. (In my experience, they are much worse in early summer at high altitudes in the West and North Woods.) During the day, keep them off with a spray or ointment containing DEET. At night, sleep in a tent protected by mosquito netting.

Ticks: Ticks are common from spring to late fall. One tick-transmitted illness, Lyme disease, has received a lot of publicity recently. It's not nearly as common here as it is in New England and states around the Great Lakes; 11 cases were reported in 1990 and 14 in 1991. Rocky Mountain spotted fever is more prevalent and just as serious, with 32 and 19 cases reported in 1990 and 1991, respectively. Both diseases are easily cured with antibiotics if the symptoms are recognized and treated early.

To avoid ticks people are usually told to wear long-sleeved shirts and pants, tucking their pants legs into their boot tops. Unfortunately this is not a comfortable way to dress during the seasons when ticks are most numerous. If parts of your arms and legs are exposed as you hike, you will need a repellent. DEET is somewhat effective against ticks. Permanone (5% permethrin) is much better. It is sold as Coulston's Permethrin Tick Repellent and is also available under other brand names. Check your body frequently during the day for ticks, and look under your clothes when convenient. Ask a friend to check your back and other parts of your body you can't see. (For more about avoiding ticks, see Drummond's *Ticks and What You Can Do About Them*, in the bibliography.)

Stings: Statistically, the most dangerous animals in Mississippi are stinging insects such as wasps, bees, and fire ants. The reason is that some people become hyperallergic after repeated stinging episodes. The normal reaction to a sting is pain and itching commensurate with the size and species of insect administering the sting. Within two hours, the pain goes away.

A few people experience a Stage 2 reaction to stings of certain species of insects. A swelling more than two inches in diameter develops around the site of the sting but remains contiguous with the site. A reaction of this kind is a warning but is not threatening in itself. Of the people who experience a Stage 2 reaction, 5% to 10% will suffer a Stage 3 reaction the next time they are stung by the same species of insect. Parts of the body separate from the sting site are affected. Itching and rashes may appear that aren't contiguous with the site. Eyes may water, or hives may develop. The affected person may have difficulty breathing (asthma) because tissues have swelled internally. In extreme cases, the victim goes into shock and could die.

Fortunately, people do not develop a Stage 3 reaction without going through a Stage 2 reaction during a previous sting. If you experience either a Stage 2 or 3 reaction to a sting, consult a physician. Doctors can prescribe a relatively inexpensive "sting kit" that you can take with you on trips.

Poison Ivy: About one-quarter of humans are immune to poison ivy, one-half are moderately allergic, and one-quarter are very allergic. Those who are immune may become allergic after repeated contact. The rash-producing substance in poison ivy, as well as in the closely related poison sumac of eastern swamps and poison oak of the Pacific Coast, is urushiol, an oil in the sap (see Frankel's book *Poison Ivy* in the bibliography).

If you know your bare skin has brushed against poison ivy leaves, you have a 2- to 6-hour grace period in which to remove the urushiol before it is absorbed into the skin and the allergic reaction begins (you won't be aware of it for at least 24 hours). Lots of cold running water may be the best and most practical way to get it off. Hot water may help spread the oil. Be careful not to spread it by hard rubbing. At least one alcohol-based lotion claims to be effective in removing urushiol, but I haven't found it so. If a rash does set in, try Benadryl spray.

At least two different research groups are developing new, effective vaccines against urushiol. In the meantime, there is a folk method of building immunity, namely eating the leaves, with which adventurous readers may wish to experiment at their own risk (I cannot vouch for its safety or effectiveness). This method was advocated by Euell Gibbons (see *Stalking the Wild Asparagus*, in the bibliography), who claimed to have tried it with success. Gibbons recommended eating three leaflets (one complete compound leaf) of poison ivy or poison oak daily for three weeks, starting in early spring when the red new leaves first begin to unfold. (To protect the lips and gums, put the leaf between pieces of bread or mix it with other food.) The leaves are growing during the treatment period and therefore contain progressively larger doses of urushiol. At the end of the three weeks, according to Gibbons, you will be immune or at least more resistant. Two friends and I have tried the treatment; it seems to work.

The immunity gained by ingesting urushiol directly or by drinking the milk of goats that are feeding on the leaves is likely to be only temporary at best. You may be able to maintain it, however, by eating a complete leaf once a week. Urushiol lasts almost indefinitely; leaves can be stored in a plastic bag in the freezer. People who want to start treatment later in the year should begin with a fraction of a single leaflet and work up to an entire leaf before the end of three weeks.

Hunters: Some form of hunting is legal in Mississippi between Labor Day and early March. In addition, a spring gobbler season occurs sometime in April or early May. The only hunting seasons that need concern nonhunters, however, are the various deer (gun) seasons, which traditionally begin on the first Saturday before Thanksgiving. More people are abroad in the woods during the first week of deer (gun) season than at any other time of the year. The chance that you will be mistaken for a deer is slight, especially if you follow the law for deer hunters by wearing, "in full view, a minimum of 500 square inches of unbroken continuous daylight fluorescent hunter orange material during all deer seasons except the archery season" (Mississippi Game Laws). You can purchase an orange cap and an inexpensive plastic vest from any store that sells hunting supplies. To avoid all the commotion, though, when you have a yen to be outside in late November and early December, you may want to explore a state park or one of the three national park areas where hunting is not allowed. If you hike at this time of year, you should wear fluorescent orange even in areas where hunting is prohibited.

Lightning: Every year four or five people on average are killed by lightning in Mississippi. During a thunderstorm, reduce your risk by being sure that you are not the highest object in the landscape or waterscape and that you are not near such an object—a large tree in a meadow, for example. If you are trapped in an open field at the height of a lightning storm, lie down. Learn cardiopulmonary resuscitation; many victims of lightning stop breathing and have no pulse but can be saved.

Appendix 2   Some Useful Names and Addresses

Defenders of Wildlife, 1101 Fourteenth St., N.W., Suite 1400, Washington, D.C. 20005 (202-682-9400). Defenders of Wildlife has been active in promoting protection of the Louisiana black bear. Its habitat is important for many other species and preserves wild areas for hiking and canoeing.

Garden Clubs of Mississippi, Trails Coordinator, Mrs. Betty Dossett, 169 D'Evereau Dr., Natchez, MS 39120 (601-446-9716). The garden clubs promote and participate in the construction of nonmotorized trails in Mississippi.

Gulf Islands Conservancy, P.O. Box 1086, Gulfport, MS 39502. The conservancy encompasses various politically active groups focused on the Mississippi Gulf coast, the Mississippi Sound, and the barrier islands. There are occasional field trips.

Mississippi Audubon Society, Jackson Chapter (601-354-7303). The Audubon Society organizes birdwatching and other nature-oriented outings and sponsors some political action on behalf of the environment.

Mississippi Endurance Riders Association, Ruth Gaddis, 1316 East 3d St., Forest, MS 39074 (601-469-2602), or Raymond Rowland, 109 W. Hamilton St., Houston, MS 38851 (601-456-3854 or 601-456-2538). The purposes of the organization are to develop and improve horseback riding trails in Mississippi and elsewhere and to promote endurance riding. The organization sponsors five endurance rides a year in Mississippi.

The Nature Conservancy, Mississippi Chapter, P.O. Box 1028, Jackson, MS 39215 (601-355-5357). The Nature Conservancy purchases ecologically significant tracts of land and usually turns them over to federal or state agencies for management. The organization also sponsors nature outings.

Recreational Equipment Inc., 1700 45th St. East, Sumner, WA 98390 (1-800-426-4840) and Campmor, P.O. Box 700-X, Sadde River, NJ 07458-0700 (1-800-526-4784). These suppliers sell backpacking and other camping gear by direct mail (ask for catalogs).

Sierra Club, Mississippi Chapter, P.O. Box 4335, Jackson, MS 39296 (601-352-1026). Delta Chapter, Sierra Club, P.O. Box 19469, New Orleans, LA 70179-0469 (504-482-9566). These politically active environmental groups sponsor hikes, canoe trips, and trail maintenance/construction outings in Mississippi.

Tennessee Trails Association, Memphis Chapter, c/o Mrs. Jerri Bull, 2995 Carvel, Memphis, TN 38118 (901-363-4408). The association sponsors hikes and trail maintenance/construction outings in northern Mississippi.

Appendix 3   Lengths and Layouts of Trails

Listed in order of increasing length in miles. Layouts: **l,** looped; **pl,** partially looped; **nl,** not looped; **ntw,** network of interconnected trails; **rt,** round trip hike involving some walking on roads. For trail networks, approx. minimum and maximum loop routes are given.

0.2 mi l:
Rocky Springs (town) Trail
Rocky Springs (springs) Trail
Falls of Mint Spring Bayou, Vicksburg National Military Park
0.2–0.3 mi nl:
Red Bluff
0.3 mi l:
Big Oak Nature Trail, Arkabutla Lake
0.2–0.5 mi nl:
Grand Gulf Military Monument
0.5 mi nl:
John W. Kyle SP Nature Trail
Burnside WP
0.5 mi pl:
Dunn's Falls WP
0.5 mi l:
Shongelo Recreation Area
Woodpecker Trail, Noxubee NWR
Picnic Area Loop, Rocky Springs
Swinging Bridge Nature Trail, Arkabutla Lake
Water Valley Rec. Area Hiking Trail, Enid Lake

Reservoir Botanical Gardens
Also see interpretive trails list in index; most are half mile loops
0.5 mi ntw:
Simmons Arboretum, Madison
0.6 mi l:
Old River Interpretive Trail, Grenada Lake
0.7 mi nl:
Magnolia Nature Trail, St. Catherine Creek NWR
0.7 mi l:
Clear Springs Nature Trail, Sardis Lake
Dorman Lake Nature Trail, John W. Starr Memorial Forest
0.8 mi l:
Marathon Lake
0.8 mi nl:
Howard-Breland Cemetery Trail
Turkey Fork Nature Trail
0.5–0.9 mi l:
Historic Jefferson College
0.9 mi l:
Clear Springs Nature Trail, Homochitto NF

1.0 mi pl:
Little Mountain Trail, Jeff Busby
Site
Haserway Wetland Demonstra-
tion Area, Grenada Lake
0.1 – 1.0 mi nl:
Pascagoula River WMA
0.2 – 1.0 mi l:
Buccaneer SP nature trails
0.5 – 1.0 mi l:
Paul B. Johnson SP nature trails
0.5 mi l, 1.0 mi pl:
Bogue Chitto WP
1.0 mi l:
Great River Road SP nature trail
Honey Island Swamp Nature Trail,
Pearl River WMA
McLeod WP Nature Trail
1.0 mi nl:
Leaf Wilderness Area
Lake Tiak-O'Khata
1.2 mi nl:
Overcup Oak Research Natural
Area
0.6 – 1.2 mi l:
Tombigbee SP nature trail
1.3 mi nl:
Trail of the Big Trees, Noxubee
NWR
0.8 mi l, 1.4 mi pl:
Holmes County SP trails
1.4 mi nl:
Pellucid Bayou, Sandy Creek
WMA
Alligator Pond trail, Yazoo NWR
1.5 mi nl:
Morgan Brake NWR
Old Natchez Trace, Rocky Springs

1.5 mi pl:
Clark Creek Natural Area
1.5 mi l:
Sandstone Interpretive Trail,
Sardis Lake
0.8 – 1.5 mi l:
Shepard SP trails
0.8 mi l, 1.8 mi rt:
Legion SP trails
1.2 – 1.8 mi ntw:
Bienville Pines Scenic Area
0.5 – 0.9 mi nl, 0.8 – 2.0 mi rt:
Trace SP nature trail
2.0 mi nl:
Shipland WMA
0.5 – 2.0 mi l:
LeFlore Trail Network, Malmaison
WMA
1.0 – 2.0 mi ntw:
Puskus Lake
1.5 mi nl, 2.0 mi rt:
Old River WMA
0.3 – 2.2 mi rt:
Leroy Percy SP trails
2.2 mi l:
Pipes Lake Nature Trail
Lost Bluff Hiking Trail, Grenada
Lake
2.5 mi nl:
Owens Creek-Rocky Springs trail
2.5 mi l:
Quail Run Nature Trail, George
Payne Cossar SP
Wall Doxey SP
0.8 mi nl, 1.3 mi nl, 2.6 mi rt:
Cypress Bayou Botanical Area
2.6 mi nl:
Dahomey NWR

3.0 mi:
Canemount Plantation
3.0 mi nl:
Sandy Creek, Sandy Creek WMA
3.0 mi l:
Wilderness Trail, Noxubee NWR
3.0 mi rt:
Sweetgum Research Natural Area
3.3 mi nl:
Beaver Dam Trail, Noxubee
NWR
0.3 mi nl, 1.9–3.4 mi ntw:
Roosevelt SP
3.5 mi nl:
Flint Creek WP
3.5 mi pl:
Tupelo Horse Trail
1.5 mi nl, 3.5 mi l:
Clarkco SP
0.3–3.7 mi ntw:
Hugh White SP nature trails
0.7–4.0 mi nl:
Delta NF trails
4.0 mi nl:
Old Robinson Road, Noxubee
NWR
0.8 mi l, 4.0 mi pl:
LeFleur's Bluff SP trails
3.0–4.0 mi ntw (proposed):
Choctaw Lake (Chata) Trail
4.5 mi pl:
Rocky Point Trail, Enid Lake
4.6 mi nl:
Old Town Overlook Trail
5.0 mi rt:
Lake Lowndes SP nature trail
Percy Quin SP nature trail

2.0–5.0 mi l:
Coldwater River Nature Trail
System, Arkabutla Lake
1.2–6.0 mi ntw:
Trace SP backcountry trails
6.4 mi nl:
Tupelo Horse Trail + Old Overlook Trail
5.5 mi l:
East Ship Island circuit
2.0–8.0 mi ntw:
Chewalla Lake (planned)
8.0 mi l:
West Ship Island circuit
3.5 mi nl, 8.2 mi rt:
Old Trace Trail
2.5 mi nl, 9.5 mi rt:
Natchez SP trails
10.0 mi rt, 6.0 mi l:
Panther Swamp NWR
1.3–2.3 mi l, 0.4–10.5 mi pl:
Tishomingo SP
12.0 mi l:
Al Scheller Scout Trail (orienteering route)
3.5–15.0 mi ntw:
Witch Dance (Tombigbee) Trail
15.0 mi l:
Petit Bois Island circuit
3.2–19.5 mi l:
Big Foot Horse Trail System
12.6 mi l, 19.7 mi pl:
Tuxachanie Trail
21.0 mi nl:
Lonesome Pine Horse Trail
23.0 mi l:
Shockaloe Trail

13.0–23.0 mi l:
Little Tiger ATV Trail
6.0–23.0 mi ntw:
Longleaf Trail System
10.0 mi l (25.0 mi l planned):
Clear Springs Trail
25.0 mi l (proposed):
Okatibee Lake Trail

25.0 mi nl (planned):
Rocky Springs to Hwy 553
2.0–26.0 mi l:
Horn Island
40.8 mi nl:
Black Creek Hiking Trail

Bibliography

REFERENCES

Anderson, Agnes Grinstead. *Approaching the Magic Hour: Memories of Walter Anderson.* Jackson: University Press of Mississippi, 1989.

Blackwell, W. H., D. M. Brandenburg, and G. H. Dukes. "The Structural and Phytogeographic Affinities of Some Silicified Wood from the Mid-Tertiary of West-Central Mississippi." In *Geobotany II,* edited by R. C. Romans. New York: Plenum, 1981.

Boy Scouts of America. *Fieldbook.* 3d ed. Irving, Tex.: Boy Scouts of America, 1983.

Brown, Calvin S. "Tishomingo State Park: Botany." 2d ed. *Mississippi State Geological Bulletin* 23 (1945).

Carroll, Thomas Battle. *Historical Sketches of Oktibbeha County.* Gulfport, Miss.: Dixie Press, 1931.

Carter, James Richard, Jr. "A Floristic Study of the Delta National Forest and Adjacent Areas." M.A. thesis, Mississippi State University, Starkville, 1978.

Conarro, Ray M. *The Beginning: Recollections and Comments.* Atlanta: USDA Forest Service, Southern Region, 1989.

Crutchfield, James A. *The Natchez Trace: A Pictorial History.* Nashville, Tenn.: Rutledge Hill Press, 1985.

Daniels, Jonathan. *The Devil's Backbone: The Story of the Natchez Trace.* 1962. Repr. Gretna, La.: Pelican Publishing, 1989.

Dockery, D. T. "Mollusca of the Moodys Branch Formation, Mississippi." *Mississippi Geological, Economic, and Topographical Survey Bulletin* 120 (1977).

Drummond, Roger. *Ticks and What You Can Do About Them.* Berkeley, Calif.: Wilderness Press, 1989.

Estes, Chuck, Elizabeth F. Carter, and Byron Almquist. *Canoe Trails of the Deep South.* Birmingham, Ala.: Menasha Ridge Press, 1992.

Federal Writers Project of the Works Progress Administration. *Mississippi: The WPA Guide to the Magnolia State.* 1938. Repr. Jackson: University Press of Mississippi, 1988.

Fletcher, Colin. *The Complete Walker III.* 3d ed. New York: Knopf, 1984.

Frankel, Edward. *Poison Ivy, Poison Oak, Poison Sumac, and Their Relatives—Pistachios, Mangoes, Cashews.* Pacific Grove, Calif.: Boxwood Press, 1992.

Futvoye, Ruby Lee Ford. "The Robinson Road." 1971. Mississippi State Archives, Jackson. Photocopy.

Gibbons, Euell. *Stalking the Wild Asparagus*. New York: David McKay, 1962.

Greenspan, Rick, and Hal Kahn. *The Camper's Companion: The Pack-Along Guide for Better Outdoor Trips*. San Francisco, Calif.: Foghorn Press, 1991.

Halbert, H. S. "Nanih Waiya, the Sacred Mound of the Choctaws." *Publications of the Mississippi Historical Society* 2 (1899): 223–34.

Hickman, Nollie W. "Mississippi Forests." In Richard Aubrey McLemore, ed., *A History of Mississippi*, vol. 2. Jackson: University and College Press of Mississippi, 1973.

———. *Mississippi Harvest: Lumbering in the Longleaf Pine Belt, 1840–1915*. University, Miss.: University of Mississippi, 1962.

Howell, Elmo. *Mississippi Scenes: Notes on Literature and History*. N.p., 1992.

Jones, Samuel B. "A Virgin Pine and a Virgin Loblolly Pine Stand in Central Mississippi." *Castanea* 36 (1971): 223–25.

Knight, E. Leslie, B. N. Irby, and S. Carey. *Caves of Mississippi*. Hattiesburg: Southern Mississippi Grotto of the National Speleological Society, 1974.

Lumpkin, Ben Gray, and Martha Neville Lumpkin. *The Lumpkin Family of Virginia, Georgia, and Mississippi*. Clarksville, Tenn.: Lumpkin, 1973.

McDonald, R. E. "Latest Research about LeFleur's Bluff." In *Jackson: A Special Kind of Place*, edited by C. Brinson. Jackson: City of Jackson, 1977.

Manning, Harvey. *Backpacking, One Step at a Time*. New York: Random House, 1986.

Maser, Chris. *The Redesigned Forest*. San Pedro, Calif.: R. & E. Miles, 1988.

Moore, Allan. "A Floristic Survey of the Noxubee Crest Region of the Tombigbee National Forest, Winston County, Mississippi." M.S. thesis, Mississippi State University, Starkville. Forthcoming.

Morse, William C. "The Geologic History of Legion State Park." *Mississippi State Geological Survey Bulletin* 35 (1937).

Phelps, Dawson A. "The Robinson Road." *Journal of Mississippi History* 12 (1950): 153–61.

Pitts, J. R. S. *Life and Confession of the Noted Outlaw James Copeland*. Introduced by John D. W. Guice. Facs. ed. Jackson: University Press of Mississippi, 1980.

Schueler, Donald G. *Preserving the Pascagoula*. Jackson: University Press of Mississippi, 1980.

Sevenair, John P., ed. *Trail Guide to the Delta Country*. New Orleans: New Orleans Group of the Sierra Club, 1992.

Sugg, Redding S., Jr., ed. *The Horn Island Logs of Walter Inglis Anderson*. Rev. ed. Jackson: University Press of Mississippi, 1985.

Toups, Judith A., and Jerome A. Jackson. *Birds and Birding on the Mississippi Coast*. Jackson: University Press of Mississippi, 1987.

Welland, Ron, et al. "Inventory and Restoration of Prairie Openings." *Blue Darter: A Newsletter for Fisheries, Wildlife, and Range, USDA Forest Service, Region 8*, no. 7 (1991): 15–16.

NATURAL HISTORY GUIDES

This list of recommended guides was compiled by Mary Stevens, librarian of the Natural Science Museum in Jackson. You can probably find other guides in your local library, but if you are going to buy your own, Mary suggests any of the inexpensive Golden Guide and Golden Field series and any of the Peterson Field Guide series. All of the Peterson guides have range maps and color paintings of species, showing field marks for easy identification in the field; they cover most species, including beetles, butterflies, other insects, fish, and birds. Some volumes in this series are listed below, with other books that Mary particularly recommends.

Conant, Roger, and Joseph T. Collins. *A Field Guide to the Reptiles and Amphibians: Eastern and Central North America.* 3d ed. Peterson Field Guides, Vol. 12. Boston: Houghton Mifflin, 1991.

Duncan, W. H. *Woody Vines of the Southeastern United States.* Athens: University of Georgia Press, 1975.

Duncan, W. H., and M. B. Duncan. *Trees of the Southeastern United States.* Athens: University of Georgia Press, 1988.

Dundee, Harold A., and D. A. Rossman. *The Amphibians and Reptiles of Louisiana.* Baton Rouge: Louisiana State University Press, 1989.

Ernst, Carl, and Roger W. Barbour. *Snakes of Eastern North America.* Lanham, Md.: George Mason University Press, University Publishing Associates, 1989.

Harrison, Colin James Oliver. *A Field Guide to the Nest, Eggs, and Nestlings of North American Birds.* Cleveland: Collins, 1978.

Lohoefner, Ren, and Ronald Altig. *Mississippi Herpetology.* NSTL Station, Miss.: Mississippi State University Research Center, National Space Technology Laboratories, 1983. (This report has distribution maps and species lists that can be used with the Peterson Field Guide on reptiles and amphibians.)

Lowery, George H. *Louisiana Birds.* Baton Rouge: Louisiana State University Press, 1974. (We do not yet have a Mississippi bird book comparable to this one. This work is a good substitute, however, since Louisiana is a neighboring state.)

————. *The Mammals of Louisiana and Its Adjacent Water.* Baton Rouge: Louisiana State University Press, 1974.

National Geographic Society. *National Geographic Society Field Guide to the Birds of North America.* Washington, D.C.: National Geographic Society, 1983.

Opler, Paul A., and George O. Krizek. *Butterflies East of the Great Plains: An Illustrated Natural History.* Baltimore, Md.: Johns Hopkins University Press, 1984.

Page, Lawrence, M., and Brooks M. Burr. *A Field Guide to Freshwater Fishes: North America North of Mexico.* Boston: Houghton Mifflin, 1991.

Peterson, Roger Tory. *A Field Guide to the Birds: East of the Rockies*. Boston: Houghton Mifflin, 1980.

Schwartz, Charles W. *The Wild Mammals of Missouri*. Columbia: University of Missouri Press and Missouri Department of Conservation, 1981. (Excellent line drawings with species accounts that are relevant to our mammals.)

Timme, S. Lee. 1989. *Wildflowers of Mississippi*. Jackson: University Press of Mississippi, 1989.

Turcotte, William H. *A Guide to Mississippi Bird Songs*. Jackson: Mississippi Department of Wildlife, Fisheries, and Parks, 1987.

———. *A Guide to Mississippi Frog Songs*. Jackson: Mississippi Department of Wildlife, Fisheries, and Parks, 1988.

Weber, Nancy S., and Alexander H. Smith. *A Field Guide to Southern Mushrooms*. Ann Arbor: University of Michigan Press, 1985.

Index